A HISTORY OF ORGANIZED LABOR IN BRAZIL

A HISTORY OF ORGANIZED LABOR IN BRAZIL

Robert J. Alexander

With the Collaboration of
Eldon M. Parker

Westport, Connecticut
London

Library of Congress Cataloging-in-Publication Data

Alexander, Robert Jackson, 1918–
    A history of organized labor in Brazil / Robert J. Alexander,
    with the collaboration of Eldon M. Parker.
      p. cm.
    Includes bibliographical references and index.
    ISBN 0–275–97738–2 (alk. paper)
    1. Labor movement—Brazil—History.   I. Title.
  HD8284.A44   2003
  331.8′0981—dc21   2002072825

British Library Cataloguing in Publication Data is available.

Library of Congress Catalog Card Number: 2002072825
ISBN: 0–275–97738–2

First published in 2003

Praeger Publishers, 88 Post Road West, Westport, CT 06881
An imprint of Greenwood Publishing Group, Inc.
www.praeger.com

Printed in the United States of America

∞

The paper used in this book complies with the
Permanent Paper Standard issued by the National
Information Standards Organization (Z39.48–1984).

10 9 8 7 6 5 4 3 2 1

To Colin Patrick Alexander

Contents

Preface

I first became acquainted with the labor movement of Brazil in 1946, about a year after the fall of the Estado Novo dictatorship of President Getúlio Vargas. I then spent six weeks in Rio de Janeiro, São Paulo, and the three southernmost states of the republic, Paraná, Santa Catarina, and Rio Grande do Sul.

This was an exciting moment in the history of Brazil. There was an aura of freedom following Vargas's long period of dominance. There was a feeling of change, for the better, and of excitement about the country's future.

This mood was reflected in the labor movement, which I was particularly interested in investigating, as well as in the society at large. I was able to learn much about the kind of organized labor system that had been constructed in the corporativist Estado Novo of the Vargas dictatorship, as well as the strong movement for change in that system that had been under way since that dictatorship had stumbled and then fallen in 1945. I was also lucky enough to encounter a number of people who had been leaders of Brazilian organized labor before the Revolution of 1930, which had brought Vargas to power, and to get some information and feeling for what the labor movement had been like in its earliest decades—as well as being able to acquire some documentary material from those years.

I was able to understand the political divisions within the labor movement that then existed and would continue to exist for several decades thereafter. I talked with labor leaders who were strong supporters of Getúlio Vargas, as well as with those who considered themselves Communists or sympathizers with the Communist Party. I was also able to meet a number of political figures who were not within the labor movement but had great influence on it, such as José Segadas Viana and Luiz Carlos Prestes.

In subsequent decades I made many more trips to Brazil, including the better part of a year that my family and I spent there in 1965–1966. In the process of those visits, I was able to get at least once to the urban centers of almost all of the Brazilian states, from the Amazon area in the north to the regions bordering Argentina, Uruguay, and Paraguay in the south. Each time I was in Brazil, I concentrated at least a substantial part of my interest and time on the organized labor movement.

Over the decades I was able to observe the changes that transpired within the workers' movement and in the conditions within which it functioned. I saw the efforts of the Dutra government to curtail the militancy that had developed after the end of the first Vargas regime, the partial renewal of that militancy during the second administration of Getúlio Vargas, the relative freedom of organized labor under President Kubitschek. I saw also the confused outburst of militancy under President João Goulart, and the imposition of rigid controls over the labor movement during the twenty-one years of military dictatorship from 1964 to 1985.

Finally, it was possible for me to observe the birth of the "new unionism" in the last years of the military regime and the early years of the return to civilian government. It was in this period that the structure of government control and in effect, domination of the workers' movement that had been instituted by the Vargas dictatorship of the 1930s and early 1940s largely disappeared. I take the story to 1990, not trying to extend it beyond that year.

I owe many debts to people who have made this work possible. One of my earliest obligations was to Plínio Barreto, the São Paulo lawyer, journalist, and political figure who during my first visit to his country was kind enough to provide me hospitality not only in his home in São Paulo but also in his apartment in Rio de Janeiro. He also introduced me in Rio to a substantial range of political and other leaders—telling me that he could introduce me, for instance, to any member of the Constituent Assembly, which was then in progress and of which he was a member, except Getúlio Vargas. The reasons for this exception will perhaps be clear from the text of this book.

Together with Plínio Barreto, I owe much to his son, Caio Plínio Barreto, whom I had met when, as an aspiring young labor lawyer, he was visiting the United States late in 1945 and who had arranged the invitation to stay with the Barreto family during my first visit to Brazil. In later years, too, Caio Plínio was often helpful in providing me with contacts among the "political class," and in 1990 he and his wife were particularly kind to me and my wife during our last trip to São Paulo.

Of course, I owe much to the many labor leaders, political figures, and other people who over the years were willing to answer my questions and discuss their work. It was from them that I learned much of what I came to know about Brazilian organized labor and Brazilian society in general. The names of at least some of these will be found in the text of this book.

A number of my trips to Brazil would not have been possible had it not been for the late Jay Lovestone, head of the Free Trade Union Committee and for long the virtual "secretary of state" of the American Federation of Labor and then of the American Federation of Labor–Congress of Industrial Organizations (AFL-CIO). For a number of years I traveled to Latin America for him on various occasions, reporting to him what I observed of the labor movements, political developments, and economic problems of the countries I visited.

Similarly, the year my family and I spent in Brazil, 1965–1966, would not have been possible had it not been financed by the Rutgers University Research Council, and an earlier trip by my wife, Joan, and me was made possible by a research project on international labor being carried out at the time by Professors John Dunlop, Charles Myers, Frederick Harbison and Clark Kerr.

Also, I have learned a lot from John French, of Florida International and then Duke University, outstanding among the more recent students of Brazilian labor and authority on the "new unionism" that so changed the Brazilian labor movement in the 1970s and the 1980s, and I owe much to his insights into the whole process of transformation of that movement.

As has been the case with several of my recent books, I am obliged to Dr. James Sabin, of the Greenwood Publishing Group, for his continuing encouragement for my research. Likewise, as with several of my more recent books, I owe a major debt to my friend and former student, Eldon Parker, who has not only prepared the camera-ready pages but has been a most expert copyeditor and proofreader for this volume. Thanks also to Katie Chase of Greenwood for shepherding the book through the production process.

Finally, as always, I am indebted to my wife, Joan, who not only accompanied me on several of my visits to Brazil, but put up with my writing about the subject when, undoubtedly, she must have thought that I might better be spending my time on doing other things.

One last word should be added, concerning what may appear to some readers as my too familiar reference to a number of the people whose names appear in this work. The Brazilians have a way of referring to many of their public figures by their first names or their nicknames. They do this not only in conversation but in print. Thus, Getúlio Vargas will appear as "Getúlio" and João Goulart as "Jango" (his nickname). Both because it makes for less sometimes dull repetition of names and because in a book about Brazil it seems to be the right thing to do, I have not infrequently adopted this Brazilian custom.

Rutgers University
New Brunswick, NJ

Introduction

The history of organized labor in Brazil divides clearly into two different segments. The first deals with the origins and early development of the movement from the last decades of the nineteenth century until the Revolution of 1930. The second is a study of the corporative state structure that President Getúlio Vargas imposed on organized labor during his first tenure in power from 1930 until 1945, and the continuation of that structure during most of the rest of the twentieth century, until it was finally dispensed with in the late 1980s.

Until 1930, the trajectory of the labor movement in Brazil was quite similar to what was happening in most of the rest of Latin America. Most of the early labor organizations were mutual benefit societies rather than trade unions, although that system had begun to change by the early 1900s. Almost from its inception, Brazilian organized labor was involved in politics, with several different political ideologies finding expression within it. The most important of these in the early years was anarchosyndicalism, although the anarchists had Socialist and Roman Catholic competitors. By the 1920s, the predominant groups contesting for leadership in the movement were the anarchosyndicalists and the Communists.

In the period before 1930, the organized workers had to deal with not only the opposition of the employers, but also that of successive governments. Although there were shades of difference in the intensity of the opposition of different government administrations on both a national and a state level, there were few if any regimes in power in this period that could be considered friendly to the labor movement.

Organized labor remained small and relatively weak before 1930. However, when individual unions did develop certain strength of members and militancy, they began to negotiate collective agreements with their relevant employers or groups of employers.

This all changed with the advent of Getúlio Vargas to power in the Revolution of 1930. First, as a means of consolidating his somewhat tenuous hold on to power, Vargas almost immediately sought to win the support of the urban working class, which until that time had had a very minor role in Brazilian politics. He set out to legalize instead of suppress the labor movement, but the cost of this legalization was that the organized workers were expected to support President Vargas.

When it became increasingly clear that by no means all of the new legal labor movement was led by supporters of his regime, and when he was faced with the unpleasant fact that his constitutional term of office was about to expire, Vargas made a coup d'état from the presidential palace in November 1937 and established what he called the Estado Novo (New State). This new regime was patterned after the fascist corporate states that were becoming prevalent at the time in much of Europe.

The Estado Novo provided that virtually all those active in the economy—employers, workers, members of the free professions—would be under the aegis of government authorized and legalized organizations. These were *sindicatos* (unions) on the lowest level, federations of *sindicatos*, and confederations of the federations.

Insofar as the working-class *sindicatos*, federations, and confederations were concerned, the Estado Novo provided for the government to determine their jurisdictions, and their activities, and to control who could hold office in them. Every worker paid an *imposto sindical* (trade union tax) of one day's pay a year. Most of this money was supposed to go to the sindicato, federation, and confederation under whose aegis the particular worker was assigned. However, the labor organization was to spend this money on social welfare projects for its members—and on the organization's own bureaucracy—rather than on negotiations with employers.

Indeed, collective bargaining between workers' organizations and employers had no place in the Estado Novo. In its stead was a system of labor courts, which would decide to what degree the employers should provide changes in working conditions that the labor organizations informed these courts that they would like to have. Clearly, since this labor court system was designed to ensure "labor peace and stability," strikes and other similar activities by the workers' organizations were completely illegal under the Estado Novo.

Although the Estado Novo supposedly came to an end with the overthrow of President Vargas in October 1945 and the adoption of a new constitution a year later, it continued largely in existence insofar as the labor movement was concerned. The Consolidaçao das Leis do Trabalho (Consolidation of Labor Laws) of 1939, which had determined the nature of labor-management relations under the Estado Novo, continued in force for more than forty years after the end of the Vargas dictatorship in 1945. Each of the governments in power during those decades decided how to apply—or whether to apply—the provisions of the Consolidaçao, but until the late 1980s none did away with the system established in that body of legislation.

In at least one respect, Brazilian labor after the Estado Novo reverted to a condition that had characterized it before 1930. Once again, there were several political currents which were seeking influence in its ranks. The two most significant of these were the Communists and those people who were loyal to Getúlio Vargas (and after his death in 1954, to his memory). However, there were also several other groups of less importance, including the Socialists and elements associated with the Catholic Church. Finally, there were those labor leaders who had no definite political allegiance but adapted themselves to whatever government was in power, so as to preserve their jobs in the labor movement.

One important modification of the Estado Novo labor system that took place in the 1960s and early 1970s was its extension to the rural sector of the economy. For their own peculiar reasons, both the administration of President João Goulart and the military regime that was in power after his overthrow in 1964 sought to extend the system of Estado Novo–legalized and government-controlled *sindicatos*, federations, and confederations to agriculture. The longer-term results of this were that the rural workers confederation, the Confederação Nacional dos Trabalhadores na Agricultura (CONTAG), became the largest of all of the trade union confederations, and after the decline and ultimate disappearance of the Estado Novo system in the 1980s, the CONTAG was one of the most militant of the country's labor organizations, not only pushing collective bargaining, but demanding new legislation, particularly agrarian reform.

It was not until the late 1970s that a major challenge was launched against the type of labor movement that Vargas had established in the Estado Novo period. That challenge originated with the autoworkers' *sindicatos* in the São Paulo area, which, through a series of strikes, demanded an end to government control of the workers' organizations and establishment of a really free labor movement. Those strikes also led to a nationwide movement to substitute collective bargaining for the labor courts.

The advent of the so-called new unionism after 1978 had two other impacts on the organized labor movement. It brought into existence for the first time since 1930 enduring central labor organizations, seeking to unite all of the trade unionists across geographical and craft-industry lines. It also gave rise to a different kind of working-class participation in politics, bringing about the rise of a mass political party with its origins in the labor movement, rather than, as in the case of Communists, Socialists, and *Getúlistas* (followers of Getúlio Vargas), an outside party seeking to win the support of and control over the labor movement.

The challenge to the Estado Novo labor system culminated in the Constitution of 1988, which proclaimed the freedom of the workers to organize, ending the requirement that there had to be government control over any *sindicatos* that were established. The constitution also proclaimed the right of the workers to go on strike. The only significant element of the Estado Novo system that persisted after the adoption of the 1988 Constitution was the *imposto sindical*, which remained in effect, although the *sindicatos* that received it were free to use the funds accumulated through it as they saw fit, rather than for purposes specified by the government, as had been the case under the Estado Novo system.

By 1990, the final year analyzed in this study, the Brazilian labor movement was larger and stronger than it had ever been. It covered a large percentage of the industrial working class, as well as many white-collar workers, government employees, and a substantial segment of the rural proletariat. Negotiation with the employers had become a standard operating procedure for most *sindicatos*, although given the runaway inflation of much of the 1980s, such negotiations tended to concentrate heavily on wage and salary issues.

1
Organized Labor Before the 1930 Revolution

Slavery persisted in Brazil until 1888. Also, Brazil's economy remained overwhelmingly agricultural, although there were some efforts to stimulate manufacturing during the last decades of the reign of Emperor Pedro II, who was overthrown in 1889. It was only after the establishment of the republic that the real beginnings of a modern proletariat appeared in Brazil, hence paving the way for an organized labor movement.

However, these circumstances did not prevent the spread, particularly among intellectuals, of various kinds of socialist ideas that were then current in Europe and dealt in one way or another with the role of the worker in society. As early as 1839, a periodical, *O Socialista*, was published in Rio de Janeiro, and in 1840 a doctor, Benoit-Jules Mure, and an engineer, Louis Leger Vanthier, began to propagate the ideas of the French utopian socialist Charles Fourier. A couple of years later, Mure undertook to establish a Fourierist colony in the southern province of Santa Catarina. He also collaborated in a newspaper, *O Socialista da Provincia do Rio de Janeiro*, which appeared between 1845 and 1847. Meanwhile, another periodical, *O Progresso*, which began to appear in the northeastern city of Recife in 1844, reported news of European revolutionary groups, including the League of the Just, which became the Communist League, for which Karl Marx and Friedrich Engels wrote the *Communist Manifesto*.[1]

One of the most widely distributed works presenting the ideas of the utopian socialists was the volume *Socialismo*, written by General Abreu e Lima, who was described as an "old general of Bolivar."[2] Although Abreu e Lima did not favor any of the utopian socialist doctrines, his work did serve to make them relatively well known.[3] He was an army officer and a staunch Catholic, but he has been described as being "filled with the spirit of '48," the year of widespread revolutions in Europe.[4]

The ideas of Karl Marx were first widely disseminated and supported apparently in the 1860s, by Tobias Barreto, Clovis Bevilaqua, and Arthur Orlando, in Recife, where St. Simonian ideas also had some currency.[5]

Three Brazilian scholars have noted: "From 1860 to 1869 there appeared in Brazil twenty working-class publications, a number which increased to 48 in the following decade. The titles, which were repeated many times, indicated the tendency of the newspaper." They included periodicals that were clearly of anarchist orientation, others of socialist tendency, and still others that just proclaimed themselves to be "working class" or "proletarian."[6]

In the last years of the empire, there were some individuals of socialist leanings, chiefly immigrants, who were in touch with the European socialist and trade union movements. Thus, in 1885, L. X. de Ricard, who said that he was the editor of *Le Courier du Brasil*, wrote to Benoit Malon, editor of *La Revue Socialiste* of Paris, declaring himself to be in complete sympathy with the program of Malon and his followers in France. He claimed that Rio was a comparatively fertile location for socialist activity.

Alfredo Gómez noted the existence for a short while after 1890 of an anarchist colony, La Cecilia, in Palmeira in the state of Parana. Consisting of some 300 Italian immigrants, who included peasants, artisans, and even people with advanced education, it sought to put into practice anarchist ideas.

Gómez noted:

In spite of the fact that few of them had experience in agricultural work, after a short while they succeeded in getting from the inhospitable soil . . . their first fruits, establishing some industries (shoe and candy making) and acquiring some cattle. To achieve this, there was no need for installing any coercive system: Without chiefs, regulations or laws, the colonists of La Cecilia organized their small society.[7]

This anarchist experiment was soon ended by the authorities. However, Gómez noted, "Thrown out by the police, some of the last members of La Cecilia moved to the great urban conglomerations of the country, and participated actively in founding the first workers' associations, constituting a Group of Social Studies."[8]

BEGINNINGS OF A TRADE UNION MOVEMENT

The first strike of which we have found notice was a "stoppage" of typographers in Rio de Janeiro in 1857. Bandeira, Melo, and Andrade noted also, "There is talk, by tradition, of another among the lamplighters."[9]

However, the trade union movement did not really get under way until the overthrow of the empire and establishment of the republic in 1889. A Liga Operária (Workers League) in Rio in 1870, which may have attempted to establish sindicatos, had a very short life.[10] During the last twenty years of the empire some labor organizations appeared from time to time, most of them mutual benefit societies. In 1888, several labor organizations in Santos formed a central body, A Internacional, which was under radical influence.[11]

At least two factors stimulated the birth of trade unionism in the early years of the republic. One was the growth of manufacturing. It is recorded that between 1890 and 1914 some seven thousand factories were established in Brazil, thus "really forming in this period the national proletariat."[12]

Another important factor was the large-scale immigration into Brazil in the early republican period of Europeans, particularly Italians, Spaniards, and Germans. Many of these workers had belonged to sindicatos of socialist or anarchist groups in their native countries. Immigrants were to play a very significant role in the labor movement in the decades before 1930.

As was the case in most Latin American countries, many of the earliest workers' organizations in Brazil were mutual benefit societies. Alfredo Gómez noted:

In this period, the workers organized in workers' leagues and associations of resistance of fundamentally mutualist and cooperative inspiration. Thus, in the State of Rio Grande do Sul there existed the União Operária, organizer of a school and a cooperative of help and mutual aid. Of this same nature were the accords of the first labor congress of Rio Grande do Sul in 1898. However, in this same congress, the Libertarian Groups succeeded in having approved the tactic of boycott as a means of struggle.[13]

Trade unions began to appear in various parts of the country. The first typographical sindicato in the city of São Paulo was organized in 1890 under the name Centro Typographico. It was notable principally for carrying out a one-day strike against the city's major newspaper, O Estado de São Paulo, but it soon disappeared. It was succeeded by another organization, of unknown name, which "disappeared without leaving its history except for the disappearance of its treasurer with the funds of the cashbox."[14]

Italian printers in São Paulo organized in 1896 the Sezione Italiana da Federação dos Trabalhadores do Livro, which published one number of a magazine called *Pensamente e Arte* and eight numbers of another, *O Trabalhador do Livro*.[15]

Metal workers, construction workers, and railroaders also formed *sindicatos* in São Paulo during the last decade of the nineteenth century.[16]

The city of Santos, the coffee exporting port of the state of São Paulo, began early to become an important center of trade union and allied activities. "Almost contemporaneously with the establishment of the Republic," the União Operário, also known as the União Socialista, was founded in that city, both to foster unionization and to spread socialist ideas.[17]

In Santos the early trade union movement took particular root among the dockworkers, many of whom were European immigrants. Eugene Ridings noted:

The Commercial Association of Santos took charge of suppressing unrest. It broke stevedore strikes in December 1889 and in May 1991 by having the governor send state armed forces and in the latter case also remove the strike leader from Santos. The association insisted that the workers were well paid and satisfied, but misled by "disorderly elements.". . . The group also prompted police to break an August 1900 strike of railroad warehouse workers and coffee wagon teamsters.

The situation was more complicated in the Santos port workers' walkout of October 1897. By that time, the large Santos Dock Company dominated much of the port. When a strike broke out as the result of an accident that wounded twelve stevedores and spread throughout the port, the Commercial Association first succeeded in getting the use of federal troops against the walkout. However, when, after five days, the independent warehouse owners settled with the *sindicatos*, and the Santos Dock Company refused to negotiate at all, the Commercial Association suddenly proclaimed that the workers' demands were "reasonable" and "just" and demanded that the Dock Company negotiate. The Rio newspaper *Jornal do Comércio* denounced the Santos Commercial Association, claiming that it was seeking to undermine the Santos Dock Company because of that organization's efforts to stop smuggling.

Ridings concluded,

The association's actions were motivated more by dislike of the Santos Dock Company than by concern for the dock workers. Like other business interest groups, it ordinarily had little empathy for workers and was affronted by their attempts to organize. Labor had no friend among Brazil's nineteenth-century business interest groups.[18]

Santos was the scene of the first citywide general strike, at the end of 1905. It was again the port workers who were principally responsible for that walkout.[19]

In Recife, the União dos Estivadores (stevedores' union) was founded as early as 1891.[20]

Some *sindicatos* also began to appear in Rio de Janeiro. In 1891, a strike took place among the cigarette workers of the city. The workers won an increase of from four to five milreis per thousand cigarettes produced, and the employers increased the price of their product.[21]

GOVERNMENT HOSTILITY TO THE EARLY LABOR MOVEMENT

The early governments were by no means friendly toward organized labor. Paulo Sérgio Pinheiro and Michael Hall noted:

Among the few local measures from the early years of the republic directly relevant to the control of the working class were three articles dealing with strikes in the Penal Code of 1890. While strikes were not precisely illegal under the terms of these articles, they included enough restrictions to make a legal strike virtually impossible. "Seducing or enticing" workers to leave their places of employment, for example, was a crime carrying a one to three month prison term and a heavy fine. However, it appears that in the severe repression directed against strikes over the years, the provisions of the Penal Code were not usually invoked. While the code served to identify strikes as illegal for almost all practical purposes, State officials did not consider themselves particularly bound by its provisions and resorted instead to a variety of highly arbitrary punishments.[22]

The embryonic labor movement had tried to prevent the adoption of this section of the Penal Code. The Centro das Classes Proletárias in Rio de Janeiro had protested strongly, but unsuccessfully, against the measure.[23]

There were also some protests in the early days of the republic by "respectable" elements against the government's persecution of workers' organizations, and especially of the anarchists, who were particularly prominent in the labor movement. Thus, R. Teixeira Mendes, the principal leader of the Positivists in Brazil, wrote a letter in 1892 to the *Jornal do Comércio* denouncing the mistreatment of the anarchists by the police. This protest was later published as a pamphlet.[24]

ORGANIZED LABOR IN THE PRE–WORLD WAR I PERIOD

Organized labor grew substantially and showed considerable militancy in the decade and a half before World War I. Many new *sindicatos* were founded in these first years of the century, particularly in Rio de Janeiro and São Paulo. Dr. Poblete Troncoso mentioned the Sociedade União dos Foguistas (firemen) and the União dos Operários Estivadores (stevedores), both founded in Rio in 1903, and the Associação da Resistência dos Cocheiros, Carroceiros e Classes Annexas (coachmen), founded in 1906.[25] What later became the single largest trade union in the country, the commercial employees of the Federal District (Rio de Janeiro), was founded in 1903 as the União dos Empregados no Comércio.[26]

At the First National Labor Congress in 1906 there were present forty-three delegates representing eighteen *sindicatos* in various parts of the country. Most of these were in Rio and São Paulo. However, an additional fourteen groups of *sindicatos* and individual organizations, including ones from Rio Grande do Sul, Alagoas, and Minas Gerais, sent greetings to the meeting, although they were unable to send delegates.[27] It is probable that the great majority of *sindicatos* that were under anarchist control, and probably a few with socialist leadership, were present at the First National Labor Congress.[28]

In 1913, the official report on the Second National Labor Congress summed up the Brazilian trade union situation in the first half-decade of the twentieth century. After commenting on the movement in Rio de Janeiro, it said:

The movement in the States was small. With the exception of São Paulo, Bahia and Rio Grande do Sul, where the foreign element contributed greatly to the diffusion of working-class propaganda, principally in São Paulo and Rio Grande do Sul. In Pernambuco, Ceará and Pará one noted also certain interest in organizing the productive classes, but without sufficient orientation to assure it continued life.[29]

There were numerous strikes during the first decade of the century. A walkout of dockworkers in Santos in 1905 brought about the declaration of a state of siege in the port city and the calling of a general strike in retaliation.[30] In the same year there was a strike of São Paulo metallurgical workers employed by the Sidgerwood Company, in which two hundred workers stayed out for six days.[31]

Two labor struggles in this period were particularly noteworthy. One was a broad struggle in Rio de Janeiro in 1904, in which the *sindicatos* of the city took an active part. The second was a widespread campaign for the eight-hour day in 1907–1908.

The passage by Congress of a Sanitary Code in 1903, and its amendment in the following year to provide for compulsory vaccination against yellow fever, was part of a much broader campaign by government and commercial interests supporting it. Teresa Meade wrote:

At one pole stood Brazil's government and urban bourgeoisie, in close alliance with British financiers, merchants and urban developers, intent on transforming Rio from a shabby disease-infested, rather dilapidated city, into a "civilized," modern center of trade and commerce. At the other pole were the popular classes—the working class, the marginalized and unemployed urban poor, and the small shopkeepers—whose homes and businesses stood in the path of the renovation/beautification project.[32]

Meade noted:

Centro das Classes Operárias . . . centralized the opposition from the trade union movement. Organized along loose syndicalist lines, the Centro united some of the more powerful labor unions in the city, including the railroad workers, dockworkers, painters, machinists, carpenters, stonemasons, plasterers and members of the maritime union.[33]

The Centro in July–August 1904 circulated a petition against the compulsory vaccination and gathered 10,000 signatures. At a meeting before the Chamber of Deputies, "the Centro representatives called on the government to rescind the obligatory vaccination code and to enact measures to upgrade the miserable living conditions in the city's poor and working class neighborhoods."[34]

Then, on November 5, a meeting of protest, with 2,000 people present, was held in the Centro's headquarters, where Vicente de Souza, president of the center, and Senator Lauro Sodre, a leading Positivist, were the principal speakers. Meade noted that in that meeting and others held in the campaign, "vaccination was opposed in relation to the government's reputation as unfeeling toward the poor."[35]

A League against Obligatory Vaccination was founded at the November 5 meeting, to pressure the government and parliament. It organized a meeting in the center of the city on November 10, which was attended by "over 3,000 people."[36] However, after this meeting, rioting broke out and continued for several days. While this was going on, the Federacão das Associações de Classe sent a protest to Congress on November 12, which "listed the painters, hatmakers, firemen, cigarmakers, carpenters, stonemasons, and plasterers' *sindicatos*, including the stevedores, [who] went out on strike to protest the Sanitary Code provisions and the harshness of the government in dealing with protesters.[37]

On November 17, the government rescinded the compulsory part of the vaccination program, restoring calm to the capital.[38] However, the rioting had sealed the doom of the Centro das Classes Operárias, which disappeared from the scene. Soon afterward, the Associações de Classe took its place.[39]

The struggle for the eight-hour day in 1907 took place particularly in São Paulo, Rio de Janeiro, Santos, and Recife, but was most notable in the city of São Paulo. The United States anarchist periodical *Mother Earth* summarized, perhaps a bit optimistically, the results of this drive, which it said showed "effective trade union organization, causing the establishment of employers associations, and a great number of strikes in many trades to obtain the eight hour day."[40]

Starting right after a May Day demonstration that *Mother Earth* reported to have been "splendid,"[41] a series of strikes broke out in the factories and workshops of São Paulo. The strikers met the usual harsh treatment from the police, provoking a strong protest from the Federação Operária de São Paulo.[42] However, in spite of employer and governmental resistance, the São Paulo labor movement was surprisingly successful in implanting, for the time being at least, the eight-hour day.

The São Paulo socialist paper *Avanti!* noted:

It is impossible for us at the moment to make a statistical chart listing the workshops in which the eight hour day was adopted, just as we cannot either know the number of workers who enjoy this improvement; but we can affirm with certainty that the eight hour day was won definitively by the bricklayers, carpenters, painters, hat workers, stonemasons, and vehicle builders.

The newspaper went on to say that "judgment of the strike would not be correct if we only refer to those categories of workers which received complete victory. To judge the importance of the road taken by the Paulista proletariat, it is necessary also to take account of the partial victories which brought notable benefits to not a few thousand workers." Among the groups who had won partial victories were the printing trades workers, who won an eight-and-a-half-hour workday, and the textile workers, who got a two-hour reduction of their very long workday.[43]

Avanti! speculated on why the São Paulo *sindicatos* had been so relatively successful in their eight-hour day campaign:

We confess sincerely that we do not know how to give the phenomenon a positive and exhaustive explanation; it is certain that the heterogeneous character of the local bourgeoisie and its lack of preparation contributed greatly to reduce the resistance. It is certain too that the spontaneity of the movement, its pacific character, and the enthusiasm that the workers showed won them the sympathy of those interests, which were not directly involved. It is also indisputable that the moment at which the movement began was singularly favorable, because the employers and entrepreneurs were enjoying a period of large sales; all this is true, but it does not adequately explain the phenomenon.[44]

These favorable conditions did not last long. Subsequent to the struggles of 1907, the trade union movement of São Paulo, and presumably of most of the rest of Brazil, suffered what Pinheiro and Hall have called "a formidable crisis." They suggest that police repression and growing unemployment, starting in 1908, were two factors explaining this decline of organized labor.[45]

The São Paulo magazine *La Scure*, in an article on "Trade Unionism in São Paulo," described the nature of this crisis in the labor movement:

Enthusiasm diminished and with this the number of members in the leagues diminished also, there remaining only a small group which had succeeded in developing consciousness. Those who stopped in the middle of the road did not return, therefore to the primitive tactics because they were convinced of their inefficacy. As trade union action showed itself contrary to their desire for egoistic peace . . . they preferred to listen to anti-organizational propaganda of those I shall call "theoreticians of convenience." Consequently, they remained at home, practically renouncing the struggle of established corporative organizations, as did the brick transporters who withdrew from the Federação Operária, since to continue the tactic of trade unionism did not seem to them to present any common interest with other workers groups. Solidarity appeared to them something noxious and so they decided not to accept any more members in their *sindicato*.

This article concluded by noting that the *sindicatos* that continued to be "more or less active" in São Paulo were the Hat Workers Union, the Bricklayers League, and the League of Woodworkers, "which were always in the vanguard of the proletariat."[46]

Leôncio Rodrigues summed up the nature of the Brazilian labor movement in the pre–World War I period:

Exact information is not available on the number of adherents of *sindicatos* or of the socialist and collectivist leagues and *sindicatos*, which in truth, were not clearly differentiated, particularly in the first years of this century. The intensity of participation of the workers must have varied greatly and not have been systematic and constant. But it must be observed that the force and the influence of the first workers associations rested most on the untiring activity of the worker activists and the anarchist and socialist militants, which was felt less or more strongly in the periods of most discontent of the masses.

Rodrigues went on:

The associations were not institutions that were firmly established, bu-
reaucratized, and their force did not come from the fact of grouping an
elevated number of adherents. The authority of the leaders, their prestige
in the class, on the other hand, did not derive from the functions which
those leaders exercised in the structure of the associations, but rather on
their individual attributes, in a phase in which the bureaucratization of
the *sindicatos* was practically nonexistent.[47]

THE CONFEDERAÇÃO OPERÁRIA BRASILEIRA (COB)

The first national central labor organization in Brazil was
formed in 1906 under the leadership of the anarchosyndicalists.
A statewide labor group had been formed by the anarchists in São
Paulo in the first years of the century,[48] and anarchist-led *sindicatos* were of importance in Rio de Janeiro, Rio Grande do Sul,
Pernambuco, Bahia, Pará, the state of Rio de Janeiro, Paraná,
and Minas Gerais.[49] Representatives of many of these groups met
in Rio to form the Confederação Operária Brasileira.

The anarchist orientation of much of the Brazilian labor
movement in this period was reflected in a number of periodicals
that appeared in those years. One of these was *Terra Livre*, established by the União dos Trabalhadores Gráficos in 1905, and
edited by, among others, Edgard Leuenroth. One of Leuenroth's
collaborators, Nenno Vasco, "considered as one of the principal
propagators of anarchism in Brazil," had earlier established the
short-lived anarchist journals *Aurora* and *Amigo do Povo*. In 1904,
an Italian language anarchist weekly, *La Battaglia*, had begun
publishing in São Paulo, and in Rio de Janeiro, *O Libertario* was
also established.[50]

The ideological orientation of the Confederação Operária Brasileira, as reflected in the resolutions of its founding congress,
might best be characterized as anarchosyndicalist or syndicalist.
Unlike the Federación Obrera Regional Argentina (FORA) of Argentina, it did not commit itself to trying to bring about the
establishment of anarchist communism, or any other kind of future society. Rather, it declared the following "objectives" of the
COB:

a) To promote the *sindicato* of the wage workers for the defense of their
interests, moral and material, economic and professional; b) To
strengthen the bonds of solidarity among the organized proletariat, giving
more force and cohesion to its efforts and revindications, both moral and
material; c) To study and propagate the means of emancipating the proletariat and defend in public the economic revindications of the workers,
using for this all of the known means of propaganda, particularly of a

journal which will be called *A Voz do Trabalhador*; d) To bring together and publish exact statistics and information about the labor movement and labor conditions throughout the world.[51]

However, the anarchosyndicalist or syndicalist orientation of the COB was reflected in the resolution to "send to the French working class the most ardent expression of its sympathies and solidarity, presenting itself as a model of activity and initiative to the worker of Brazil." At that point, the French central labor organization, the Confederation Génerale du Travail (CGT), was the outstanding representative of syndicalism, in contrast to doctrinaire anarchist labor groups such as the FORA of Argentina and socialist-oriented ones that were predominant in most of Europe at the time.

The anarchosyndicalist orientation of COB was also reflected in the fact that the Congress never specified a line of action that its affiliates were obliged to follow, but rather "advised" them or "counseled" them to take one kind of position or another. Also, it showed great reluctance, as was characteristic of anarchist and anarchosyndicalist groups, to have paid *sindicato* officials. It resolved, "The Labor Congress strongly counsels the workers organizations to reject paying officeholders, except in cases in which the great amount of service requires peremptorily that a worker dedicate himself entirely to it, but then he should not receive payment beyond the normal wage of the craft to which he belongs."

The meeting also resolved, "The Confederation does not belong to any political school or religious doctrine, cannot take part collectively in elections, party or religious demonstrations, nor can any member whatever use the name of the Confederation or function of the Confederation in any electoral or religious act."

The First Congress of the COB dealt with a wide range of matters. It resolved that the COB would be made up of industrial and craft federations, local or state groupings of *sindicatos*, and isolated *sindicatos* where there were no federations, indicating a preference for industrial *sindicatos*. It provided for the COB to be led by a Confederal Commission between congresses, which were to be held every year, although such annual meetings proved impossible in practice.

Although counseling its affiliates to have nothing to do with cooperatives or mutual benefit activities, the First Congress of the COB did urge them to establish "lay" schools for their members' children. It urged that the foremen be excluded from *sindicato*, except under very exceptional circumstances. It urged a campaign to win the eight-hour day, as we have seen that many of its affiliated groups did in the year after the congress. It urged member *sindicatos* to organize women workers on the same basis as men and to seek abolition of labor by children. It expressed opposition to piecework.[52]

Pinheiro and Hall noted that the COB "maintained a precarious existence during most of the following decade" and that "it was the first national labor organization of some consequence. The COB, especially through its periodical *A Voz do Trabalhador*, permitted for the first time a certain coordination and exchange of information in the interior of the labor movement, on the national level."[53]

For the first few years of its existence, the COB had a fairly active life. A report to the Second COB Congress in 1913 stated that during the 1906–1908 period it had maintained contact with about fifty *sindicato* groups. These included the Federação Operária of Rio de Janeiro as well as statewide federations in Bahia, Alagoas, and Rio Grande do Sul, and citywide organizations in São Paulo and Santos, each of which had several individual *sindicatos* in its ranks.[54]

In 1908, the COB carried on an extensive campaign against the military draft. At that time, there were rumors of a possible war between Brazil and Argentina, with a considerable fanning of patriotic fires in Brazil, which the COB sought to counteract. On December 1, the COB organized "a stupendous demonstration of protest," attended by 10,000 people.[55]

In 1909, the Confederation organized demonstrations of protest against the execution of Francisco Ferrer, the Spanish anarchist educator, after the so-called Tragic Week in Barcelona, in which Spanish anarchist *sindicatos* had provoked strikes and demonstrations against drafting of soldiers to fight in the continuing war in Morocco. Some 5,000 people were reported to have participated in the COB demonstration in Rio de Janeiro.[56]

However, by 1912, the Confederação Operária Brasileira had fallen into inactivity. The initiative to revive it was taken by the Federação Operária do Rio de Janeiro, and "in accord with various federations and associations of the interior," it established a Reorganizing Commission of the Confederação Operária Brasileira, with the objective of calling a Second Brazilian Labor Congress. That body renewed publication of the COB paper *A Voz do Trabalhador* and sent out a series of circulars to organizations throughout the country, asking them to provide information about themselves, to name delegates to the Second Congress, and to send funds to help pay for that meeting. It also sent invitations, which were accepted, to the FORA of Argentina and the Federación Obrera Regional Uruguay (FORU) of Uruguaya, to send fraternal delegates.

The Second Congress of the COB finally met September 9–13, 1913. According to the official records of that meeting, there were fifty-nine "associations" represented. The great majority came from Rio de Janeiro, São Paulo, Minas Gerais, and Rio Grande do Sul. Other *sindicatos* sent messages of support, although they could not send delegates. These included organizations in Ceará, Mato Groso, and Pará. Telegrams of greeting were received from several organizations, including the Argentine FORA and the French CGT.

The Second COB Congress more or less reiterated the ideological positions taken by the First Congress. It resolved to "invite the working class of Brazil, repelling the dissolving influence of politics, to dedicate itself to the work of trade union labor organization which . . . is the most efficacious and powerful way to make immediate conquests which are needed to strengthen the struggle for its complete emancipation."

Another resolution indicated the same general orientation. Dealing with the question of how workers should guarantee the prompt payment of wages, it reiterated support for the resolution of the First Congress on the subject, except for dropping "including the tribunals" as a means of assuring such payment.

The Second Congress adopted a long resolution that, aside from setting forth the kind of trade union structure the COB was seeking to establish, sketched the kind of society that it hoped would evolve. On both counts, this resolution was clearly anarchosyndicalist.

The resolution proclaimed that

the government or the State, with its institutions of force and violence, constitutes an enormous barrier between the working class and the capitalist class, a barrier that is necessary to destroy through an economic transformation that will make disappear the class antagonisms that convert men into devourers of men, and free of any kind of centralizing or authoritarian organism, and bring about the establishment of a people of free producers, so that at last the servant and the master, the aristocrat and the plebian, the bourgeois and the proletarian, the owner and the slave, who with their economic and social differences have bloodied history, will finally embrace as true brothers.

In setting forth the principles of trade union organization, this resolution was equally anarchosyndicalist. It said that it considered

the only method or organization compatible with the irrepressible spirit of liberty and with the imperious necessity of workers action and education, the federative method—the largest autonomy of the individual in the *sindicato*, of the *sindicato* in the federation and of the federation in the confederation, and with there only being permissible simple delegation of function without authority.[57]

This Second Congress also adopted a number of resolutions dealing with specific problems. These included propaganda for trade unionism, the stimulation of a trade union press, education of the workers, the fight against alcoholism, health and safety problems in the workplace, the fight against militarism, and various other matters.[58]

The Second Congress also endorsed the idea of organizing a South American Workers Congress. It called for cooperation with the FORA of Argentina and the FORU of Uruguay to this end.[59]

One of the decisions of the Second COB Congress was to try to inform European workers' organizations about the true state of labor conditions in Brazil, to counteract the propaganda of the steamship agents and others who were trying to attract European workers to the country. The COB did get out a circular, which it sent to various European *sindicato* groups. This was a "warning to all foreign workers to keep away from the country." It warned that the masses of workers from the Northeast were migrating to the south central area of Brazil, "in order to escape from certain death by starvation." It also said, "The workers have made desultory attempts to improve their condition by united action, but invariably have been beaten back by the rifles and sabers of the soldiery and imprisonment and exile on the part of the judges." The COB, according to the circular, "calls upon the workers of the world to aid and support the Brazilian workers in their bitter and difficult struggle."[60]

The Second Congress was no more successful than its predecessor in establishing a durable labor confederation in Brazil. In spite of renewed labor militancy during World War I, the COB languished. Finally, a new effort to reactivate the Confederation was taken when the Third Workers Congress met in April 1920.

The 1920 Congress of the Confederação Operária Brasileira drew up an elaborate scheme for effective central direction of the labor movement. Labor federations were supposed to be established in all of the states. National industrial federations were to be organized, including a Federation of Land Transport; a Federation of Port, Maritime and River Workers; and a Federation of Industrial Workers, all with their headquarters in Rio de Janeiro.

As an intermediate step, the country was to be divided into five sections: Central, Southern, Extreme Southern, Northern, and Extreme Northern, and appropriate secretaries were to be established in Rio de Janeiro, São Paulo, Pôrto Alegre, Recife, and Belem. Each secretariat was to consist of a permanent secretary and a traveling secretary, the latter to keep in close touch with the General Secretariat in Rio de Janeiro.[61] Finally, the Commissão Executiva do Terceiro Congresso Operário was established as the highest organization between congresses, with secretary general, treasurer, four regional secretaries, and five traveling secretaries.[62]

Edgard Leuenroth, printing trades worker and journalist of São Paulo, the founder of the graphic arts workers' organization of that city, became secretary general of the Executive Committee. Leuenroth had worked since he was fifteen years old and had been active in the anarchist and labor movements about as long. He was one of the founders of the Centro Typographico of São Paulo in 1903 and was the guiding spirit of the printing trades workers' organizations there down to the advent of the Vargas regime in 1930.[63]

For a short while, the reestablishment of the COB seemed to augur a new unity and strength for the labor movement in general. Domingos Passos, the traveling secretary of the Central Section of the Confederação, undertook an organizing tour in the state of Rio de Janeiro in August 1920, with promising results.[64]

However, by May 1921, it was clear that the new organizational structure of the COB was not functioning. As a consequence, some of the principal COB leaders in Rio, with Edgard Leuenroth and several others from São Paulo, Recife, and elsewhere, met to discuss the situation. Leuenroth reported that the new COB organization "had failed." José Elias da Silva, the traveling secretary of the Northern Section, attributed the problem to the loose federative nature of the COB.

For his part, Astrojildo Pereira, one of the younger leaders based in Rio, agreeing with da Silva's analysis, suggested that the Brazilian anarchosyndicalist *sindicato* leaders study the organization of the Industrial Workers of the World (IWW) in the United States. He said that the IWW had "one great *sindicato* of all the workers, with a single secretariat, a propaganda fund, a single center of coordination."[65]

However, nothing seems to have come of these efforts to give more vitality to the COB. The timing was unfortunate, since the labor movement was suffering a retrogression after the intense activity of 1917, 1918, and 1919. For all practical purposes, the COB went out of existence.

THE 1912 LABOR CONGRESS

The anarchosyndicalists were not the only ones to try to establish a national central labor group. In November 1912 there met in Rio de Janeiro what called itself the Fourth Labor Congress; the meeting was sponsored by the Liga do Operariado do Distrito Federal.[66]

This meeting was sponsored, in fact, by Mario Hermes, a federal deputy and son of President Hermes de Fonseca. The sessions met in the Congress building, and some of the delegates were provided by the government with free passage on the Loide Brasileiro steamship line.[67]

The antianarchist point of view of those attending was shown in the call issued by the Liga do Operariado: "The direct action urged by the workers' *sindicatos* is good in theory but in practice fails, lacking force, and only adds to existing discontent." It was claimed that more than eighty organizations from Bahia south to Porto Alegre were represented. Most of these seem to have been craft groups, although workers' cultural groups such as the Lyceu de Artes e Officios de Bahia were also represented. The Congress resolved to launch a labor political party to be called Confederação Brasileira do Trabalho; there is little evidence that such a party was in fact established. The meeting also adopted various other resolutions, dealing with such elements as unemployment insurance, obligatory weekly wage payments, maximum hour and minimum wage legalization, pure food laws, and universal free education.[68]

Understandably, the anarchosyndicalist *sindicatos* did not participate in the November 1912 meeting. The Federação Operária de Rio de Janeiro wrote:

In the beginning, this Federação thought that the organization of this congress showed a thoughtful orientation, we were disposed to attend it, in case we were invited, and were ready to defend the orientation that guides us and which we propagate. Soon, however, we were aware of the character and objectives of this meeting . . . organized by suspicious individuals who had pretensions of developing themselves into political leaders of the working class.[69]

The report of the Second Congress of the COB noted that the November 1912 meeting had somewhat confused the efforts of the COB leaders to organize their own meeting:

The work of the sappers continued to undermine the foundations of our edifice. A meeting in the Monroe Palace, financed by the government, had produced its bad effects, dividing still further the working class. The foundation of a labor party—creation of individuals paid to speak in the name of the workers—was strongly advocated.[70]

TRADE UNION MILITANCY DURING WORLD WAR I

The ranks of organized labor expanded precipitously, and the unionists exhibited a high degree of militancy, during World War I. There were at least two reasons for this. On the one hand, with Brazil to a large degree cut off from its accustomed sources of industrial goods, there was as a consequence rapid expansion of domestic manufacturing, and a consequent increase in the ranks of the wage earning working class. On the other hand, there was substantial inflation during the war, which stimulated the workers' demands for wage increases and other concessions.

Some idea of the rise of the labor movement during the second decade of the century can be gained from the case of Rio de Janeiro. According to José Oiticica, who emerged during this period as one of the principal anarchist leaders, there were only three anarchist-controlled *sindicatos* in the city when he entered the labor movement in 1912, with only 3,000 or 4,000 workers subject to their influence. There were some other *sindicatos*, dominated by politically minded people, but all the organized workers together were neither numerous nor very militant.[71]

However, by 1918, there were, according to Oiticica, 150,000 organized workers in the capital city, of which 30,000 were in textile *sindicatos*.[72]

Santos, the country's principal coffee port, presented another instance of the spread of *sindicatos* during World War I. By the end of the conflict, the organized workers of that city included those in construction, coffee, textiles, beverages, bakeries, and trolley cars, as well as the port workers.[73]

Many new *sindicatos* were organized during the war years, and in other cases, organizations that had become inactive in the earlier period were revived. Thus, for example, the graphic arts workers of São Paulo reorganized their *sindicato* in 1916, with the name of Sindicato Graphico do Brasil, and in 1919 it was once again renamed as União dos Trabalhadores Graphicos. The União was more successful than any of its predecessors. It succeeded in winning collective agreements with several of the leading newspapers and printing establishments, although it lost a strike against the *Estado de São Paulo*. In 1920, the União had some 1,250 members, including typographers, bookbinders, lithographers, and linotypists. It was one of the most important *sindicatos* in the country.[74]

Labor organization spread even to the far northern Amazonian state of Para. In Belem, capital city of that state, a number of *sindicatos* under anarchist leadership were established. One of the more important was the União dos Empregados no Comércio (Commercial Employees Union), organized in April 1919, which gained general enforcement in that city of the regulations making Sunday a day of rest for commercial employees.[75]

Militancy, as well as numerical expansion, characterized the labor movement during World War I. This was particularly the case in the years 1917, 1918, and 1919.

Late in February 1917 there were marches and demonstrations in Rio de Janeiro against the rising cost of living. The police retaliated by closing the headquarters of the Federação Operária. Then on March 1, the workers in the Moreira Mesquita & Cia. furniture factory went on strike for wage adjustments, and a picket line was established outside the plant, whereupon the police arrested four of the strike leaders. On May Day, the workers of the textile plant Fábrica Corcovado stayed off the job to celebrate the workers' holiday, and the strike soon spread to other plants. A mass meeting of the strikers on May 10 was broken up by charges of mounted policemen, and on May 12 the police forbade all outdoor meetings.

Bandeira, Melo, and Andrade noted: "Those strike movements never ended completely and in October they expanded. The causes were always the same: hard working conditions and constant increase in the cost of living."

The situation was complicated when the textile plant Fábrica Aliança declared a lockout, and several other plants followed suit. The Shoemakers Union declared a strike at one large plant, announcing, "The strike has its principal reason the following: the cutters cannot maintain themselves with the amount which is paid them for piecework."

The textile workers' organization, the União dos Operários em Fábricas de Tecidos, declared a boycott of the Aliança firm. Meanwhile, the textile and shoe workers' strikes received widespread support from the other *sindicatos* in Rio de Janeiro and in nearby cities, such as Petrópolis. When the *sindicatos* organized a march to the presidential palace, Catete, to seek an audience with the president of the Republic, the police broke up the demonstration.

Bandeira, Melo, and Andrade noted: "These two strikes only terminated at the end of the month of December, and in spite of the workers' demands being met, the workers lost the leaders of the movement, who were later dismissed, one by one, from their jobs."[76]

However, it was in São Paulo that the most militant strike movement of 1917 took place, as described by Bandeira, Melo and Andrade:

The largest movement, which took on an insurrectional character, occurred in the month of July. The workers of a factory had a sit-down strike. Others joined it in solidarity and, like a chain reaction. São Paulo was totally paralyzed a week later. Commerce closed. Transport stopped. . . . The strike spread to the interior of the State. There were some disturbances in some wards and the workers raised barricades to impede the passage of the police. The population showed its sympathy for the strikes. The women threw soap on the streets to overturn the horses of the police.

The government was helpless in the face of all of this. At one point, the state government left São Paulo, and the "workers took over the city. They only permitted milk and meat to be delivered at the hospitals."

Many years later, Edgard Leuenroth, one of the leaders of the movement, recalled, "The general strike of 1917 was a spontaneous movement of the proletariat, without the interference, direct or indirect, of anyone. It was an explosive manifestation, after a long period of tempestuous living suffered by the workers."

On June 9, the strike became general after a conflict with the police in front of the Mariangela factory during which one worker was killed. There were mass gatherings in front of the home of the dead worker and at his funeral. Some 15,000 workers were estimated as participating in the strike.

The *sindicato* leaders then formed the Comité de Defesa Proletária, which called a meeting in one of the largest sports arenas in the city. At the same time, a Commission of Journalists was formed to try to arrange a meeting of the *sindicato* leaders, the public authorities, and the principal employers. A majority of the city's newspaper supported the strikers.

The Comité de Defesa Proletária drew up a series of demands. These included the freeing of all those jailed because of the strike movement, full respect for the right of assembly, effective application of laws regarding children employed in the city's factories. They demanded: "The public authorities will study immediately all possible means within their competence to check the rise in living costs, using unofficially their authority with representatives of the large retailers so as to assure the consumers a reasonable price for goods of prime necessity;" they further proposed that the government take steps to prevent the adulteration of food products.

An agreement was reached between the governor and the secretaries of justice and agriculture, on the one hand, and the Comité de Defesa Proletária, on the other, concerning the issues that had been raised. However, later, Edgard Leuenroth was arrested on charges connected with the general strike, charges of which a jury completely absolved him.[77]

The strike wave of 1917 was not confined to Rio de Janeiro and São Paulo. The workers of the South Railway struck successfully. In Belem, the trolleycar workers closed down transportation.[78] In Rio Grande do Sul, the railroad workers also walked out, gaining considerable wage increases and other benefits.[79] Bandeira, Melo, and Andrade summed up the situation: "From north to south in the Country, during the months of 1917, the revolt broke out in strikes and demonstrations of the masses."[80]

In the light of the labor militancy of 1917, the reaction of the workers to Brazil's formal entry into World War I on the side of the Allies in October of that year might appear somewhat surprising. The COB in its Second Congress had passed a resolution calling for a revolutionary general strike should Brazil become involved in a foreign war.

However, such an event did not occur. Alfredo Gómez noted: "The expected mobilization did not take place. On the contrary, the internationalist nuclei remained isolated in the face of the patriotic fervor which took control of many workers' sectors and which contributed to weakening the wave of strikes of 1917."[81]

CONTINUING LABOR MILITANCY

Workers' unrest and numerous strikes continued in 1918. Bandeira, Melo, and Andrade noted:

The center of the trade union struggle in 1918 was the eight-hour day. . . . The prefect Paulo de Frontin conceded the eight hours to the workers of the Municipality. The maritime workers obtained it after great struggles in the Loide and Costereira lines. President Venceslau Bras, mediating between shoe industrialists and workers, decided for eight hours and a half. Some owners, to avoid problems with their employees and to win their sympathy, adhered "spontaneously" to the campaign.[82]

Early in the year, the government, taking advantage of the existing state of siege throughout the country, closed all of the Federações Operárias in Brazil. But new organizations soon took their place, such as the União Geral dos Trabalhadores in Rio and the Federação das Classes Trabalhadoras in Recife.[83]

Bandeira, Melo, and Andrade noted:

The method of struggle was, fundamentally, anarchist: direct action. This expression included everything: the strike, the boycott, sabotage, the bomb. It also included the speech, the march, the meeting. The idea of the general strikes was in everyone's head. And the boycott (and sometimes it drove firms into bankruptcy) against the industrialist and the merchant, principally the small ones, produced its results.[84]

But the most spectacular event of the year was the effort of the anarchists and anarchosyndicalists of Rio de Janeiro to organize an insurrection. This took place on November 18, against the background of the influenza epidemic, which had aroused particular working-class unhappiness, because of the widespread feeling that, in dealing with the epidemic, the authorities had concentrated on trying to help middle- and upper-class segments of the population.

A committee had been established to lead the insurrection. Its most important figure was José Oiticica, an anarchist journalist and teacher. It included representatives of major trade union groups in Rio and neighboring cities. The committee also had some contacts within the military, particularly an army second lieutenant, José Elias Anjus, who promised to rally support within the armed forces, but in fact was a government spy within the group.

The plan for the insurrection was that it would begin with a general strike in Rio de Janeiro, Niterói, Petrópolis, and Mage, to begin at 4 p.m. on November 18. The strikers would then attack a key police station in the São Cristovão working-class area and the nearby army supply center, where large quantities of arms were thought to be deposited.

The strike broke out on time, and most of the textile factories in the four cities were affected. There were also metal workers, construction workers, and some other groups who walked out. However, the electric workers and the municipal employees in charge of the water supply did not strike.

Although the workers were able to seize the São Cristovão police station, they were unable to take the army installation. Lieutenant Anjus had informed his superiors of the insurrection plans, and so they had heavily reinforced the army base. The government also quickly moved in substantial army units into the São Cristovão area, and within a few hours the uprising had been totally suppressed.[85]

A few days later, the government closed down the headquarters of the União Geral dos Trabalhadores and the textile, metal, and construction workers' federations in Rio de Janeiro. However, the textile strike that had been part of the insurrection attempt continued for ten days more.[86]

Meanwhile, there had been widespread arrests. Most important were those of José Oiticica, Astrojildo Pereira, João da Costa Pimenta, and Agripino Nazaré, who the government claimed were the leaders of the insurrectionary attempt.[87]

Certain militancy continued in 1919, particularly in the city of São Paulo and its environs, where a second general strike, in May, was, if anything, more widespread than that of 1917. It was reported that in 1919, there were thirty-seven large strikes, of which twenty took place in the city of São Paulo and seventeen in the interior of that state. This was more than all of the walkouts in São Paulo that had occurred between 1915 and 1918.[88]

According to a report on the São Paulo general strike of 1919 in the anarchist newspaper *A Plebe*, "It arose in an unexpected way, with a spontaneity that left everyone surprised. . . . From the third day it was seen that the strike movement would grow and the police would not hesitate in employing their old inquisitorial procedures."[89]

The strikers drew up a series of joint demands, including the eight-hour day and uninterrupted thirty-six–hour weekly rest period, prohibition of work by children of less than fourteen years of age, establishment of a minimum wage, equal pay for men and women, and "complete respect on the part of the public authorities for working class associations." They also demanded "effective reductions" of prices of articles of prime necessity, and immediate reduction of rents.

The writer in *A Plebe* estimated that about 50,000 workers had participated in the strike, which affected not only the center city but also its suburbs. Soon after it began, a General Council of Workers was organized to coordinate the walkout. However, particularly in the face of severe persecution by the police, the Council declared its own dissolution. Apparently the estimate of the success of the walkout was at best inconclusive.[90]

REGIONAL AND INDUSTRIAL LABOR ORGANIZATIONS

Although no effective national central organization of the anarchist-led trade union movement was ever established in Brazil, on the state level there did exist a number of groups that maintained themselves over more or less extended periods. These included the following:

- Federação dos Trabalhadores do Rio de Janeiro, which included *sindicatos* of both the Federal District (city of Rio de Janeiro) and the state of Rio de Janeiro.[91]
- Federação Operária Mineira, with headquarters in Juiz da Fora, the principal industrial center of the state of Minas Gerais.[92]
- Federação Operária Paulista, succeeded sometime before 1930 by the União Geral dos Trabalhadores, which covered *sindicatos* of the state of São Paulo.[93]
- União Geral dos Trabalhadores Cearenses, which reached its peak right after the end of World War I, when a number of

sindicatos were established in the state of Ceará, but declined soon afterward.[94]

- Federação Operária do Rio Grande do Sul, in the southernmost state.[95]
- Federação das Classes Trabalhadoras de Pará, centering on the Amazonian city of Belem.[96]
- União Operária de Paraná, in the state just south of São Paulo and centering on the capital city of Curitiba.[97]
- União Operária Amazonense, with headquarters in Manaus, the capital of the state of Amazonas.[98]
- Federação das Classes Trabalhadoras de Pernambuco, which was for a while divided, with a dissident group calling itself Federação Sindicalista. Unity was restored to the labor movement of Pernambuco during the sessions of the Third Labor Congress of COB in 1920.[99]
- Centro Operário do Estado de Espírito Santo, which later took the more limited title Centro Operário de Vitória (the state capital of Espírito Santo) and was described as "not purely libertarian," but in which the anarchists had considerable influence.[100]

All three national anarchosyndicalist labor congresses urged formation of national industrial labor federations. The first congress called specifically for the establishment of maritime, construction, and factory workers' federations.[101] A few industrial federations were actually organized, including the Federação dos Conductores de Veículos.[102] In the early 1920s, a national textile workers congress was held in Rio, and the Federação Têxtil was launched.[103] However, it is not certain to what extent these organizations were really national in scope, although it is likely that some of them did not extend beyond the borders of Rio de Janeiro or São Paulo.

ANARCHISTS AND SOCIALISTS IN LEADERSHIP OF ORGANIZED LABOR

Until foundation of the Communist Party of Brazil in March 1922 by former anarchosyndicalists who had been won over to Leninism, leadership of the organized labor movement was principally in the hands of libertarians (anarchists and anarchosyndicalists). Socialists played a very secondary role.

From the early 1890s, through their press and their activity in *sindicato* organizing, the anarchists played a major role in bringing into existence the Brazilian labor movement. However, the Brazilian anarchists were much less doctrinaire and sectarian than their counterparts in Argentina and Uruguay. For instance, although the anarchists had a clear majority within the Confederação Operária Brasileira, they never sought, as did the leaders of the Argentine FORA, to commit that organization to the establishment of "anarchist communism."[104]

The United States anarchist periodical *Mother Earth*, edited by Emma Goldman, noted the lack of dogmatism among the Brazilian anarchists:

The vain discussions about Individualism and Communism which are responsible for much waste of time in the movements of other countries have been practically eliminated. The majority of the comrades consider divergent opinions underlying such discussions as questions of individual temperament. Instead of wasting energy in never-ending debates, they employ their time more profitably by carrying on revolutionary propaganda.[105]

Nor was there in Brazil a split in the anarchosyndicalist labor movement between the anarchists and syndicalists, such as occurred in Argentina and Uruguay. There was widespread sympathy in the pre–World War I period with the French syndicalists of the CGT, as was indicated by resolutions of the First and Second National Labor Congresses of the COB.

The Brazilian anarchists, like their confrères in other countries, were militantly antimilitarist. In 1908 and 1916 the COB organized demonstrations against militarism, and in 1915 they organized resistance to compulsory military training. They published an antimilitarist journal, *Não Mataras!* (Thou Shalt Not Kill!).[106]

The anarchosyndicalist labor movement had a very active press. In São Paulo, its principal periodicals were *O Amigo do Povo* (Friend of the People), *A Terra Livre* (The Free Land), *A Vanguarda* (The Vanguard) and *A Plebe* (The Plebeian). In Rio de Janeiro appeared, among others, *A Greve* (The Strike), *Novo Rumo* (New Directions), and *A Voz do Povo* (The Voice of the People), the last of which was the organ of the Federation of Workers of Rio de Janeiro.[107] *O Trabalho* (Work) also was published in Rio as the organ of the construction workers.[108] In Porto Alegre in Rio Grande do Sul appeared *A Luta* (The Struggle); *Nosso Verbo* (Our Message), organ of the Federação Operária of that state; and *A Voz da Estiva* (The Stevedores' Voice), organ of the stevedores' *sindicato*.[109] In the late 1920s, the Labor Federation of Rio Grande do Sul published a periodical called *O Sindicalista*.[110]

These were only a fraction of the anarchosyndicalist press. Many individual *sindicatos* had their own periodicals for a longer or shorter period. There were undoubtedly many periodicals that as a result of economic problems or punitive action by the authorities appeared for only a few issues.

As we have noted, the Brazilian anarchosyndicalists tried to establish and maintain relations with their counterparts elsewhere in Latin America, as well as in Europe. However, the anarchists never succeeded in establishing any effective Latin American or even South American trade union organization, although there was a notice that one Brazilian was a member of the South American Federation of Hat Workers (Federação Sul Americano dos Operários Chapeleiros).[111]

In 1919, the anarchosyndicalist leaders, unaware of the nature of the organization, decided to send a delegation to a meeting in Bern, Switzerland, to reorganize the International Federation of Trade Unions (IFTU), the pre–World War I socialist-controlled group. One Brazilian, Antonio Canellas, after great difficulties with the Brazilian police, finally arrived in Switzerland, but only after the IFTU congress had adjourned.[112]

Throughout the first three decades of the Brazilian labor movement the socialists also had some influence. However, they were very much less influential than the anarchosyndicalists.

The first Socialist Party to be established was the Partido Operário, set up in Rio de Janeiro in 1890. A throwaway with the heading "Partido Operário" and starting off with the salutation "Citizens!," announced its formation. It noted that independent labor political action had been discussed in labor meetings since 1870 but that theretofore the restriction of the franchise had prevented its establishment. Now, with the Republic and nearly universal male suffrage, the time had come to launch a labor party.[113] The party published a newspaper, *O Partido do Operário*, for some time. It elected a deputy, Murcio Paixão, who in August 1892 presented to the Chamber of Deputies a petition demanding the eight-hour day.[114]

The Partido Operário called a national conference, which met in August and September 1892. Later, the party reported to the Zurich Conference of the Socialist International in August 1893:

The States where we have the largest number of affiliates are Ceará, Pará São Paulo and Rio de Janeiro. In Rio Grande do Sul, for which we had high hopes, the movement is paralyzed by the political reaction of the bourgeois parties. Santa Catarina and Paraná are preparing to propagate the idea. In a good number of States the idea already exists, but not the organization.[115]

In 1894 there was another national congress of Socialists. It adopted the resolutions passed at the Zurich conference as its own, particularly the idea of celebrating May Day as the workers' holiday.[116] We have no further information on this first Brazilian Socialist Party.

In 1902, there was established in Rio de Janeiro the Partido Socialista Coletivista, headed by Dr. Vicente de Souza and Gustavo de Lacerda. Lacerda later took an active part in the antianarchist labor congress of 1912. The leaders of the party campaigned against anarchist direct action and particularly against strikes, saying that they actually cost more than the workers gained from them. They advocated a general program of social reforms.[117]

Immigrants played a major role in the early socialist organizations. There existed in São Paulo Allgemeiner Arbeiterverein (General Association of Workers) among German immigrants. There were also Italian socialist groups. These all collaborated in calling what is generally referred to as the Second Socialist Congress, which met in 1902, and had forty-four delegates from seven states. São Paulo, Rio Grande do Sul, Paraná, Bahia, Pernambuco, Paraíba, and Pará. It proclaimed the establishment of the Socialist Party of Brazil.[118]

This Second Socialist Congress adopted a program that, among other things, called for imposition of a progressive income tax and inheritance taxes; abolition of indirect taxes, particularly consumption taxes and tariffs; the eight-hour day for adults and six hours for minors between ages fourteen and eighteen; a prohibition of work by children of less than fourteen; a continuous thirty-six-hour compulsory rest period each week; workers' compensation; and recognition of Brazilian citizenship for all immigrants with one-year residence in Brazil. It also demanded "effective" separation of church and state, a divorce law, abolition of the standing army, a social security system, and recognition of the right to strike with the state remaining neutral in labor disputes.[119]

The existence of this Socialist Party was "ephemeral." It apparently never named candidates in elections. The only lasting result of the congress was the newspaper *Avanti!*, published in São Paulo for many years in Italian.[120]

Leôncio Rodrigues noted, "After 1902, other Socialist 'parties' were founded, all of short duration, disappearing without leaving any profound evidence of their existence."[121]

During and right after World War I, several socialist parties were established in various parts of the republic. Thus, on May 1917 a group of intellectuals and students, headed by Nestor Peixoto de Oliveira, founded a new Partido Socialista do Brasil. "Its orientation was clearly social-democratic, perhaps most influenced by the line of Jean Jaurès." It proclaimed that it was "not

Maximalist" (Bolshevik). It published a periodical, *Folha Nova* (New Sheet), the name of which was subsequently changed to *Tempos Novos* (New Times), which appeared every two weeks. The party ran Evaristo de Morais as candidate for deputy in the 1918 federal election, but he was not elected. The party was unsuccessful in obtaining affiliation with the revived Socialist International and apparently expired after about two years.

There was also a Socialist Party in São Paulo in this period. Likewise, in August 1920 there was founded in Salvador the Partido Socialista Baiano, some of whose leaders were construction workers, shoemakers, and metal workers. It was founded in the headquarters of the Furniture Workers Union. It named candidates for congress in 1920, although there is no indication as to whether its nominees were successful.[122]

In Ceará there was formed in 1918, the Partido Socialista Cearense, which met with considerable initial success. This party had considerable influence in the local labor movement, and took the leadership in a number of strikes against the high cost of living. It also strongly supported a walkout of cigarmakers that at first gained those workers the eight-hour day, but as a result of a fight between the leaders of the party and those of the *sindicato*, these gains were lost, and the cigarmakers were alienated from the party. Other Socialist-led strikes included those of needle trades workers, who gained the eight-hour day, and metal workers, who lost their walkout. Internal quarrels within the Partido Socialista Cearense resulted in its demise.[123]

Finally, in the State of Rio de Janeiro there existed for a number of years the Partido Socialista of the city of Campos, led by Saturnino Brito. It put out a paper, *Amigo do Povo* (The People's Friend); published a number of pamphlets; and continued in existence during much of the 1920s.[124]

Dr. A. Piccarolo, an Italian Socialist who participated in several of the ephemeral Brazilian Socialist parties, said of them:

The various attempts at socialist organization in Brazil always failed. The Centro Socialista Paulistano . . . died a physiological death, as a doctor would say. After that, every period had its attempts. Little groups, usually foreigners, often moved by nostalgia for the past, would meet, discuss, draw up projects, plans for the future and these groups would be called Socialist Circles, Groups or Centers. The action of these groups was not felt outside their own circle, and after a while all activity ceased until some new group came along. The whole development was much like the concentric circles produced by a stone falling in a lake. Individuals coming from Europe, especially Italy, brought with them the socialist ideals and convictions, founded a Brazilian Socialist Party. . . . These people were almost all foreigners, socialists before coming to Brazil.[125]

IMPACT OF THE RUSSIAN REVOLUTION ON BRAZILIAN LABOR MOVEMENT

The Bolshevik Revolution in Russia was greeted with very wide support by the leaders and rank and file of the dominant elements in the Brazilian labor movement. Bandeira, Melo, and Andrade reported of the May Day demonstrations of 1918 that they "differed from those of previous years. The workers commemorated the triumph of their brothers in Russia. They converted the day of protest into a fiesta of solidarity and fraternization with the first proletarian Republic."[126]

The anarchists were, in the beginning, particularly attracted to the Bolshevik regime, as was the case with their counterparts in Spain and various other countries. Astrojildo Pereira, the principal founder of the Brazilian Communist Party, wrote many years later, "The anarcho-syndicalist periodicals favorable to the Bolshevik revolution—and all were until at least 1920—published in their columns articles and authentic documents about the revolution, collected from the working class press of Europe and America."[127]

Thus, *A Plebe* carried an appeal by Maria Gorki in favor of the Russian Revolution in its February 22, 1919, issue. The same issue carried the reprint of a letter to a Rio paper from one "Kessler," who described himself as "Delegate of the Socialist Republic of the Russian Soviets to the Workers of the Bourgeois Republic of the United States of Brazil," consisting of a long defense of the Russian regime. Announcements of the contents of future issues indicated that they would include among others, an article by Lenin on the Treaty of Brest-Litovsk; an article by the Argentine Socialist José Ingenieros, "The Historical Significance of Maximalism" (which was then a favorite name for Bolshevism); the "The Figure of Carl Liebknecht;" and another letter by "Kessler." A good part of the paper was taken up with praise, outspoken or implied, of the Russian Revolution.[128]

Some of the anarchosyndicalist *sindicatos* dramatized their support of the Bolshevik regime. Thus, the União dos Metalúrgicos do Rio de Janeiro proclaimed a general strike in 1919 "against imperialist intervention and in solidarity with the Workers and Peasants Republic."[129]

There was obviously considerable confusion and lack of real information about the new Soviet regime in the ranks of the Brazilian anarchosyndicalists. Astrojildo Pereira, the founder of the Communist Party, wrote:

What was not known for sure was that the Communists who were leading the Russian Revolution were Marxists and not anarchists. Only later were these differences clarified, producing then a rupture between the anarchists labeled "pure" or "intransigent," who began to criticize and have reservations about the Russian Communists, coming finally to struggle openly against the Soviet State, and the anarchists who remained loyal to the working class, who came finally to understand that in Marxism is to be found the correct theoretical definition of the ideology of the proletariat.[130]

Meanwhile, a group of anarchosyndicalist leaders, at a meeting in Rio de Janeiro on March 9, 1919, established what they called the Partido Comunista do Brasil (PCB). Three months later the libertarian leaders in São Paulo established what they also called the Partido Comunista.[131]

The PCB established in Rio drew up a "basic accord" as the ground rules of the organization. It proclaimed the "immediate objectives" of the party: "To promote the propaganda of Libertarian Communism, as well as to organize Communist nuclei throughout the country."[132]

Astrojildo Pereira noted that this PCB organized several commemorative meetings in the headquarters of various *sindicatos* in Rio. These included the anniversary of the Paris Commune, the anniversary of the abolition of slavery in Brazil, and the 14th of July, the day of the fall of the Bastille.[133]

Edgard Leuenroth, one of the anarchosyndicalist leaders who remained loyal to libertarian principles, wrote of this Communist Party:

It had no political objectives, in spite of being called a party, which characterizes political organizations carrying on electoral activities. Being an organization of the moment, without the discipline of Bolshevism, and without the objective of being the organic expression of anarchism in Brazil, it ceased its activity as the motives that had given it origin were disappearing.[134]

THE ANARCHIST-COMMUNIST SPLIT

As we have noted, the Brazilian anarchosyndicalists greeted the Bolshevik Revolution with great enthusiasm. In 1919, Hélio Negro and Edgard Leuenroth, two of the country's leading anarchist labor leaders, wrote, "The present regime in Russia is an organization of defense and reconstruction, the road to libertarian communism, which will bring peace, well-being and liberty to all." Their book then went on outline in some detail a possible libertarian communist regime for Brazil—decentralized government based on the trade unions, abolition of jails, parliaments, and judges, and so on.[135]

As late as August 1920, the organ of the COB proclaimed:

We defend with the greatest energy, without fear of persecution and violence, the Russian Revolution. We see in the Muscovite movement an insurrection of markedly social character, which has innumerable points of contact with us, being the first revolution that had the courage to inscribe on its banner of the land and the instruments of work to the wage earners.[136]

However, as time passed, most Brazilian anarchists became convinced, as did their fellows in most other countries, that the Bolshevik Revolution was not headed down an anarchist road. By early 1922, a group of leading anarchists published a statement in *A Plebe* that, although beginning "As the revolutionary anarchist communists that we are we feel leagued by our sympathy and solidarity to the Russian revolutionary movement," went on to note the existence in Russia of a Bolshevik dictatorship.

The statement continued:

Supported in this so-called proletarian dictatorship, Bolshevism maintains its state as its administrative machine and continues its centralist policy, imposing its orders upon the masses in an authoritarian way, and preventing by force the Federalist libertarian tendencies of the revolution, destroying the proletarian individuals, groups and organizations. . . . In appreciation of what is passing in Russia, we shall always point this contradiction in principles, exercising our criticisms, however severe, with the necessary serenity, to always point out that our doctrinary divergences should in no way be confused with the campaign of defamation by the international bourgeoisie, whose objective is to demoralize the revolution.

This statement was signed by Edgard Leuenroth, Rodolpho Felipe, Antonio Domingues, Ricardo Cipolla, Antonio Cordon Filho, Emilio Martines, João Pérez, José Rodrigues, and João Penteado.[137]

As Paulo Sérgio Pinheiro and Michael Hall noted, the statement "was quite moderate in its criticisms; the tone of the debate soon became much more virulent."[138]

In the meantime, a small group of the anarchosyndicalist leaders had become converts to Bolshevism. Leoncio Basbaum attributed this, in part at least, to the fact that by 1921 the distribution in Brazil of French and Spanish translations of some of the works of Lenin, as well as those of Marx and Engels, had become rather widespread. He commented, "Thus were established the theoretical bases for the formation of the Communist Party of Brazil."

Small Communist groups were established in various Brazilian cities. The oldest of these was the União Maximalista, established in Pôrto Alegre in Rio Grande do Sul in 1918 by Abilio de Negrete, who had made contact with Communist groups in Montevideo and Buenos Aires.[139] In 1921, it changed its name to Grupo Comunista de Pôrto Alegre.[140]

On November 7, 1921 a Grupo Comunista was also established in Rio de Janeiro. It began to publish a monthly, *Movimento Comunista*, which in its first issue, of January 1922, stated:

With reference to party organization, we desire and propose the *sindicato*, solidly based on the same ideological, strategic and tactical program, of the most conscious elements of the proletariat. Our own experiences and those of others counsel unity and concentration of efforts and energies, to coordinate, systematize, make more methodical, the propaganda, the organization and the action of the proletariat.[141]

The founding congress of the Partido Comunista do Brasil took place in Rio de Janeiro and Niterói March 25–27, 1922. Nine people participated in this meeting: Abilio de Nequete, a barber; the journalist Astrojildo Pereira; Cristiano Cordeiro, a public employee; Hermogenio Silva, an electrician; João da Costa Pimenta, a printer; Joaquim Barbosa, a tailor; José Elias da Silva, a government employee; Luis Peres, a street cleaner; and Manuel Cendón, a tailor.

These nine men represented directly groups in Pôrto Alegre, Recife, São Paulo, Cruzeiro, Niterói, and Rio de Janeiro. Abilio Nequete also had credentials from the South American Bureau of the Communist International and the Uruguayan Communist Party.[142] All of these people except Manuel Cendón, a Spaniard, who was a Marxist of long standing, had been anarchosyndicalists.[143] These delegates represented a total party membership at its foundation of seventy-three.[144]

Clearly, the principal leader in the formation of the Communist Party was Astrojildo Pereira, who became its secretary general and served until 1929.[145] He had emerged during and right after World War I as one of the principal anarchosyndicalist leaders. He was one of the principal contributors to the anarchist periodical *A Plebe* and had been one of those arrested after the anarchist insurrection attempt in November 1918.

Pereira became increasingly frustrated with the inability of the anarchosyndicalists to establish and maintain a central labor organization to give leadership to the trade union movement. We have noted that in May 1921, he had suggested to a meeting of anarchosyndicalist leaders that they seek to restructure the COB on the model of the IWW of the United States. However, he quickly moved entirely away from anarchism and anarchosyndicalism and took the lead in establishing a Marxist-Leninist party on the model of the Russian Bolsheviks.

Several other original members of the Communist Party were to play major roles in the labor movement, the Party, or both, for several decades. One of these was Roberto Morena, who had been one of the younger anarchosyndicalist labor leaders in Rio de Janeiro, was one of the founding members of the Communist Party in the Rio de Janeiro area, and remained with the Party for the rest of his life, becoming one of its most important trade union leaders. He joined the International Brigades during the Spanish Civil War, and after the fall of the dictatorship of Getúlio Vargas in 1945, he emerged as the single most important trade union figure in the Communist Party.[146]

Octavio Brandão was also one of the younger anarchosyndicalist leaders in the post–World War I period. He early showed his pro-Soviet sympathies when he wrote in *A Plebe*, "I believe that the only program of the journal should be this: The intense propaganda of bolshevism, for the glorification of Russia of the Soviets."[147] In the late 1920s, he went to Moscow, where he became one of the most important leaders of the Latin American section of the Comintern.

On the other hand, Antonio Canellas, who also joined the Communist Party at its inception, and was its delegate to the 1922 Congress of the Comintern, on returning from Moscow resigned from the party, of whose Central Committee he was at the time a member.[148]

With the formation of the Communist Party, a bitter struggle broke out in the labor movement between the party members and their anarchist former comrades and continued for the rest of the 1920s.

Alfredo Gómez noted some of the anarchist-Communist clashes. An attempt by the anarchists to establish a Federation of Workers of the Central Region was broken up by the Communists, with the result that two rival groups emerged. In 1927 there was a violent clash in the Graphic Arts Workers Union of Rio de Janeiro, in which two workers were killed. In April 1929, a strike called by the anarchists' construction workers' *sindicato* of Rio de Janeiro was sabotaged by the Communists, who published in to newspapers calls for the workers not to go on strike.[149]

ORGANIZED LABOR IN THE 1920s

The early 1920s was marked by a general decline from the high point of labor activity that had been reached during and immediately after the First World War. Characteristic of the situation was the necessity in 1922 to constitute a Comité de Reorganização da Classe Trabalhadora in São Paulo. The princi-

pal *sindicatos* in São Paulo at the time were the União dos Trabalhadores em Calzados (shoemakers), União dos Trabalhadores
Graphicos, A Internacional, União dos Empregados em Cafes (cafe
and restaurant workers), União dos Operários em Construção Civil
(construction workers), and União dos Metalúrgicos, which took
the lead in forming the Reorganization Committee.[150] *Sindicatos* also
existed among hat makers, textile workers, bakers, and commercial
employees.[151]

A few *sindicatos* were formed in this period, such as the Syn-
dicato de Resistência de Pintores (painters), the formation of
which brought forth the comment, "This profession, always the
most combative, has decided to organize itself."[152] There was a
widely observed May Day demonstration in 1922, sponsored by
the most important *sindicatos* in São Paulo.[153]

One Communist source noted that there was a decline in *sindicato* strength from about 1920 until 1923, when there began a
new upsurge of *sindicato* activity, with the organization campaigns
of the construction workers, commercial employees, printing trades
workers, bakers, coffee workers, and employees of the railway.[154]

The Confederação Operária Brasileira, which still maintained
a precarious existence, was credited in 1924 with having only
seventeen *sindicato* groups affiliated with it, including some transport
workers, shoemakers, quarrymen, building trades workers, printers, lithographers, and weavers.[155] In a report submitted to the
Second Congress of the anarchosyndicalist International Workingmen's Association in 1925, the Federação Operária do Rio Grande
do Sul reported that it had 2,380 members, and that its member
sindicatos included organizations of bakers, shoemakers, restaurant employees, miners, agricultural workers, and small peasants, as
well as local labor leagues and groups among German immigrants.[156] In 1927, the COB informed the International Workingmen's
Association that it had but 4,000 members.[157] The Communists
claimed that by 1925 the COB existed "only on paper."[158]

The anarchist segment of the labor movement was particularly subject to persecution by the Brazilian government. Alfredo
Gómez noted:

The libertarian organizations suffered severe blows at the time of the
failed military uprisings of July 1924 in Rio and São Paulo. Under the
state of siege, which was extended until 1926, the arrests, deportations,
searches and closing of workers headquarters multiplied. *A Plebe*, closed
by the regime of President Bernardes, did not reappear until 1927. Hundreds of prisoners were taken to concentration camps situated on
inhospitable islands and territories. The agricultural colony of Clevelandia in the region on the border of French Guiana received between 1924

and 1925 about one thousand prisoners, of whom, as a consequence of bad treatment and unhealthy conditions, about one-third died.[159]

A U.S. observer wrote in 1925:

Organization of labor unions in Brazil has been very naturally limited to the larger cities such as Rio de Janeiro, São Paulo, Pernambuco, Bahia and Santos. At the city of Santos, the world's largest coffee port, every group of workers has its own association or guild to which the members pay fees, receiving in return medical attention, part pay during illness, and other benefits. In certain of these organizations the directorate has the power to call the members out on strike, usually after a favorable vote by a majority of the members, in order to force an increase in wages or to secure some other reform. Strikes have been called by the dock company laborers, by the teamsters, by the independent stevedores, by laborers in building operations, by certain groups of laborers on the São Paulo Railway, and by others. While the associations of workers in Santos have been more active, perhaps, than those elsewhere in the country, they are not actually strong labor unions, and so far as is known, are not united into any strong federation.[160]

Michael Conniff noted, with special reference to Rio de Janeiro, "Repression is well documented for the years 1920–24, a time when strikes were brutally put down and *sindicatos* infiltrated by police. Since all but wildcat strikes were impossible, workers' organization concentrated on building monetary reserves and member loyalty. The 1920s were not a time of *sindicato* expansion, then, but of consolidation." However, he did note establishment of a few new *sindicatos*, among skilled workers "who could afford the luxury of paying dues."[161]

A late 1928 report to the Communist periodical *El Trabajador Latino Americano*, published in Montevideo, gave an overall view of the state of the Brazilian labor movement at that time. It noted that in Rio de Janeiro, after a period of "ferocious capitalist reaction" in 1920–21, the labor movement had substantially recovered. It noted that the principal *sindicatos* in that city were those of maritime workers, printing trades, metal workers, construction workers, restaurant and hotel employees, shoemakers, textile workers, bakers, marble workers, tailors, employees of soft drink plants, stone workers, barbers, and municipal employees. The report estimated that there were about 40,000 *sindicato* members in all, not including the commercial employees, who had an additional 10,000 members.

This report noted that *sindicato* organization in the state of São Paulo was "relatively weaker." In the city of São Paulo there were *sindicatos* of the printing trades, shoemakers, hotel and restaurant employees, drivers, and commercial employees, with a total of more than 10,000. In Santos there were an estimated 5,000 organized workers, whereas in other cities of the state there "exist mixed leagues of workers" with about 5,000 workers in all.

There were, according to this report "various *sindicatos*" in Pôrto Alegre, Pelotas, Rio Grande, and other urban centers of Rio Grande do Sul, with approximately 5,000 members. Likewise, in Pernambuco there were about 5,000 *sindicato* members, principally in Recife, where the largest organization was that of port workers.

There were about 10,000 workers in other states, particularly Minas Gerais, Bahia, Rio Grande do Norte, Amazonas and Santa Catarina: *sindicatos* of port workers, transport employees, textile workers, printers, and mixed *sindicatos*. The report added, "Aside from these, in the small cities of the interior there are frequently encountered Mixed League of Workers, without a clearly trade union character, but which in any case organize and unify the workers for defense of their common interests, and which bring together another 10,000 workers."

In all, this report concluded, there were about 100,000 organized workers of all kinds in Brazil in 1928.[162]

The *American Labor Yearbook* of 1929 reported approximately the same number of organized workers, although its breakdown of the labor movement was considerably different from that of the Communists. It said that there were 116,600 workers in Brazilian trade unions, of whom 14,000 were classed as "bona fide unionists," 98,000 were listed as "neutral or state controlled," 3,500 were Communist-controlled, and 3,000 were anarchosyndicalists.[163] It seems possible that the majority of the 96,000 "neutral or state controlled" workers were members of mutual benefit societies, rather than of trade unions. Dr. Moisés Poblete Troncoso, writing in 1929, listed most of the important labor organizations in Brazil as mutual benefit societies, citing only a small number of *sindicatos*.[164]

Michael Conniff said that, at least insofar as the *sindicatos* of Rio de Janeiro in the 1920s were concerned, a major function was

promotion of brotherhood and solidarity among workers. Most unions met frequently and created a sense of participation and belonging for members. Virtually every group purchased its own building during the 1920s as a symbol of stability and union hall loyalty. Meetings generally were held between 7 p.m. and 9 p.m. on weekdays, and the minutes of many were summarized in the press. Most big dailies carried a section for labor news, and on special dates, such as general assemblies and anniversaries, they often ran articles of up to five columns, with historical background on the group, Labor Day (May 1) celebrations receiving extra attention in most papers. Such coverage probably sold newspapers, but it also contributed to the identity of the workers as union member and citizen.[165]

Conniff also argued that

unions' participation also promoted a broader vision of working class problems. Many groups, for example, published or contributed to labor newspapers and magazines. Larger unions occasionally sent observers to national and international labor conferences, such as those of the ILO. By maintaining formal and informal ties with sister unions and confederations elsewhere, unions helped create labor cosmopolitanism.[166]

ANARCHIST-COMMUNIST CONFLICTS IN ORGANIZED LABOR

The 1920s was marked by bitter conflicts between the anarchists and Communists for control of the labor movement. One of the earliest clashes took place late in 1923 in the Federação dos Trabalhadores do Rio de Janeiro, which until then had been under anarchist leadership. When the Communists proved to have a majority in that conference, the anarchist-controlled *sindicatos* withdrew to form their own federation.[167]

The anarchist construction workers' leader Adolfo Marques da Costa commented of that split in the Rio labor movement that the new anarchist-controlled group, the Federação Operária do Rio de Janeiro,

is today categorical affirmation of the revolutionary spirit—and of characteristically libertarian tendency—of the workers of Brazil. The divisionist campaign of the false Communists achieved nothing. The decisive attitude of the União dos Operários em Construcão Civil, courageously seconded by the Aliança dos Operários em Calçado, União Geral dos Trabalhadores em Hotéis, Restaurantes e Similares, União Geral dos Metalúrgicos and other *sindicatos* was the deatblow of the centralizing and dictatorial pretensions of the *Moscowized*.[168]

Through much of the decade, the Communists worked to establish their own national central labor organization. A congress of Communist-led *sindicatos* of the Federal District and the state of Rio was held in April 1927. The congress claimed to include representatives of thirty-six *sindicatos*, twenty-three factory committees not belonging to *sindicatos*, and three "revolutionary minorities" from anti-Communist *sindicatos*. It was claimed that the meeting represented 80,000 workers, certainly a gross exaggeration. At that time, the Communists also claimed to have a trade union following in Recife, São Paulo, Santos, and Pôrto Alegre, as well as those in Rio de Janeiro.[169] The meeting in Rio "laid the basis for a provisional committee of organization of the CGT."[170]

In April 1929, the Committee for a Confederação Geral do Trabalho Brasileiro (CGTB) sponsored a congress that finally established the CGTB. It was attended by representatives of *sindicatos* in the principal states, and claimed that some 60,000 workers were represented. This conference named a delegation of five people to attend the founding congress of the Confederación Sindical Latino Americana (CSLA), the Communist-controlled central labor organization for Latin America, which met in Montevideo in the same year. The Communists by 1929 had organized minority groups in the anarchist-controlled state labor federations in São Paulo, Rio Grande do Sul, and Pernambuco, as well as the *sindicatos* that formed the CGTB.[171]

Leoncio Basbaum claimed, "In 1929 the great majority of the workers' *sindicatos* were led by Communists or sympathizers with Communism."[172]

GOVERNMENT HOSTILITY TO ORGANIZED LABOR BEFORE 1930

The attitude toward organized labor of the Brazilian government and the government of the states was generally one of hostility in the four decades before the Revolution of 1930. We have earlier noted the passage in the early 1890s of a penal code that, for practical purposes, outlawed strikes. In subsequent decades, the government used a great variety of measures not only to curb strikes but also to cripple the labor movement in general.

This attitude of hostility toward organized labor existed in spite of the fact that in 1907 Law 1637 was passed; its Article 2 proclaimed, "Professional *sindicatos* may be freely formed, without authorization of the Government, it being sufficient for them in order to obtain the favors of the law that they be listed in the mortgage registry of their respective districts." This curious means of recording the *sindicatos*' existence reflected the fact that there did not exist a Ministry of Labor or any other similar government institution.

Article 8 of this same law provided:

The *sindicatos* that are constituted with the spirit of harmony between employers and workers, as are those lined by permanent councils of arbitration, destined to settle the divergences and arguments between capital and labor, will be considered to be legal representatives of the whole class of men of work and, as such, can be consulted in all matters of the profession.

The word *profession* in this context is best translated as "craft" or "trade."[173]

It is doubtful that any of the anarchist-controlled *sindicatos*, which strongly opposed government in principle, sought registration under this law. In any case, the law did not in fact reflect the attitude of the governments of the early twentieth century toward organized labor.

Michael M. Hall and Paulo Sérgio Pinheiro have noted the observation of José Maria dos Santos, whom they categorize as "a conservative Brazilian observer," concerning

the habits of grossness and unlimited brutality which particularly characterize our police in their relations with the Poor. Police imprisonment, without legal charges, for an indeterminate period, made worse by the application of physical abuses, became the usual means of instilling good conduct. . . . The process of purging the proletarian milieu by deportations to distant localities was permitted as normal, even when there had been no disturbance of public order.[174]

Hall and Pinheiro went on to note:

Repression directed specifically against the labor movement, rather than toward the working class generally, also reached notable levels of brutality. The Brazilian case admittedly was not the most murderous in Latin America. . . . Nevertheless, the intensity of repression in Brazil could be very great indeed. While trade unions, for example, were not illegal, in practice their existence remained highly precarious. The *Voz do Trabalho* had noted in 1909: "This is already the third time in São Paulo that the *civilista* police have assaulted the headquarters of the Workers' Federation and stolen its books and furniture. . . . The bourgeoisie has firmly decided to kill the movement of proletarian emancipation, and in order to do so employ all manner of violence."[175]

Hall and Pinheiro said:

The regime repressed even more consistently than it sought to crush the organizations of the working class. Brazilian strikes often proved particularly violent, although as a foreign police agent observed, "one must admit that provocative action, with some exceptions, comes more from the police than from the workers." The arrest and beating of those on strike took place with considerable frequency; there are various accounts of the police going from door to door in working class districts and arresting anyone who did not return to work. Owners routinely fired strikers when the labor market permitted, as it almost always did.[176]

If anything, government repression of the labor movement was worse in the 1920s than it had been before. Hall and Pinheiro noted:

Despite the various efforts after 1917 to develop new forms of control, the major thrust of bourgeois policy was toward improving the effectiveness of repression . . . the major legal changes of the 1920s occurred not in the area of social legislation, but in that of repression. The state found it expedient to bring the law into closer accord with practice. A decree of January 1921 for the "Repression of Anarchism" authorized the closing of associations, unions and societies when they bring on "acts harmful to the public good" and provided for the arrest of their officers. To provoke crimes aimed at "subverting the existing social organization" by the written or spoken word carried a penalty of one to four years of imprisonment.[177]

Another law passed in this period made it legal for the government to deport any labor leader who happened to be an alien.[178] Previous to the passage of this law there had been instances in which legal deportation proceedings against labor leaders had been instituted, but there had been only a few cases of actual expulsion. Perhaps the most famous of these cases occurred in 1909, when the Italian anarchist Eduardo Rossoni had been sent back to his native land because of his activities in organizing in Rio a "free school" patterned after that of Francisco Ferrer in Barcelona.[179]

In the years following passage of the 1922 law a number of prominent anarchist and trade union leaders were expelled from Brazil. The most famous was Rodolfo Marques da Costa, who was returned to Portugal in 1924.[180] The leader of the shoe workers *sindicato* of São Paulo, Antonio Rodrigues, was expelled from the country in 1923, although he had lived in Brazil for twenty years.[181]

Internal exile was frequently resorted to by the government. Hall and Pinheiro noted:

The government of Artur Bernardes (1922–1926) became particularly notorious for the summary deportations it carried out of militants and others. To be sent to Clevelandia, the major detention camp located in a remote part of Amazonia, represented something close to a death sentence. A report sent to Bernardes noted that in 1925, 946 prisoners had been deported to Clevelandia and 444 had died. . . . During the Bernardes government, police vigilance of the labor movement remained quite intense. The president of the Republic even detailed daily reports on the activities of the working-class organizations of Rio de Janeiro. The police also attempted to undermine their operations during the 1920s. By 1928, the Secretary of Justice and Public Security in São Paulo reported that the "Division of Political and Social Order" had managed to identify and register 102,654 of the estimated 300,000 workers in the state.[182]

It was during this period that Washington Luiz, a prominent conservative politician and later president of the Republic, is reported to have said, in discoursing on his political program, "The Social question is a Police problem."[183]

Late in 1928 and in the early months of 1929 there was, at least in Rio de Janeiro, an upsurge of labor militancy. Michael Conniff noted a month-long strike in the shipyards of the capital in September 1928, as well as walkouts in a shoe store and textile factory. In December, the workers of the large Brahma Brewery struck. Early in 1929 there were walkouts of the Union of Textile Factory Workers, "which reached a settlement." Finally in April 1929 there was a month-long walkout of the Bakery Workers Union, as well as one of the construction workers, both of which were the more or less successful.[184]

However, Conniff noted:

After mid–1929 no more strikes occurred, but both labor and business turned their attention to the presidential election of March 1930. The two paramount issues from their points of view were a labor code and an end to coffee price support programs which drained off credit; from early in the campaign both candidates agreed to these positions. A hiatus in industrial strife ensued, therefore, as associations threw themselves into politics to an unprecedented degree.[185]

SUMMARY OF THE PRE-1930 LABOR MOVEMENT

Leôncio Rodrigues has very well summarized the situation of the organized labor movement of Brazil in the decades before the 1930 Revolution: It was characterized by

asymmetry and lack of organizational uniformity. Along with dual unionism, it adopted in various places and economic sectors the type of association that was most convenient: union of various trades, craft unions, and associations grouping all the workers of a given industrial sector. These associations, when it came to forming organizations on a higher level, such as federations and central labor organization, affiliated to them directly.[186]

Rodrigues went on:

In the economic sectors in which the process of capitalist production was most advanced, as in the establishment of large factories, there began to appear organization by industry, that is, grouping all the workers in an industrial sector, independently of their specific skills. The point of reference was not the craft, but the firm. In addition to the railroad workers, those in textile chose early on this type of unionism.[187]

Rodrigues also noted the basic weakness of the labor movement in this period:

In Brazil . . . within a traditional and agricultural society, scarcely industrialized, the proletariat, constituting a very weak and heterogeneous social group, did not succeed in structuring a solid social movement, capable of carrying out an important role in the formation of the industrial society. The influence of the *sindicatos* in terms of organizations to protect the labor force and obtain a less unequal distribution of national income was very small.[188]

NOTES

1. Moniz Bandeira, Clovis Melo, and A. T. Andrade, *O Ano Vermelho: A Revolução Russa e Seus Reflexos no Brasil*, Editora Civilização Brasileira, Rio de Janeiro, 1967, pages 6–7.

2. Ibid., page 9.

3. General Abreu e Lima, *Socialismo*, Typographia Universal, Recife, 1955.

4. *Le Mouvement Socialiste*, Paris, October 15, 1899.

5. Bandeira, Melo, and Andrade, op. cit., page 9.

6. Ibid., page 10.

7. Alfredo Gómez, *Anarquismo y anarcosindicalismo en América Latina: Colombia, Brasil, Argentina, Mexico*, Ruedo Ibérico, Madrid, 1980, page 117.

8. Ibid., page 118.

9. Bandeira, Melo, and Andrade, op. cit., page 12.

10. *Le Mouvement Socialiste*, October 15, 1899.

11. Stephen Naft, "Labor Movements in South America," unpublished manuscript.

12. Bandeira, Melo, and Andrade, op. cit., page 12.

13. Gómez, op. cit., page 118.

14. Paulo Sérgio Pinheiro and Michael M. Hall, *A Classe Operária no Brasil 1889–1930: Documentos*, Vol. 1—*O Movimento Operário*, Editoria Alfa Omega, São Paulo, 1979, page 152.

15. *O Trabalhador Graphico*, organ of Sindicato dos Trabalhadores Graphicos, São Paulo, May–June 1936.

16. Interview with Paulino Humberto De Fazio, ex-president of Sindicato dos Trabalhadores nas Indústrias Gráficas de São Paulo, in São Paulo, August 22, 1946.

17. Bandeira, Melo, and Andrade, op. cit., page 14.

18. Eugene Ridings, *Business Interest Groups in Nineteenth-Century Brazil*, Cambridge University Press, New York, 1994, page 274–275.

19. Gómez, op. cit., pages 119–120.

20. Unpublished manuscript on Brazilian labor by Mrs. Barbara Hadley Stein.

21. Gustavo de Lacerda, *O Problema Operário no Brasil (Propaganda Socialista)*, Rio de Janeiro, June 1901.

22. Michael Hall and Paulo Sérgio Pinheiro, "The Control and Policing of the Working Class in Brazil, A Paper for the Conference on the History

of Law, Labour and Crime, University of Warwick, 15–18 September 1983."

23. Bandeira, Melo, and Andrade, op. cit., page 15.

24. R. Teixeira Mendes. *A Ordem sociale e o comunismo anarchista*, Rio de Janeiro, 1893.

25. Moisés Poblete Troncoso, *El Movimiento Obrero Latinoamericano*, Fondo de Cultura Económica, Mexico, 1946, page 107.

26. Interview with Nelson Motta, president of Sindicato dos Empregados do Comércio of Rio de Janeiro, in Rio de Janeiro, August 14, 1946.

27. Pinheiro and Hall, 1979, op. cit., pages 44–46.

28. *La Correspondencia Sudamericana*, publication of South American Secretariat of Communist International, Buenos Aires, November 30, 1926.

29. Pinheiro and Hall, 1979, op. cit., page 207.

30. *La Correspondencia Sudamericana*, November 30, 1926.

31. *El Libertario*, publication of anarchist group "Centro Internacional," Montevideo, Uruguay, March 5, 1905.

32. Teresa Meade, " 'Civilizing' Rio de Janeiro: The Yellow Fever Campaign, 1889–1904" (manuscript), page 2.

33. Ibid., page 39.

34. Ibid., page 40.

35. Ibid., page 43.

36. Ibid., page 44.

37. Ibid., pages 50–51.

38. Ibid., page 52.

39. Pinheiro and Hall, 1979, op. cit., page 207.

40. *Mother Earth*, anarchist magazine published by Emma Goldman, New York City, July 1907.

41. Ibid.

42. Pinheiro and Hall, 1979, op. cit., pages 64–66.

43. Ibid., pages 69–70.

44. Ibid., page 71.

45. Ibid., page 114.

46. Ibid., pages 115–116.

47. Leôncio Rodrigues, *Conflito Industrial e Sindicalismo no Brasil*, Difusão Européia do Livro, São Paulo, 1966, pages 127–128.

48. *Diário da Noite*, Rio de Janeiro, April 6, 1945.

49. *Jornal de São Paulo*, April 28, 1945.

50. Gómez, op. cit., page 119.

51. Pinheiro and Hall, 1979, op. cit., page 42; see also Gómez, op. cit., pages 120–121.

52. Ibid., pages 41–58.

53. Ibid., page 41.

54. Ibid., pages 208–209.

55. Ibid., page 209.

56. Ibid., page 210.

57. Ibid., pages 192–193.

58. Ibid., pages 194–200.

59. Ibid., page 201; see also Gómez, op. cit., pages 126–127.

60. *The Call*, Socialist Party newspaper, New York City, April 22, 1913.

61. *A Plebe*, anarchist newspaper, São Paulo, June 28, 1924.

62. *Boletim da Commissão Executiva do 3° Congresso Operário,* publication of Confederação Operária Brasileira, Rio de Janeiro, page 2; see also Gómez, op. cit., page 136.

63. Interview with Edgard Leuenroth, onetime leader of Confederação Operária Brasileira, in São Paulo, September 2, 1946.

64. *Boletim da Commissão Executiva do 3° Congresso Operário,* op. cit., page 9.

65. Pinheiro and Hall, 1979, op. cit., pages 249–251.

66. *Conclusões do 4° Congresso Operário Brasileiro Realizado no Palacio Monroe no Rio de Janeiro de 7 a 15 de Novembre de 1912,* Typographia Leuzinger, Rio de Janeiro, 1913.

67. Jornal do Brasil. *Cademos JB de IV Centenario, December 16, 1965,* Rio de Janeiro, 1965, page 311.

68. *Conclusões do 4° Congreso Operário Brasileiro etc.,* op. cit.

69. Pinheiro and Hall, 1979, op. cit., pages 170–171.

70. Ibid., page 214; see also Gómez, op. cit., pages 125–126.

71. Interview with Jose Oiticica, old-time anarchist and labor leader, director of *Acão Direta,* in Rio de Janeiro, august 30, 1946.

72. *Acão Direta,* Rio de Janeiro, May 7, 1946.

73. Interview with João Francisco da Rocha, president, Sindicato dos Empregados no Comércio Hoteleiro e Similares do Rio de Janeiro, in Rio de Janeiro, August 27, 1946.

74. *O Trabalhador Graphico,* São Paulo, May–June 1946; see also *Boletim da Commissão Executiva do 3° Congresso Operário,* op. cit., pages 10–12.

75. *Boletim da Commissão Executiva do 3° Congresso Operário,* op. cit., pages 12–13.

76. Bandeira, Melo, and Andrade, op. cit., pages 52–55.

77. Ibid., pages 56–63.

78. Ibid., page 52.

79. Ibid., pages 64–65.

80. Ibid., page 52.

81. Gómez, op. cit., page 27.

82. Bandeira, Melo, and Andrade, op. cit., page 118.

83. Ibid., page 119.

84. Ibid., page 120.

85. Ibid., pages 122–134.

86. Ibid., pages 134–136

87. Ibid., page 137.

88. Ibid., page 178.

89. Ibid., page 238.

90. Ibid., pages 238–243.

91. *A Plebe,* June 25, 1921.

92. Ibid.

93. *A Plebe,* May 27, 1922.

94. *A Plebe,* October 7, 1922.

95. *A Plebe,* November 18, 1922.

96. *A Plebe,* January 27, 1923.

97. *A Plebe,* March 24, 1923.

98. *A Plebe,* June 28, 1924.

99. *Boletim da Commissão Executiva do 3° Congresso Operário,* op. cit.

100. *A Plebe*, August 25, 1922.
101. *A Plebe*, June 28, 1924.
102. *A Plebe*, January 22, 1921, and *Boletim da Commissão Execitiva do 3° Congresso Operário*, op. cit.
103. *A Plebe*, September 1, 1923.
104. Interview with Edgard Leuenroth, op. cit., September 2, 1946.
105. *Mother Earth*, June 1908.
106. *A Plebe*, July 1, 1947.
107. *Jornal de São Paulo*, April 28, 1945.
108. *A Plebe*, June 24, 1922.
109. *A Plebe*, November 18, 1922.
110. *A Plebe*, February 26, 1927.
111. *A Plebe*, July 21, 1923.
112. *A Plebe*, March 18, 1922.
113. Throwaway of Partido Operário, Rio de Janeiro, 1890.
114. *Le Mouvement Socialiste*, October 15, 1899.
115. Pinheiro and Hall, 1979, op. cit., page 29.
116. Ibid., page 26.
117. *Conclusões do 4° Congresso Operário etc.*, op. cit.
118. Pinheiro and Hall, 1979, op. cit., page 27.
119. Leôncio Rodrigues, op. cit., pages 134–135.
120. Ibid., page 135.
121. Ibid., page 136.
122. Bandeira, Melo, and Andrade, op. cit., pages 155–158.
123. *A Plebe*, February 24, 1923.
124. José Saturnino Brito. *Socialismo Pátrio*, Rio de Janeiro, 1920.
125. A Piccarolo, *O Socialismo no Brasil-Esboço de um programma de acão socialista*, 3ra Edição, Editoria Piratininga, São Paulo, 1922, page 4.
126. Bandeira, Melo, and Andrade, op. cit., page 115.
127. Astrojildo Pereira, *Formação do PCB*, Editorial Vitória Limitada, Rio de Janeiro, n.d., page 28.
128. *A Plebe*, February 22, 1919.
129. Pereira, op. cit., page 30.
130. Ibid., pages 43–44.
131. Bandeira, Melo, and Andrade, op. cit., page 158.
132. Pereira, op. cit., page 42.
133. Ibid., page 43.
134. Bandeira, Melo, and Andrade, op. cit., page 159.
135. Hélio Negro and Edgard Leuenroth, *O Que e o Maximismo ou Bolchevismo*, São Paulo, 1919.
136. *Boletim da Commissão Executiva do 3° Congresso Operário etc.*, op. cit., August 1920, page 16.
137. Pinheiro and Hall, 1979, op. cit., pages 258–265.
138. Ibid., page 258.
139. Leoncio Basbaum, *História Sincera da República, de 1889 a 1930*, Vol. 2, Editoria Fulgor Limitada, São Paulo, Terceira Edição, 1968, page 212.
140. Pereira, op. cit., page 51.
141. Ibid., pages 51–52.
142. Ibid., page 46.

143. Basbaum, op. cit., page 212.

144. Pereira, op. cit., page 46.

145. Basbaum, op. cit., page 212.

146. Interview with Roberto Morena, leading Communist trade unionist, in Rio de Janeiro, August 28, 1946.

147. *A Plebe*, March 5, 1921.

148. *A Plebe*, May 7, 1924.

149. Gómez, op. cit., pages 139–140.

150. *A Plebe*, July 8, 1922.

151. *A Plebe*, June 25, 1921 and July 30, 1921.

152. *A Plebe*, March 28, 1922.

153. *A Plebe*, May 13, 1922.

154. *La Correspondencia Sudamericana*, November 30, 1926.

155. *American Labor Year Book 1923–24*, Rand School Press, New York, 1924, page 339.

156. Unpublished manuscript of Stephen Naft, op. cit.

157. *American Labor Year Book 1927*, Rand School Press, New York, 1927, page 200.

158. *International Press Correspondence*, February 2, 1928.

159. Gómez, op. cit., page 140.

160. James A. Rowan, "Trade Union Movement and Wages in Brazil," *Monthly Labor Review*, Washington, DC, September 1925, page 467.

161. Michael L. Conniff, *Urban Politics in Brazil: The Rise of Populism, 1925–1945*, University of Pittsburgh Press, Pittsburgh, 1981, page 47.

162. Pinheiro and Hall, 1979, op. cit., pages 286–287.

163. *American Labor Yearbook 1929*, Rand School Press, New York, 1929, page 226.

164. Moisés Poblete Troncoso, "The Labor Movement in Brazil," *Monthly Labor Review*, Washington, DC, July 1929.

165. Conniff, op. cit., page 48.

166. Ibid., page 49.

167. Pinheiro and Hall, 1979, op. cit., pages 298–299.

168. Ibid., page 275.

169. *International Press Correspondence*, February 2, 1928.

170. Pinheiro and Hall, 1979, op. cit., page 297.

171. Stephen Naft, *Fascism and Communism in South America*, Foreign Policy Reports, Foreign Policy Association, New York, December 15, 1937.

172. Basbaum, op. cit., page 215.

173. *Decreto N. 1637 de 5 de Janeiro de 1907: Crea Sindicatos Profissionais e Sociedades Corporativas*, Soc. Coop. Resp. Limitada, Banco de Petrópolis, Rio de Janeiro, 1928.

174. Hall and Pinheiro, 1983, op. cit., page 4.

175. Ibid., page 5.

176. Ibid., page 6.

177. Ibid., page 14.

178. Interview with Roberto Morena, op. cit., August 28, 1946.

179. *Mother Earth*, January 1910.

180. *A Plebe*, February 25, 1927.

181. *A Plebe*, May 12, 1923.

182. Hall and Pinheiro, 1983, op. cit., page 15.

183. *A Plebe*, May 10, 1924; see also Conniff, op. cit., page 54.
184. Conniff, op. cit., page 58.
185. Ibid., page 59.
186. Rodrigues, op. cit., page 153.
187. Ibid., page 154.
188. Ibid., page 155.

2
Organized Labor in the Vargas Era (1930–1945)

In October 1930 there took place a revolution in Brazil that put an end to the so-called Old Republic and created a profound transformation of the Brazilian economy, politics, and society. It brought to power Getúlio Vargas, who was to remain in the presidency for fifteen years, and who in many ways was to continue to dominate the country's politics until the Revolution of 1964 (although he had died a decade earlier).

THE REVOLUTION OF 1930

The Revolution of 1930 began as a quarrel among members of the country's political elite. It had been customary for the presidency of Brazil to alternate between the states of São Paulo and Minas Gerais. But as the 1930 election approached, President Washington Luiz, a Paulista (resident of São Paulo), decided to have another Paulista, Julio Prestes, as his successor. The governor of Minas Gerais, Antonio Carlos, greatly resented this, feeling that he was in line to succeed. However, instead of announcing his own candidacy, he threw his support to Governor Getúlio Vargas of Rio Grande do Sul and to João Pessoa, of the northeastern state of Paraíba, as nominee for vice president.

Although under the political system of the Old Republic the victory of the outgoing president's choice in the 1930 election was all but certain, the opposition candidate, Getúlio Vargas, campaigned extensively. In a major speech, delivered in Rio de Janeiro in January 1930, he outlined his governmental program, emphasizing economic nationalism, but also stressing the need for extensive social legislation benefiting the country's workers.[1]

Michael Conniff noted:

Vargas's labor promises went beyond the conventional platform, calling for a comprehensive labor code covering the welfare and working conditions of urban and rural laborers. The code would grandly address the social question by legislating on additional issues as education, hygiene, housing, nutrition, social security, and even sports and cultural activities.[2]

The government candidate, Julio Prestes, also (if in somewhat vaguer terms) promised a labor code. Michael Conniff pointed out that, at least in Rio de Janeiro, most *sindicatos* supported Prestes and the government ticket in general. In those parts of the city in which union labor was more or less strong, Prestes carried the day, although in other segments of the capital where nonunion wage earners predominated, Getúlio Vargas won. Even after the election, "on Labor Day a large number of unions reiterated their support for Prestes but pointedly reminded him of his preelection pledge of a labor code."[3]

As was expected, Júlio Prestes was elected, with the only states supporting Vargas being Minas Gerais, Rio Grande do Sul, and Paraíba. At first, Vargas accepted his defeat, but after his vice presidential running mate was murdered on July 26, 1930, Vargas finally accepted the idea being urged by many of his supporters, to attempt to overthrow the Washington Luiz government before Júlio Prestes was inaugurated.

The Revolution of 1930 was the work of two different military forces. One was the so-called military police of the state of Rio Grande do Sul, under command of Vargas's successor as governor, Osvaldo Aranha, which soon took control not only of that state, but of the two states to the north, Santa Catarina and Paraná.

The second military element in the 1930 Revolution were the so-called *tenentes* (lieutenants), who in a few days seized control of the Northeastern and Amazonian states. The *tenentes* were a military-civilian conspiratorial group that had been organized after two unsuccessful military insurrections of junior officers in the early 1920s.

The *tenentes* began as a conspiracy among young officers in the Rio de Janeiro garrison. They were particularly upset by the arrest of the ex-president, Marshal Hermes da Fonseca, for insubordination. They planned an uprising on July 5, 1922, in which the Vila Militar just outside Rio, the Military School, and the Fort of Copacabana were supposed to revolt. Although the conspirators in the Vila Militar were arrested and so could not participate, the young officers did lead insurrections in the other two posts. The mutiny in the Military School was quickly suppressed, and the rebellious officers in Fort Copacabana finally marched down the beaches of Copacabana to confront troops from the center of the city; a few were killed and the rest surrendered.[4]

Exactly two years later, on July 5, 1924, a much more serious *tenente* uprising occurred in São Paulo. Some of the young officers of 1922 were among the leaders, as were an army veteran, General Isidoro Dias Lopes, and Major Miguel Costa of the São Paulo state "military police." After holding the city of São Paulo for several days, they retreated westward toward the Iguassu Falls, where they were joined by another group of rebels from Rio Grande do Sul, led by Captain Luiz Carlos Prestes.

For the next two and a half years, this rebel contingent, which became known as the Prestes Column, after Luiz Carlos Prestes, its chief of staff, although the commander was actually Miguel Costa, wandered around the interior of Brazil, engaging in countless battles with the federal army and state police forces. They finally retreated into Bolivia.

However, the young officers continued to conspire, both inside Brazil and from abroad. Several of them were jailed for a while, but then most were assigned to the Army Personnel Bureau in Rio, without specific duties, but with the obligation to sign in every afternoon. Thus they met regularly, thereby facilitating their conspiracy. They recruited members of the Military Academy, who in due time became conspiratorial leaders in various parts of the country, particularly in the Northeast and Amazon areas. They also recruited a number of civilians as part of their conspiracy, including Pedro Ludovico Teixeira, a doctor from Goiás, who organized his own branch of the conspiracy in that state. Coordinating it all was Major Antonio Siqueira Campos, who lived in Buenos Aires but made frequent trips incognito to São Paulo.

The great majority of the *tenentes* supported Getúlio Vargas's presidential campaign. After he lost, they urged him to organize a revolt against the regime, which he agreed to do after the death of João Pessoa.

When the Revolution broke out, it was the *tenentes* who seized control of the Northeast and Amazon areas, eleven states in all. Only in Pernambuco and Bahia was there any serious fighting—in the other states, the conspirators merely sent in people to take command of the local garrisons and received no resistance.[5]

By the end of October, with the three most southern states and most of the Northeast and Amazonas areas in the hands of the rebels, the armed forces high command finally took action. They put the president and president-elect on a ship to Europe and invited Getúlio Vargas to Rio de Janeiro to assume control of the government.[6]

BEGINNING OF ESTABLISHMENT OF THE VARGAS SYSTEM

Once he was settled into the presidential palace in Rio de Janeiro, Getúlio Vargas faced a serious quandary. He was very beholden to the *tenentes*, who had brought about the revolution in more than half of Brazil. Yet, at the same time, they were still very junior officers, and Vargas had to deal with the senior officers who were still in at least nominal control of the armed forces. So long as the *tenentes* remained a more or less organized group, there was serious potential for a clash between the junior and senior officers. Furthermore, the *tenentes*, if they remained united, always constituted a potential danger to the new president.

Vargas handled the *tenente* problem with great political skill. He named many of them to be "interventors" (appointed governors) in the various states, where, as he certainly was sure they would, they set to work to build up their own individual bases in the eventuality of the elections that sooner or later would be held. Others were given other jobs in the administration.

Vargas also set up a vaguely defined "superintendency of the Northeast," putting Juarez Tavora, the senior *tenente* (since Major Siqueira Campos had died in an airplane accident shortly before the revolution), in charge, seconded by two other *tenentes*, Juracy Magalhães and Agildo Barata.[7] Subsequently, Magalhaes was made interventor in Bahia, where he established the basis for a long political career.

Vargas also owed a considerable debt to such old-line political leaders as Governor Antonio Carlos of Minas Gerais. Although the Minas Gerais Republican machine had supported Vargas's presidential campaign and had supported the rebellion led by him, Vargas undoubtedly knew that they would sooner or later present him with a "bill" for this help. He may well also have expected that Antonio Carlos (correctly) would see himself as the natural successor to Vargas.

Vargas also faced problems with the labor movement. The *sindicato* leaders and rank and file were delighted with the overthrow of the "old regime," and in some cases, the Communists and others sought to take advantage of it. In São Paulo, there was for a short while an unsuccessful effort to organize a kind of "soviet," to present the new regime with a "dual power" in the city and state.[8]

In this complicated situation, the only continuing political support of which he could be more or less certain was that of the "political class" of Rio Grande do Sul. Indeed, he recruited a considerable number of people from the "gaucho" state into this new administration immediately. However, if he were to remain in power for a considerable period, Vargas had to develop a new constituency.

To garner this new support, Vargas turned to the group who had been regarded as a "problem for the police" by all previous administrations, that is, organized labor. Except to a very limited degree in Rio de Janeiro and a handful of other cities the worker, organized or unorganized, had played at most a very marginal role in Brazilian politics in the Old Republic. Vargas clearly hoped to provide them with a major role, but one in which they would be loyal to him and he would be in control.

Therefore, within only a few weeks of taking office, President Vargas took the first steps in constructing what is sometimes known as the Vargas System. In broad terms, the Vargas System, as it developed over the next fifteen years, consisted of three major elements. The first was the deliberate decision to leave the economic, social, and political system of rural Brazil alone, to leave in place the large landholdings, the local and state political bosses, and the traditional patron-client relations that characterized rural Brazil.

The second aspect of the Vargas System was the strong encouragement of economic development, and particularly the industrialization of Brazil. This conformed to Vargas's belief in economic nationalism—one of the few ideas to which he held firm in his long political career. It also might be expected over the long run to strengthen the political power of urban Brazil and undermine the pre-1930 status quo.

Finally, the Vargas System involved creation of a system of control of the inevitable social conflicts arising from rapid economic and social development. This involved establishment of a system of workers' and employers' organizations and relations between them that would be thoroughly under the control of the state, and would permit adaptation of the traditional patron-client relationship so as to make Vargas appear as the "great patron" of both parties in labor-management relations, but particularly of the workers.

THE COLLOR LAW

It is doubtful that Vargas had clearly in mind in 1930–1931 the full outlines of the Vargas System. However, it is clear that he set out soon after taking office to try to win the support of the hitherto marginalized urban working class, as a major basis of his political support.

One of his first acts was to establish the Ministry of Labor and Industry. He named to that post one of his closest Rio Grande do Sul colleagues, Lindolfo Collor. In one of his first pronouncements, the new minister announced, "The Ministry of Labor is specifically the Ministry of the Revolution. The mentality of the deposed government, that in Brazil social conditions are mere problems for the police, susceptible of solution *ultima ratio* by repressive measures, has long been opposed by the liberal conscience of the nation."[9]

On March 19, 1931, Labor Minister Collor issued Decree 19,770, which "regulates unionization of employers and workers and has other provisions." This became known as the Collor Law.

This law provided for legalization of *sindicatos* composed of at least thirty individuals, two-thirds of whom had to be Brazilian citizens. Only native-born Brazilians, naturalized citizens of at least ten years' standing, or foreigners who had lived in the country at least twenty years could be *sindicato* officers. The *sindicatos* had to file their statutes and the biographies of their officers with the Ministry of Labor, after which they could be recognized by the government and receive "legal personality." The employers would be required to negotiate with legally recognized *sindicatos*.

This decree provided for three types of trade union organization—professional or craft unions, plant or one-company unions, and industrial unions. Industrywide *sindicatos* (the Textile Workers Union of Recife, for instance) became predominant in textiles, although there were some one-company *sindicatos* in this field; in the metal trades; in the shoe and leather industry, and in the construction field. One-company *sindicatos* came to predominate in public utilities and on the railroads. In the latter field, the ministry recognized a few dual *sindicatos*, although generally one *sindicato* in a particular jurisdiction was recognized. Craft unions predominated in the maritime industry.[10]

The first *sindicato* to be legally recognized under the new decree was the Sociedade União dos Operários Estivadores do Rio de Janeiro (Stevedores Union of Rio de Janeiro). It was officially registered on June 4, 1931.[11]

Old-time *sindicato* leaders were quick to express their opposition to the "legalization" of *sindicatos* by the Vargas government, protesting that it was a fascist method of labor organization.[12] Their fears were confirmed when the government passed another decree calling for each worker to have a "professional card" listing the jobs he or she had held, and his or her record on those jobs.

The anarchosyndicalist *sindicatos* took the lead in the name of the Confederação Operária Brasileira in calling a general strike against this regulation. The walkout was centered principally in São Paulo and was broken. The Communists were the first of the nongovernment *sindicato* groups to accept the "professional card," and the anarchosyndicalists accused them of breaking the movement against this law. A União Geral dos Trabalhadores do Brasil, formed in 1931 and claiming 15,000 members a year later, was established with the avowed aim of fighting the system of legally recognized *sindicatos*.[13]

The reasons why the old *sindicato* leaders were fearful of growing government control of the *sindicatos* can be judged from the case of the Liga dos Empregados do Comércio (League of Commercial Employees) of the city of Santos. This organization was established right after the 1930 Revolution and in its early years was a decidedly left-wing group. Its periodical, *O Commerciario*, carried such articles as "Socialismo e os Trabalhadores" (Socialism and the Workers); was full of quotations from Lenin, Marx, and others; and had articles ostensibly signed by "Marat," "Danton," and other French revolutionary leaders. Its main article on May 8, 1932, was "The Sindicalization Decree is Anti-Social."

However, late in 1932 the *sindicato* began to modify its left-wing sentiments. By early 1934, it had received legal recognition and the whole character of its publication changed. Long articles were now devoted to feting the minister of labor, who was visiting the city; it was noted that the *sindicato's* "White Collar Workers' Day" had been presided over by an inspector of the Ministry of Labor.[14]

SPREAD OF LEGALIZED UNIONS

In spite of opposition by old-line *sindicato* leaders, the government-recognized *sindicatos* grew rapidly in number and size. By the last half of 1934 it was reported that more than one thousand *sindicatos* throughout Brazil had been recognized, 200 of these in the state of São Paulo, 143 in the states of Rio Grande do Sul and Rio de Janeiro, and fewer than 100 in all of the other states. Only three *sindicatos* had been recognized in each of the states of Mato Grosso, Paraíba, and Piauhí. It was reported that 1,5000 more *sindicatos* that had applied for recognition were not recognized by the government because they were dual *sindicatos*. It was the official policy to recognize only one *sindicato* in one trade or industry in a given area. It was said that in some cases as many as ten or fifteen *sindicatos* in the same trade and town had asked for recognition.[15]

A considerable variety of *sindicatos* had been given legal recognition. These included *sindicatos* of motor vehicle drivers, coffee workers, stevedores, shoe workers, packing house employees, flour millers, railroaders, street cleaners, and barbers that had been recognized by 1932.[16]

Labor organization had even spread into fields that in most Latin American countries were considered of doubtful eligibility for formation of *sindicatos*. Thus, in October 1931, the Associação dos Funcionarios Públicos do Estado de São Paulo was founded among the state government employees of São Paulo. This was apparently predominantly a mutual benefit organization but owed its foundation tó the general spread of labor organizations at that time.[17]

In some trades, federations of government-recognized *sindicatos* were formed. Among the commercial employees, the first convention was held in February 1935, when *sindicatos* of Rio de Janeiro, Itajuba, and Juiz da Fora in Minas Gerais; in Cachoeira and Bage in Rio Grande do Sul; in Florianópolis in the state of Santa Catarina; in Aracajú in Sergipe; Recife in Pernambuco, João Pessôa in Paraíba; and in several São Paulo cities joined to form the Confederação Nacional dos Empregados do Comércio.[18] A previous unsuccessful attempt to launch a commercial employees federation had been made just before the 1930 Revolution on the initiative of the Association of Commercial Employees of Rio de Janeiro.[19]

In 1933 and 1934, the Ministry of Labor fostered the establishment of regional federations of labor and was reportedly preparing the organization of a Confederação Nacional do Trabalho, a national central labor body of legally recognized *sindicatos*.[20] However, subsequent events prevented these plans from coming to fruition, and a central labor body under the aegis of the Ministry of Labor was never organized during the Vargas regime.

On July 12, 1934, the Ministry of Labor issued a decree to take the place of the Collor Law, a decree on "professional *sindicatos*."[21] In this law:

sindicatos are defined . . . as organizations of the economic and vocational groups of the population. Their function will be to defend the interests of the group or trade and those of their members, to coordinate the rights and the obligations of employers and workers in relation to economic and social conditions and to cooperate with the Government in the study and solution of problems directly or indirectly affecting the interests of particular groups.

However, only workers with "professional cards" could form *sindicatos*.

This decree provided that "As organs of the coordination of the rights and obligations of employers and workers, the trade unions will have the right to conclude or approve collective agreements and to cooperate in conciliation boards and labor courts, in settlement of disputes between employers and workers."

The decree specifically provided for formation of "local councils of *sindicatos* representing different occupations and federations of *sindicatos* belonging to the same occupational group and for the right to combine three or more federations in a confederation, which must have its headquarters in the capital of the republic."

Finally, employers were forbidden by this decree to dismiss workers for *sindicato* activity. But it added that a worker so fired had to receive "as many months' wages as he has years of service."[22]

COMMUNIST INFLUENCE IN THE EARLY 1930s

Not only the legalized *sindicatos* gained during the early 1930s. The anarchosyndicalist- and Communist-controlled *sindicatos* also saw their organizations expand under the comparatively free conditions then prevalent. The Communists worked inside many of the government-recognized *sindicatos*, some of which, such as the Commercial Employees Union of São Paulo, they succeeded in controlling.[23] In the city of Santos, the Communist-controlled Federação Sindical included in 1932 *sindicatos* of construction workers, railroaders, vehicle conductors, public utility workers, and printing trades employees. Also affiliated with this federation were an organization of the unemployed with six hundred members and a Juvenil Proletário Futebol Club, as well as a "recreational" youth group. Finally, the Santos federation had Communist opposition groups in four *sindicatos* that the party did not control. The federation organized a May Day demonstration in 1932.[24]

The Confederação Geral do Trabalho Brasileiro (CGTB), which the Communists had launched in the late 1920s, continued in existence during the early Vargas period and in 1932 was reported by the International Labor Organization to have 8,600 members.[25] Its influence was confined largely to Rio de Janeiro and São Paulo.[26] In the early 1930s, Socialist elements got control of the CGTB and Communist-led *sindicatos* withdrew. Then, with a change of the International Communist line to favor the Popular Front, a number of Communist and non-Communist *sindicatos* were joined in May 1935 to form the Confederação Sindical Unitária (CSU).[27]

The formation of the Confederação Sindical Unitária was preceded by a series of local trade union unity conventions. The *sindicatos* involved in the CSU were described by the Communists as having "the greatest mass character."[28] Three hundred delegates attended the founding congress of the confederation, claiming to represent half a million workers.[29] This was certainly a gross exaggeration.

STRIKES AFTER THE 1930 REVOLUTION

Strikes were numerous during the first years of the administration of Getúlio Vargas. According to the Communist leader Octavio Brandão, there were in 1931 some fifty-six strikes, involving 96,576 workers; in the next year there were some thirty-one walkouts, involving 124,980 workers. The textile workers had the largest number involved in these strikes, some 45,426 in 1931 and 31,400 in 1932. In 1931 there were also walkouts involving some 15,950 motor vehicle drivers, and smaller numbers of strikers on the railroads and trolley car systems; in the leather, glass, and tobacco industries; and in the maritime trades. In 1932 there were important walkouts in the food and printing trades.

During these two years, strikes occurred in eleven states, although 57 percent of the strikers were in the city of São Paulo, and others were in other cities in that state. Additional important strike centers were Rio de Janeiro and Niterói, right across Guanabara Bay from the capital, and Recife.[30] Even bank employees went out on strike in São Paulo in April 1932.[31]

There was a further strike wave in the state of São Paulo early in 1933, which involved, among others, workers of the São Paulo Railway, and a general strike of shoemakers.[32]

Some of the strikes during this early Vargas period were political. A wave of walkouts in July–August 1931 in the state of São Paulo had the purpose of preventing the prospective appointment by Vargas of a well-known lawyer and copublisher of the newspaper *Estado de São Paulo*, Plínio Barreto, as interventor of the state. The movement was inspired by General Miguel Costa, a commander of the state's military police and onetime leader of the Prestes Column, who sought the appointment of another *tenente*, João Alberto, as interventor.[33] This wave of strikes achieved its aim.[34]

During the three-month revolt of São Paulo against the Vargas regime in 1932, there were strikes and antiwar demonstrations in Rio de Janeiro under the leadership of the Communists. These were suppressed with considerable violence by the police.[35]

In 1934 and 1935 there was a further series of strikes, inspired at least in part by the formation of a "popular front," the National Liberation Alliance. The most important walkouts during the 1934–1935 period were a strike on the Great Western Railroad, which resulted in a 30 percent wage increase but that the pro-Communist leaders of the *sindicato* seem to have continued even after this favorable settlement; and a series of Communist-led general strikes in the state of Espírito Santo and the cities of Santos, Bahia, and Recife, to protest conventions of the Brazilian fascist party, Acão Integralista.[36] In Santos, there was a general strike in January 1935 to protest a national security bill then being considered by Congress.[37]

Violence frequently accompanied walkouts during this period. Michael Hall and Paulo Sérgio Pinheiro noted:

Even before the Estado Novo, physical violence against the independent labor movement intensified. The leading figures of the regime made it clear that the new labor legislation in no way precluded police action against unacceptable mobilizations of the working class. Repression of militants soon became quite violent and aggressive. In 1934, for example, the United Sates military attaché, after describing the demolition of a union headquarters by the police, remarked that it was "a typical example of police excess. There was no justification for it, but there will be no redress. In Brazil, certainly in Rio de Janeiro, only the simple minded appeal for 'police protection'—unless it is protection from the police."[38]

LABOR POLITICAL ACTIVITY AFTER 1930

Various labor political groups were active during the early Vargas years. One of these was the Partido Trabalhista (PT, or Labor Party), which had been founded in 1928 in Pôrto Alegre but grew rapidly after the advent of the Vargas movement. It was patterned after the British Labour Party, and its declared aim was to form "a federation of workers' *sindicatos* without distinction of classes, races, nationalities and religions to fight for the interests of the Brazilian proletariat."[39]

In 1930, it was reported that there were 600 affiliated organizations in the PT, of which it was claimed that 134 were trade unions, with a total membership of 862,400. In the *sindicato* groups said to be affiliated with the party, the largest number represented were the commercial employees, with 80,000 members; the railroaders and the maritime workers, who it was said had together 40,000 members. There were also textile *sindicatos* and transport workers organizations. Finally, the party claimed to have about 20,000 agricultural workers as well as eighty-six societies of foreign workers, with some 63,800 members.[40]

The second congress of the Partido Trabalhista in October 1930 passed resolutions favoring workmen's compensation legislation, and a motion in favor of suspending immigration was dropped after opposition from the delegates representing the Socialist Party of Polish Jews in Brazil.[41] The third, and last, convention of the party met in October 1931, with eighty-nine constituent groups represented, and a claimed membership of only 23,000. This congress reorganized the party and the União Geral do Trabalho (UGT), which was apparently controlled by it. It was agreed that the party would apply for admission to the Labor and Socialist International, and the UGT would join the International Federation of Trade Unions.[42]

Little more was heard of the Partido Trabalhista after the first year of the Vargas Revolution.

In a quite different category was the Partido Socialista do Brasil, founded under the leadership of Major Juarez Távora, the *tenente leader*. The congress that launched that party was said to have included delegates who were Communists, anarchists, fascists and Catholics, and it drew up a declaration of principles saying that the party would follow "a general line tending to socialism, subordinate to Brazilian conditions." It saw in the drive to organize pure workers' trade unions a tinge of Bolshevism and said that it would try to unionize not only workers, but also employers and the liberal professions. It stated: "Unionization and representation by classes in parliament are the two fundamental things which we write upon our banner."[43]

This Partido Socialista was basically an attempt of some of the *tenentes* to establish their own political organization. However, it failed because the *tenentes* who had been appointed to be state interventors and to hold other positions in the Vargas administration were too much concerned with building their own local power bases to be really interested in building up a national political party. Typical was Juracy Magalhães, the interventor in Bahia, who admitted that he was going to have to work with the local political bosses in that state (the so-called colonels) and who had absolutely no interest in socialism of any kind. As a consequence, he organized his own Autonomist Party in Bahia and with its help was elected governor in 1934.[44]

The Communists were very active during the early 1930s. A *New York Times* correspondent reported in December 1934, "This development of labor's power under government guidance . . . brought other movements in its wake. Communism, which for many years had been peeking through the keyhole, now advanced openly, favored strikes right and left and stirred up further turmoil."[45]

The Vargas regime had no sympathy for the Communists, whom they frequently persecuted. Communist *sindicato* strength was reported to be largely among the workers in small factories serving the needs of the urban population.[46] Much Communist activity occurred outside the *sindicatos*, however. For instance, in 1934 the Communists engaged in a propaganda campaign in support of the *cangaceiros*, bands of armed landless peasants and agricultural workers,[47] although the Communists in fact had very little general contact with peasants and agricultural workers.[48] They also carried on a vigorous propaganda campaign against the Vargas regime, especially against the Law for the Security of the State, which was passed early in 1935 and which the Communists thought was aimed particularly at them and at the *sindicatos* that they controlled.[49]

In elections of 1933 for a constitutional assembly, and in 1934 for the regular Congress, various elements in the organized labor movement in Rio de Janeiro sought to play an independent role. One such effort was the formation of the Carioca Proletarian Convention (CPC), which Michael Conniff said "was founded in late March 1933 by the Labor Federation, a union coalition with loose ties to the Ministry of Labor, and by the Maritime Federation, a powerful seamen's association. Thirty-five of Rio's major unions participated in the formation of the CPC, representing a large electoral potential." The CPC put up ten candidates and organized thirteen campaign rallies.

But the CPC was faced with the Brazilian Socialist Party, which we have already noted, which for this campaign took the name Brazilian Socialist Party–Proletarian Political Union (PSB—UPP). However, neither of the labor-based groups did very well in the 1933 election. The CPC came in fourth, and the PSB-UPP got only about half as many votes as the CPC.

Then in 1934, a new Socialist Party of Brazil, headed by two *tenentes*, Roberto Sisson and Heroclinio Cascardo, was organized, "but the group did not prosper." As the October 1934 elections approached, a new labor political group, the Proletarian United Front, was established, drawing together various small radical and labor groups, including the Partido Trabalhista.

The effort to form a single labor party for the 1934 election failed, since "by polling time the labor vote was hopelessly divided among a dozen minor parties. The União Operáia Camponesa (UOC), a descendant of the 1920s Bloque Operário Camponês (BOC) received almost four thousand votes and was the third largest party, but it did not have sufficient ballots to complete one quotient" (elect one member of Congress), and "the rest of the labor parties received less than one thousand votes each."[50]

Another kind of election, which directly involved the legally recognized *sindicatos*, also took place in 1933. The decree calling for a new constituent assembly had provided that 40 of the 254 members of that body should be chosen by "syndicalized groups." Of these, legal labor unions had eighteen, employers' groups seventeen, the liberal professions three, and civil servants two. Michael Conniff noted with regard to the labor delegates, "Seventeen of the eighteen delegates eventually chosen were from traditional unions in large cities, with a pre-determined regional distribution of at least four from the north, four from the south and three each from Rio and São Paulo. The Rio delegates were from the warehouse, banks and store employees unions." Conniff added, "The *bancada trabalhista*, as the labor delegation was known, was supplied with an advisory committee by the Ministry of Labor, and throughout the ten months of the ANC [National Constitutional Assembly] they voted in accord with the government's wishes."[51]

The new constitution that went into effect in 1934 incorporated most of the changes that Vargas had made with regard to organized labor. According to Hobart A. Spalding, Jr.:

It guaranteed the right to join unions, although it did not make membership compulsory. Unions could not support political parties or candidates nor issue political propaganda, but they could draw up labor contracts and maintain a variety of services such as schools, clinics, and cooperatives. The ministry retained extensive control over unions. It could recognize or withhold recognition, it had access to all records, and its officials could attend meetings. Most important, the government agency could intervene in any union and replace elected officers with its own agents.[52]

THE NATIONAL LIBERATION ALLIANCE

The high point of radical and *sindicato* activity in the 1930s was the organization of the National Liberation Alliance (Aliança Nacional Libertadora, or ANL). The ANL fitted in with the Popular Front line that the Communist International was adopting at the time. It ultimately included in its ranks a wide range of groups and individuals in addition to the Communists, including the remains of the Partido Socialista Brasileiro originally established by Juarez Távora several years before, many *tenentes* disillusioned with the Vargas regime, trade unionists of a variety of ideological persuasions, and liberals who were fearful of the increasing strength of the Brazilian fascist party, Acão Integralista.

The ALN was formally established at a congress in March 1935. At that meeting, Carlos Lacerda, who was at the time a leader of a generally left-wing youth group that had been organized when the Communists dissolved their party youth affiliate in conformity with the Popular Front line, moved that Luiz Carlos Prestes be named honorary president of the ALN, a motion accepted by acclamation.[53] Prestes, of the famous Prestes Column, had refused to support the 1930 Revolution and subsequently gone to Moscow, where he was co-opted into the Executive Committee of the Communist International. He returned to Brazil late in 1934.

Although the ALN was to remain a legal organization for only about four months, it was extremely active in that period. It sponsored the trade union unity conference that established the Confederação Sindical Unitária in May 1935. It held meetings all over the country that were attended not only by very large numbers of civilians but also by military officers of all three services. It carried out a campaign against the profascist Integralistas and pushed for passage of a minimum wage law. At one point, the Alliance threatened to call a general strike if President Vargas tried to effect a coup d'état.[54]

There was considerable friction between the formal leadership of the ALN, including its president, Heroclinio Cascardo, and its secretary general, Roberto Sisson, both old *tenentes*, on the one hand, and the Communist Party leadership on the other. Cascardo and Sisson were particularly outraged when, on July 5, Luiz Carlos Prestes, in his capacity as honorary president of the ALN, issued a very provocative proclamation. Among other things, it stated that "with the Aliança are the best officers of the armed forces of the country, all those who would be incapable of leading their soldiers against the liberators of Brazil." Prestes's statement called, among other things, for repudiation of the foreign debt, the seizure of property "without indemnization to the imperialists, the most reactionary large proprietors and elements of the Church." It ended by calling on "workers, peasants, soldiers, Northeasterners and Northerners and honest democrats," to join "the struggle for national liberation, for a popular, national and revolutionary government."[55]

A few days later, on July 12, 1935, the Vargas government outlawed the ANL and its headquarters were seized by the police in Rio and other cities. Thereafter, the Aliança virtually ceased to function as an ongoing organization. However, the Communists continued to agitate in the name of the ALN.

This agitation culminated in military insurrections between November 23 and 27, under Communist leadership. Troops first revolted in Natal, the capital of the state of Rio Grande do Norte, but were quickly suppressed on November 23. The next day, the revolt spread to Recife and Olinda in Pernambuco, where after considerable fighting it was also suppressed. Then, on November 27, on the direct orders of Luiz Carlos Prestes, two parts of the garrison of Rio de Janeiro rose in rebellion. Prestes issued a proclamation:

The Revolutionary Committee under my direction, in the face of events in the north of the country and the menace of the installation of a reactionary dictatorship, decides that all the forces of revolution are ready to fight for the popular freedoms, and to give the definitive blow to the government of national betrayal of Getúlio Vargas.[56]

Although these uprisings took place in the name of the Aliança Nacional Libertadora, they were carried out only by the Communists, without any consultation with those who were supposedly the leaders of the ALN. It has been claimed by, among others, John W. F. Dulles, that "plans for an insurrection in Brazil were reached in Moscow in 1934 at meetings attended by a few Brazilian Communists and leaders of the Comintern."[57] However, Luiz Carlos Prestes flatly denied that:

The official history says that Moscow ordered the uprising. That is not the truth. It is a lie. It was the CC of our party that opted for and decided in favor of the uprising. Our party concluded that the conditions existed for our coming to power, particularly since the ANL had great prestige and had arbitrarily been illegalized by Getulio.[58]

The November 1935 Communist uprising was disastrous not only for the Communist Party, but for all the left-wing opposition to Vargas, and particularly for the organized labor movement.[59] For the following two years the country was kept under a constant state of siege, which was renewed periodically by Congress. Trade union rights, and civil liberties in general, were drastically curtailed. This situation culminated on November 10, 1937, with the open establishment of a dictatorship by President Vargas.

With the suppression of the November 1935 uprising, the Communists lost much influence in the labor movement. The government roughly treated the Communist-dominated *sindicatos*. In the case of the Communist-controlled São Paulo Sindicato dos Empregados no Comércio, for instance, the *sindicato* disappeared at the end of 1935, after having "subordinated itself to political ends." The fate of many other Communist *sindicatos* was similar.

The Communist Party continued some activities, although underground. It sporadically published *A Classe Operária*. However, the Communists were seriously hampered by government persecution. Between November 1935 and the middle of 1937, some 7,056 Communists were jailed.[60] These included Luiz Carlos Prestes. The Communists, of course, were very much opposed to Vargas, spoke bitterly of "the toadies of the Vargas government," and claimed that the Brazilian president was Hitler's ally.

THE ESTABLISHMENT OF THE ESTADO NOVO

By 1937, President Vargas was faced with a serious problem. His term as constitutional president was due to expire in the following year, and the Constitution of 1934 did not permit reelection. However, Vargas had little desire to give up power.

In spite of President Vargas's distaste for relinquishing office, by the second half of 1937 there was under way a campaign to choose his successor. The unofficial government candidate was the northeastern novelist José Américo de Almeida; his principal opponent was Armando de Salles Oliveira, who resigned as governor of São Paulo to launch his candidacy.

However, Getúlio had his own plans. His daughter, Alzira Vargas do Amaral Peixoto, recounted mysterious conferences in the presidential palace in Rio involving Francisco Campos, leader of a fascist-type party in Minas Gerais; Plínio Salgado, head of Acão Integralista; and top military officers of the regime. At the time, she did not understand the significance of these meetings.

However, on November 10, 1937, their meaning became clear. That morning, troops turned members of Congress away from the legislative buildings. A bit later in the day, President Vargas announced by radio the suspension of the Constitution of 1934, and its replacement by a new constitution, which established the Estado Novo (New State).

LABOR UNDER THE ESTADO NOVO

That the economic and social organization established by Vargas was patterned after fascist models of Italy and Portugal was at the time even admitted by government spokesmen. For instance, such an admission was made in an article by Cavalcanti de Carvalho in the *Revista do Trabalho* in April 1941.

The 1937 Constitution dealt extensively with labor problems. Its Article 136 proclaimed that labor "constitutes a treasure which it is the duty of the state to protect by providing conditions favorable to its defense." It then set forth a list of labor reforms that would be instituted under the Estado Novo.

The outline of labor legislation set forth in the 1937 Constitution included an obligatory day of rest on Sundays and holidays; vacation after a year's uninterrupted employment; indemnity in cases of unjust dismissal, proportional to length of service of the worker; minimum wages, fixed according to the conditions of the particular locality; a working day of eight hours which can be reduced, but which can be extended only in certain cases prescribed by law; extra pay for night work; prohibition of work by minors of fourteen years and under; prohibition of work in unhealthy industries for minors under eighteen and for women; medical and hygienic assistance for workers; hygienic and medical aid for pregnant women, and a period of rest from work before and after pregnancy without deduction from the woman's wage; insurance for old age, invalidity, accidents and life insurance; workers' associations to provide mutual benefit in other cases.

Strikes and lockouts were declared "anti-social activities, harmful alike to labor and to capital, and incompatible with the superior interests of national production." Ostensibly, there was no restriction on the functioning of any labor organization. However, a *sindicato* had to be recognized by the government before it could appear before the Labor Tribunals or otherwise take part in legal procedures.[61]

For a *sindicato* to be recognized by the Ministry of Labor, its president had to be a native-born Brazilian and its other officers had to be Brazilian citizens. It had to agree to abstain from "all propaganda of doctrines incompatible with the institutions and the interests of the nation, such as participation in election campaigns."[62]

The system established by Vargas under the Estado Novo envisaged a corporate state hierarchy of employers' and workers' organizations. According to the revision and codification of the system established in a decree of May 1, 1943, the *Consolidação das Leis do Trabalho*, "confederations" of workers were to be formed by workers in industry; commercial employees; maritime, river and air transport workers; land transport employees; workers in communications and publicity; credit institutions; educational and cultural institutions. Counterparts of these confederations were to be formed among the employers of the same broad groups. In addition, the National Confederation of the Liberal Professions was to be organized.[63]

Beneath the confederations in the hierarchy envisioned by the Estado Novo were the federations. To be formed in the individual states, these consisted of five or more *sindicatos* in the same general trade. The confederation had to consist of at least three such state federations.[64]

In actual practice, no labor confederations were formed during the Estado Novo period. There were formed a number of state federations, particularly among textile workers and commercial employees. There also existed a National Maritime Federation. There was no provision at all in the Estado Novo hierarchy for a central labor organization comparable to the American Federation of Labor–Congress of Industrial Organizations (AFL-CIO) or the British Trade Union Congress.

On the employers' side, there were only two confederations established during the Estado Novo period, the Confederação Nacional da Indústria and the Confederação Nacional do Comércio. In the case of the first of these, an already existing organization, the Centro da Indústria, which dated its remote origins to the early years of the empire, was transformed into a part of the Estado Novo hierarchy.[65]

The individual *sindicatos* that were the base of this corporative pyramid were subject to a great deal of government interference. They had to submit to the Ministry of Labor a list of all their elected officers and acquire the same authority's approval to elect new officials.[66] There were various classifications of individuals not eligible to election to office in the *sindicatos*, including those "who profess ideologies incompatible with the institutions or interests of the Nation," and those "who had bad conduct, well proven."[67] The *sindicato* officials could not take office without approval of the ministry.

The Vargas regime used these provisions to bar all those from holding office in the *sindicatos* who might be considered unfriendly to the regime. For instance, as late as the middle of 1944, the election of officers in the Union of Port Workers of Santos was thrown out by the ministry on the grounds that two of those elected were listed on the register of the Public Delegation for Political and Social Order as "undesirables."[68] The government several times moved to step in to void elections in that staunchly anti-Vargas group, the printing trades *sindicato* of São Paulo.[69]

Another form of control by the state was over *sindicato* funds. No *sindicato* could sell any real estate without approval of the Ministry of Labor.[70] Each *sindicato*, federation, or confederation had to submit to the ministry by June 30 each year its budget for the following calendar year.[71] If actual expenditures were much out of line with this estimate, the *sindicato* leaders had to get special dispensation from the ministry or were liable to imprisonment. Recognized *sindicatos* were authorized to receive a part of what was known as the "trade union tax." This consisted of one day's pay a year, deducted from the wages and salaries of all workers in Brazil and deposited by the employers in the Banco do Brasil during the month of March. In case there existed a trade union with jurisdiction over a particular worker, that local *sindicato* received 40 percent of the *imposto sindical* (trade union tax). If that *sindi-*

cato belonged to a federation, the federation received 15 percent. Had there existed a confederation to which that federation was affiliated, that confederation would have received 5 percent of the tax. The remaining 20 percent (plus what might have gone to federations and confederations that did not yet exist) was put aside for a special Trade Union Social Fund, which was to be used for "objects in the general interest of national trade union organization."[72] The exact use to which this "social fund" was put remained something of a mystery long after the end of the Estado Novo.

The Ministry of Labor also determined the category of workers who could form an individual *sindicato*. In theory at least, a group of workers could request recognition for a *sindicato* covering two or more of the categories set forth in the Consolidação. However, as the Ministry of Labor official in charge of deciding *sindicato* jurisdictions conceded to me more than a decade after the Estado Novo supposedly had disappeared, the objectives of Brazilian labor legislation enacted during the Estado Novo period were to organize workers by professional or craft category and to have the narrowest possible jurisdiction for any given *sindicato*.[73]

ABOLITION OF COLLECTIVE BARGAINING

The labor-management relations system set up by the Estado Novo had little or no room for collective bargaining between workers' *sindicatos* and employers' organizations, let alone with individual employers. Although there were a few collective contracts negotiated during the Estado Novo period, such as one between the chauffeurs of Rio de Janeiro and the *sindicato* of the passenger transport employers,[74] this was the exception that proved the rule.

In place of the collective bargaining there was substituted a system of labor courts. This labor judiciary was created in conformity with Decree Law 1,237 of May 12, 1939.[75]

There were three steps established in the labor tribunal hierarchy. The lowest of these consisted of so-called boards of conciliation (*juntas de conciliação*). These consisted of three judges, one a "togaed" judge, that is, a professional magistrate; one member named by the workers' *sindicato* of the jurisdiction; and one named by the employers' *sindicato* in that area. Their function was to handle complaints that would normally be dealt with in a grievance procedure in a collective bargaining system. The role of a local *sindicato* leadership in the functioning of such a "junta" was to present the workers' cases before it.

The second level of the labor court system of the Estado Novo was the Regional Labor Tribunal. It consisted of one workers' representative, one employer representative, and three professional judges. The Regional Labor Courts covered a state (in the cases of the larger ones) or several states. They could handle appeals from the boards of conciliation, but such cases of appeal were rare.

The principal task of the Regional Labor Tribunals was to act as a substitute for collective contract negotiation. A *sindicato* that wanted changes in the working conditions of its members submitted a list of these to the appropriate Tribunal Regional do Trabalho. That body then asked the appropriate employers' group for a counterproposal. The judges then decided what the employers must concede, if anything, and embodied this decision in a judgment known as *dissidio coletivo*.

The highest level of the labor court hierarchy of the Estado Novo was the Superior Labor Tribunal, located in the national capital. It consisted of seventeen members, three representatives of the workers, three of the employers, and the rest professional judges. It handled appeals from the regional labor courts and in a few instances was the court of first instance for the determination of *dissidios coletivos*. The only appeal from its decisions was to the Supreme Court.[76]

UNION SOCIAL WELFARE ACTIVITIES

Deprived of the right to bargain collectively, the *sindicatos* under the Estado Novo had their principal role in the field of social welfare. The Consolidation of Labor Laws provided that only one *sindicato* in a given industry in a given locality could be recognized by the Ministry of Labor and that one of the factors that the ministry should use in deciding which *sindicato* should receive recognition (if more than one sought recognition) was "the social services founded and maintained."[77]

What these social service activities could mean is demonstrated by the case of the Sindicato dos Officiaes Alfaiates, Costureiras e Trabalhadores na Indústria de Confecções de Roupas de Pôrto Alegre (Dressmakers and Tailors Union of Pôrto Alegre), which in 1946 had two dental clinics and four medical clinics for its members and ran a technical school and an employment agency. This *sindicato* got its members a 10 percent discount for x-ray treatments, it paid its members 100 cruzeiros on the birth of each child, and paid 300 cruzeiros to survivors on the death of a member. It also paid hospital costs of members.[78]

The cargo checkers' *sindicato* of the port of Santos late in 1946 was paying 8,000 cruzeiros on the death of any member; a subsidy of 30 cruzeiros a day to sick members; 2,000 cruzeiros to a member ordered by a doctor to take a trip for recuperation; and 200 cruzeiros a month on retirement. The *sindicato* employed five doctors full time and retained a lawyer to defend the members against anyone except the *sindicato* itself.[79]

The truck drivers' *sindicato* of São Paulo provided that after six months' affiliation a member could receive visits from a doctor in the member's own home; that after twelve months the members would get hospital services and 10 cruzeiros a day while in the hospital, as well as six months' disability pay at 200 cruzeiros a month. The *sindicato* also paid funeral expenses. A novel feature of this *sindicato's* social aid program was the provision of legal aid to its members who got in trouble with the police as a result of traffic incidents.[80]

The services of the *sindicatos* we have cited were being provided about a year after the end of the Estado Novo. However, it is doubtful that the services provided had been changed drastically in the interim.

A survey of the Statistical Service of Social Welfare and Labor indicated that the *sindicatos* surveyed, covering about 49 percent of all those then legally in existence, had in 1944 provided various services to 731,961 members. Of these, 333,875 members had received medical aid and 212,668 dental help. Others had had hospital service, prescriptions, funeral subsidies and legal aid. This service also reported that in 1945 the *sindicatos* reporting had maintained seventy-two schools, with average attendance of 5,144 children.[81]

Sindicato membership was not compulsory under the Estado Novo, although all workers had to pay the *imposto sindical*. In order to be a member of a *sindicato* a worker had to pay an extra amount for *sindicato* dues. Although the dues payments were usually not very large, the great majority of the workers did not consider membership in "their" *sindicato* to be worth paying the extra amount.

What happened as a result of this situation is demonstrated by the case of the graphic arts workers *sindicato* of São Paulo, which continued to be one of the more militant labor groups. Its membership fell to below 1,000 among the city's 15,000 printing trades workers.[82] The tobacco workers' *sindicato* of Rio de Janeiro in 1944 had only 800 members of 5,000 workers in the trade.[83] Among the hotel workers of Rio, only 720 members of about 60,000 eligible workers were in the *sindicato*.[84] The metallurgical workers *sindicato* of Rio in 1944 had only 8,000 members of a total of 40,000 possible unionists.[85] In 1944 it was reported that there were 327,000 members in 2,381 *sindicatos*, or about 20 percent of all industrial workers.[86]

However, given the total control of the mass media—newspapers, magazines, and radio—Vargas succeeded in convincing many of the workers who did belong to and were active in the organized labor movement that that movement had originated with him. Perhaps a typical attitude of many of the trade unionists in Brazil was expressed by the president of the Commercial Employees Union of Rio de Janeiro when I interviewed him in August 1946, less than a year after the end of the Estado Novo. This young man, when asked about the founding of his organization, replied that it was established during the regime of Vargas, although he was not sure of the exact date. However, a few minutes after telling me this, while glancing over the statutes of his *sindicato* before handing them to me, he read in the first article that the organization had in fact been established in 1908.[87]

THE SOCIAL SECURITY SYSTEM

Another important part of the Vargas System, particularly from the point of view of the average worker, were the social security institutions established under it, which provided health care and retirement benefits for those covered by them.

However, the social security institutions did not constitute a single system. Rather, each large group of workers had its own social security organization. There were six major social security funds, and a large number of smaller ones. The six principal social security organizations were the Instituto dos Industriários (industrial workers), Instituto dos Comerciários (commercial employees), Instituto dos Empregados Marítimos (maritime workers), Instituto dos Empregados do Transporte e Carga (transport workers), Instituto dos Bancários (bank workers), and Instituto dos Servidores do Estado (government employees).

The first five of these "institutes" were under the jurisdiction of the Conselho Superior de Previdência Social (Superior Council of Social Security). Its main function was to act as a court of last appeal for workers who felt that they were not getting the benefits to which they were entitled. Such complaints were first lodged with the director of a particular institute, from which there would be appeal to the governing board of that particular fund, and thence to the Conselho Superior. This council was not considered to be part of the general judicial system, although the Labor Tribunals were.

The social security system was supposed to be financed by three sources—a contribution from the individual worker, deducted from his or her pay by the employer; a contribution from the employer; and a contribution from the government. However, this system of payment suffered from at least two major defects. One was that a substantial number of employers, although deducting the prescribed amount from their workers' pay, failed to turn over these funds to the appropriate social security institute and likewise did not pay their own contribution. As a consequence, not infrequently a worker who applied for the benefits to which he or she was entitled found that he or she was not in fact registered with "his" or "her" institute.

An additional problem was that the government itself was frequently laggard in paying what it was supposed to contribute to the social security system. This fact, as well as the delinquency, continued to be a problem for many years after the end of the Estado Novo.[88]

PERSISTENCE OF THE VARGAS SYSTEM

Insofar as the organized labor movement was concerned, the Vargas System persisted for four decades after the end of the Estado Novo, and three decades after the death of Getúlio Vargas himself. The Ministry of Labor continued to have the right rigidly to control the jurisdiction, funds, elections, and other aspects of the *sindicatos*. Decisions of labor courts rather than collective bargaining continued to predominate. Although the successive governments varied considerably in the degree to which they enforced the Vargas System rules, it was not until the late 1980s that these controls were officially eliminated and a more or less independent labor movement began to emerge.

NOTES

1. Getúlio Vargas, *As Diretrizes da Nova Política do Brasil*, Libraria José Olympio Editora, Rio de Janeiro, 1942, pages 115–116 and 223–224.

2. Michael L. Conniff, *Urban Politics in Brazil: The Rise of Populism, 1925–1945*, University of Pittsburgh Press, Pittsburgh, 1981, page 80.

3. Ibid., pages 82–83.

4. Glauco Carneiro, *História das Revoluções Brasileiras*, Volume I, Edições O Cruzeiro, Rio de Janeiro, 1965, pages 228–242.

5. Interviews with Agildo Barata, onetime *tenente*, onetime treasurer of Partido Comunista, in Rio de Janeiro, August 20 and September 6, 1965; Felinto Muller, senator, onetime *tenente*, in Brasilia, March 18, 1966; Pedro Ludovico, governor of Goiás, onetime *tenente*, in Goiânia, October 3, 1965; see also Virginio Santa Rosa. *O Sentido do Tenentismo*, Civilização Brasileira, S.A., Rio de Janeiro, 1933.

6. For an overall view of the Revolution of 1930, see Jordan Young, *The Brazilian Revolution of 1930 and the After*math, Rutgers University Press, New Brunswick, NJ, 1967.

7. Interview with Agildo Barata, op. cit., August 20, 1965.

8. Interview with Plínio Mello, a leader of Partido Socialista Brasileiro, ex-Communist, ex-Trotskyist, in São Paulo, June 16, 1953.

9. Michael M. Hall and Paulo Sérgio Pinheiro, "The Control and Policing of the Working Class in Brazil, A Paper for the Conference of the History of Law, Labour and Crime, University of Warwick, 16–18 September 1983," page 16.

10. W. Niemeyer, *Movimento Syndicalista no Brasil*, Rio de Janeiro, 1933; see also Alfredo Gómez, *Anarquismo y anarcosindicalismo en América Latina: Colombia, Brasil, Argentina, Mexico*, Ruedo Ibérico, Madrid, 1980, page 143.

11. Jornal do Brasil. *Cadernos JB de IV Centenario*, December 16, 1965, Rio de Janeiro, 1965, page 311.

12. Niemeyer, op. cit.

13. *Acão Direta*, May 7, 1946; see also article by Max Levin and Joseph J. Santuria, "Trade Unions in Latin America," in *Encyclopedia of the Social Sciences*, The Macmillan Company, New York, 1937.

14. *O Commerciario*, publication of Liga dos Empregados do Comércio of Santos, November 30, 1934.

15. *O Commerciario*, October 30, 1934.

16. *O Commerciario*, April 23, 1932; January 7, 1933.

17. *Revista da Associação dos Funcionarios Públicos do Estado de São Paulo*, São Paulo, February and March 1933.

18. *O Commerciario*, August 11, 1934 and February 26, 1935.

19. *American Labor Year Book 1931*, Rand School Press, New York, 1931, page 257.

20. Augusto Machado, *A Caminho da Revolução Operária e Camponesa*, Calvino Filho, Rio de Janeiro, 1934, page 93.

21. *Organização Sindical*, Ministério do Trabalho, Indústria e Comércio, Serviço de Estatística da Previdência e Trabalho, Rio de Janeiro, 1948, page 7.

22. *The Labour Gazette*, monthly periodical of Ministry of Labour of Canada, Ottawa, November 1934, pages 1021–1022.

23. *O Commerciario*, July 18, 1936.

24. *O Commerciario*, May 1, 1932.

25. *Encyclopedia of the Social Sciences*, op. cit.

26. Stephen Naft, "Labor Movements of South America," unpublished manuscript.

27. Stephen Naft, *Fascism and Communism in South America*, Foreign Policy Reports, Foreign Policy Association, New York, December 15, 1937, page 230.

28. *Communist International*, official English-language magazine of Communist International, May 20, 1935.

29. *International Press Correspondence*, news periodical of Communist International, December 2, 1935.

30. *International Press Correspondence*, January 5, 1933.

31. *O Commerciario*, April 23, 1932.

32. *O Commerciario*, May 8 and 15, 1933.

33. Machado, op. cit., page 76.

34. Interview with Caio Plínio Barreto, son of Plínio Barreto, in São Paulo, August 22, 1946.

35. *International Press Correspondence*, January 26, 1935.

36. *International Press Correspondence*, December 21, 1935.

37. *New York Times*, January 30, 1935.

38. Hall and Pinheiro, op. cit., page 18; see also Conniff, op. cit., page 139.

39. Moisés Poblete Troncoso, *El Movimiento Obrero Latinoamericano*, Fondo de Cultura Económica, Mexico, 1946, page 110.

40. Ibid., pages 112–113.

41. *American Labor Year Book 1931*, op. cit., page 267.

42. *American Labor Year Book 1932*, Rand School Press, New York, 1932, page 254.

43. Reid Peraigão, *Manifesto do Partido Socialista Brasileiro*, Rio de Janeiro, 1933.

44. Interview with Heroclinio Cascardo, ex-*tenente*, onetime president of Aliança Nacional Libertadora, in Rio de Janeiro, February 3, 1966.

45. *New York Times*, December 1, 1934.

46. *American Labor Year Book 1931*, op. cit., page 267; and *Los Partidos comunistas de america del Sur y del Caribe y el Movimiento Sindical Revolucionario*, Publicaciones 'Edege,' Barcelona, 1933, page 31.

47. *Diário da Noite*, Rio de Janeiro, December 3, 1936.

48. Machado, op. cit., page 140.

49. *International Press Correspondence*, May 25, 1935.

50. Conniff, op. cit., page 111.

51. Ibid., page 131.

52. Hobart A. Spalding, Jr., *Organized Labor in Latin America: Historical Case Studies of Workers in Dependent Societies*, New York University Press, New York, 1977, pages 179–180.

53. Interview with Carlos Lacerda, ex-governor of Guanabara, onetime leader of Brazilian Communist youth organization, in Rio de Janeiro, February 6, 1966.

54. *International Press Correspondence*, December 2, 1935.

55. Felix de Morães and Francisco Viana, *Prestes: Lutas e Autocriticas*, Vezes Petrópolis, 1982, page 68.

56. Ibid., page 77.

57. John W. F. Dulles, *Brazilian Communism 1935–1945: Repression During World Upheaval*, University of Texas Press, Austin, 1983, page 1; see also Eudocio Ravines, *The Yenan Way: The Kremlin's Penetration of South America*, Charles Sribner & Sons, New York, 1951, page 146.

58. Morães and Viana, op. cit., page 70.

59. Foregoing information on Aliança Nacional Libertadora from Morães and Viana, op. cit., pages 66–77; and interviews with Heroclinio Cascardo, op. cit., February 3, 1966 and Roberto Sisson, onetime secretary of Aliança Nacional Libertadora in Rio de Janeiro, September 8, 1965.

60. *O Commerciario*, July 18, 1936, and International Press Correspondence, July 24, 1937.

61. *Brazil 1939–1941*, published by the Ministry of Foreign Affairs, Rio de Janeiro, 1941, pages 67–69.

62. *Revista de Trabajo*, Ministry of Labor, Santiago, Chile, March 1940.

63. *Consolidação das Leis do Trabalho*, Comissão Técnica de Orientação Sindical Ministério do Trabalho, Indústria e Comércio, Rio de Janeiro, 1944, Article 357.

64. Ibid., Article 535.

65. Interview with Ernesto Street, economist of Confederação Nacional da Indústria, in Rio de Janeiro, March 6, 1966.

66. Consolidação das Leis do Trabalho, op. cit., Article 532.

67. Ibid., Article 530.

68. *Diário Oficial*, official publication of Government of Brazil, Rio de Janeiro, August 18, 1944.

69. Interview with Paulino Humberto De Fazio, ex-president of Sindicato dos Trabalhadores nas Indústrias Gráficas de São Paulo, in São Paulo, August 22, 1946.

70. Interview with Vicente Gamboa, Venezuelan trade union leader recently returned from Brazil, in Caracas, July 21, 1947.

71. Consolidação das Leis do Trabalho, op. cit., Article 550.

72. Ibid., Sections 1–3 of Chapter 3.

73. Interview with Celio Dinardo L. Lacerda, head of Registration Section of Serviço de Organizacão e Registro Sindical of Ministry of Labor, in Rio de Janeiro, April 5, 1956.

74. Sindicato dos Operário Nos Serviços Portuários de Santos. *Convenção Coletiva do Trabalho*, Rio de Janeiro, 1943.

75. Geraldo Montedonio Bezerra de Meneses, *Justiça do Trabalho no Brasil, Relatório das Actividades de 1950*, Rio de Janeiro, 1951, page 8.

76. Interviews with Dr. Raimundo Maura, president of Tribunal Regional do Trabalho, in Belem, February 8, 1956; and Delfim Moreira Jr., president of Tribunal Superior do Trabalho, in Rio de Janeiro, March 13, 1956.

77. *Consolidação das Leis do Trabalho*, op. cit., Article 519.

78. Interview with José Lopes Careja, administrative secretary of Sindicatos dos Oficiais Alfaiates, Costureiras e Trabalhadores na Indústria de Confecções de Roupas de Pôrto Alegre, September 19, 1946.

79. Interview with Francisco Ramon Vico, secretary general, Sindicato dos Conferentes de Carga e Descarga do Porto de Santos, in Santos, September 4, 1946.

80. Interview with Alvaro Gonçalves Casador, president, Sindicato de Condutores de Veículos Rodoviarios e Campos de São Paulo, in São Paulo, September 3, 1946.

81. *Organização Sindical*, op. cit., page 42.

82. Interview with Paulino Humberto De Fazio, op. cit., August 22, 1946.

83. Interview with José Soares Sampaio, president, Sindicato dos Trabalhadores na Indústria do Fumo de Rio de Janeiro, in Rio de Janeiro, August 30, 1946.

84. Interview with João Francisco da Rocha, president, Sindicato dos Empregados no Comércio Hoteleiro e Similares do Rio de Janeiro, in Rio de Janeiro, August 27, 1946.

85. Interview with Manuel Lopes Coelho Filho, official of Metallurgical Workers of Rio de Janeiro, later secretary general of Confederação Geral do Trabalho Brasileiro, in Rio de Janeiro, August 29, 1946.

86. *CIO News*, periodical of Congress of Industrial Organizations, Washington, DC, March 27, 1944.

87. Interview with Nelson Motta, president, Sindicato dos Empregados do Comércio of Rio de Janeiro, in Rio de Janeiro, August 14, 1946.

88. Interview with Octavio de Sousa Leão, president of Conselho Superior de Previdência Social, in Rio de Janeiro, March 12, 1956.

3
Unionism in the Democratic Interregnum (1945–1964), Part I

The formal end of the Estado Novo may be dated from the overthrow of President Getúlio Vargas by the military on October 29, 1945. However, for almost a year before that date, the corporative state that Vargas had established on November 10, 1937, had been unraveling.

By the last year of World War II, fascist-like corporative states were out of fashion. This was peculiarly the case in Brazil, which had joined the antifascist side in the war and in the last months of the conflict had a contingent of troops fighting with the American forces in the last struggle against the German and Italian fascists in Italy. It grew increasingly incongruous for a government modeled on the 1930s fascist regimes of Europe to be fighting a "war against fascism."

In the later months of 1944, opposition to the Vargas regime became increasingly open. The União Democrática Nacional (UDN) was formed by the democratic opposition in the principal states of São Paulo, Minas Gerais, and Rio Grande do Sul and in Rio de Janeiro. It included industrialists, students, landowners, workers, part of the old *tenentes*, as well as remnants of the National Liberation Alliance and the Communist Party. There were some two hundred former deputies and senators connected with the movement. A *pronunciamento* issued by the UDN announced its intention "to coordinate all democratic currents in a united front and reestablish constitutional democracy" and proclaimed the candidacy of General Eduardo Gomes, former chief of the air force, for president of the Republic.[1]

It is important to note that the Communists were enthusiastically part of the UDN when it was first formed and for several months thereafter. The New York Communist newspaper *Daily Worker* noted, "This coalition organization is supported by leading democratic figures throughout the country."[2] Two months later, the *Daily Worker's* Latin American expert, Juan Antonio Corretjer, said: "It is important to see who is this man who appears as Brazil's future presidential candidate. General Eduardo Gomes proceeds from the tenentista, a movement that has written so many great pages of democratic history."[3]

President Vargas finally had to concede to the growing opposition. General Eurico Dutra, his minister of war, reportedly advised him to put an end to the Estado Novo.[4] On February 22, 1945, censorship of the press was ended, and on February 28, Vargas announced an amendment to the Constitution of 1937 that opened the way for general elections of both the president and Congress.

In April, the UDN was converted into a political party. On April 18, Vargas signed a decree of amnesty of 148 political prisoners, including the most famous of them all, the Communist leader, Luiz Carlos Prestes.[5]

Thus, by the end of April 1945, an election campaign was under way. For this purpose, the Vargas administration organized its own political parties. These were the Partido Social Democrático (PSD), which encompassed particularly the traditional political bosses in the more rural states (the "colonels"), some industrialists who had prospered under Vargas, and some considerable middle-class elements. The other was the Partido Trabalhista Brasileiro (Brazilian Labor Party, or PTB), which was designed particularly to rally Vargas's working-class supporters.

ORGANIZED LABOR AND THE APPROACHING END OF THE ESTADO NOVO

The organized labor movement was greatly influenced by the approaching end of the Estado Novo. In 1946, various trade union leaders informed me that they became aware of the loosening of the bonds of the dictatorship during the latter half of 1944, when the government began to permit more or less free elections in the *sindicatos*. It was at this time, for instance, that José Soares Sampaio was elected president of the Tobacco Workers Union of Rio de Janeiro, although he was at the time labeled, a bit recklessly, a "Communist," and about the same time a distinctly anti-Vargas administration was allowed to take office in the Printing Trades Union of São Paulo.[6]

Organized labor was particularly influenced by a tacit alliance between the Communists and the supporters of President Vargas during the months before the ouster of the president. In the period preceding this, the underground Communist Party had been the scene of a bitter internal struggle between those who insisted on maintaining the hitherto unrelenting opposition to the Estado Novo and those who sought a rapprochement with President Vargas. On his release from jail, Luiz Carlos Prestes sided with the latter group and took most of the party members with him.[7]

In his first speech after getting out of prison, before 70,000 people in the Vasco de Gama stadium in Rio de Janeiro, Prestes astounded other leftists who had been demanding that Vargas resign by saying that resignation of the president would be a "desertion" and would cause confusion and chaos. He said that the Communist Party, "loyal to the principles of national unity," would ask all good Brazilians to join in support of a progressive program.[8] In another speech, two weeks later, Prestes said that the fight was for the reform of existing legislation and not against the Ministry of Labor. He said that the question of the presidential succession should not have arisen until a national program had been developed.[9]

A year and a half after his release from prison, in answer to my questions, Luiz Carlos Prestes denied that during the last months of the Vargas regime the Communists had had any "alliance" with the dictator. He denied that he had ever met Vargas until after his release from jail. Prestes said that any similarity in tactics between the Communists and Vargas in 1945 had been merely a coincidence of short-term interests. Both Vargas and the Communists wished to avoid a military coup d'état, since it would be directed against both of them, so they had both worked to keep Vargas in power temporarily. The Communists had wanted a constitutional convention to abolish the fascist constitution of 1937 before new elections were called.[10]

As a result of this sudden shift in the Communists' position, they had to withdraw from the UDN, and soon they were attacking their old allies. Rodolfo Ghioldi, the Argentine Communist leader who was an old friend of Prestes, after a visit to Brazil undoubtedly was reflecting the Brazilian Communist leaders' view when he wrote:

The oppositionists are not against the Estado Novo. . . . They were the theoreticians of corporatism while Fascism was in the ascendancy throughout the world and were admirers of Vargas from 1936 to 1942. But now, when Vargas established relations with the USSR and granted amnesty as well as freedom of the press and association and of labor and announced that elections will be held, they are furiously anti-Vargas. . . . They resent democratization and their new techniques consist in appealing to the opposition candidate to assume a dictatorship. They are using the honorable name of Brigadier General Eduardo Gomes in this way as a smokescreen for their reactionary intrigues.[11]

Whether or not there was a formal alliance between the Communists and Vargas, there was clearly a de facto arrangement. Vargas legalized the Communist Party and permitted it an almost free hand to operate in the labor movement, and the Communists in return supported Vargas's efforts to stay in office.

The Communist Party expanded with great rapidity after the release of Prestes from jail. Communist organizations sprang up all over the country. The Executive Committee of the São Paulo party was inaugurated with a message from Prestes in June.[12] Prestes was elected general secretary of the party in a convention held in the middle of August 1945.[13]

GROWTH IN UNION MEMBERSHIP AND MILITANCY

With the return of substantial freedom, the labor movement revived rapidly. Membership in the sindicatos increased at a quick pace. The Rio de Janeiro tobacco workers' organization, for instance, grew from 800 in 1944 to 3,200 by August 1946.[14] The Rio de Janeiro hotel workers' *sindicato* membership jumped from 720 to between 12,000 and 13,000 in about the same period.[15] Membership in the metallurgical workers *sindicato* in Rio more than doubled between 1944 and 1946.[16] This same general tendency was manifested throughout the country.

The renaissance of the labor movement was not only in numbers but also in militancy. For the first time in ten years, there were numerous strikes. Many walkouts occurred in Santos, where the Communists quickly got control of the key *sindicatos*. Strike fever throughout Brazil began about the middle of March 1945 and increased in volume as time went on. By the end of May, for instance, strikes had occurred in the Goodyear factory; the coffee machinery manufacturing plant of Martins, Ferreira & Co.; and the metal works of the Albion Manufacturing Co., all in São Paulo. All São Paulo commercial employees threatened a strike for a wage rise. The São Paulo Railway workers had a strike for the first time in many years, seeking a 40 percent wage increase.[17]

The increasing boldness of at least some of the workers was shown on May Day 1945. In São Paulo, although the "official" May Day celebration was held in the Municipal Theater, with the Regional Labor Delegate Fernando Nobre Filho the principal speaker, a rival meeting was organized in the headquarters of the Classes Laboriosas, by several political groups, as well as the Journalists Union. On that day, the *Jornal de São Paulo* published an article by the old anarchosyndicalist leader Edgard Leuenroth on the origins of May Day as the workers' holiday to commemorate the "martyrs of Chicago," that is, the anarchist leaders executed in the wake of the Haymarket massacre in 1886.[18]

The Communists were very active in the revived *sindicatos*. They adopted the policy of fighting within the *sindicatos* that had been legalized by the Ministry of Labor, rather than trying to form independent organizations under their own leadership. This method of working was designed to arouse less opposition from the government and had the advantage that when they got control of a *sindicato*, they had at their disposal the funds provided by the *imposto sindical*. The effectiveness of the Communist penetration of the government-recognized *sindicatos* is shown by the extent of control they had by August 1946 in almost all of the thirty-seven *sindicatos* in the port city of Santos,[19] as well as decisive control of the *sindicatos* of the northeastern city of Recife; they were also very powerful in Rio de Janeiro and in the city of São Paulo, where they had control of about half of the legally recognized *sindicatos*.[20]

THE MOVIMENTO UNIFICADOR DOS TRABALHADORES

In addition to the rapid growth in militancy of the legally recognized *sindicatos*, there began to appear as early as the last months of 1944 a number of extralegal labor groups, many of them under Communist leadership and control. In several states, congresses were held to establish statewide labor organizations. For instance, in Minas Gerais, the Congresso Sindical dos Trabalhadores met in November 1944 with delegates reportedly present from fifty-two *sindicatos*.[21] Other kinds of extralegal labor groups appeared, such as the Comité Operário Contra a Carestia da Vida (Workers' Committee against the High Cost of Living) in São Paulo.[22]

The culmination of this drive to establish labor groups outside the Estado Novo legal framework culminated in April 1945 in the establishment of the Movimento Unificador dos Trabalhadores (Unifying Movement of the Workers, or MUT). According to one pro-Communist United States source, the leaders of the MUT included "those who fought in existing *sindicatos* in the interests of labor and who are now participating in the MUT as individuals, and those trade unionists of great prestige and militant background who until recently found it impossible to join the government-controlled *sindicatos*."[23]

In fact, the MUT was largely the creation of the Communist Party. Arnaldo Spindel, a student of the Brazilian labor movement, said that that the objective of the MUT was "not only to support the dictator in order to achieve legalization of the Communist Party, but also to place Communists in positions of leadership within the labor union structure."[24]

John W. F. Dulles asserted that the MUT "flourished with the permission of the Vargas government although it lay outside of the arrangements prescribed by the labor laws."[25] Clearly, the MUT could not have assumed the importance it did if President Vargas had been strongly against it. However, there is evidence that the minister of labor was unhappy about the MUT and the general direction the labor movement was taking by April 1945.

In that month, the ministry issued a document urging that workers continue to cooperate with the ministry and not try to settle labor disputes outside legal channels. This was signed by a number of *sindicato* leaders, including heads of the food workers of Rio de Janeiro, the Motor Vehicle Conductors Federation, the Rio de Janeiro Commercial Employees Federation, and the National Maritime Federation.[26]

In the months between its establishment and the fall of Vargas, the MUT followed the then-current policy of the Communist Party. By September, its emphasis had shifted from economic demands to agitation in favor of a constitutional assembly. In the middle of September, MUT organized a parade of 40,000 workers in Rio de Janeiro on Brazilian Independence Day, to demand full restoration of trade union freedom and the calling of a constituent assembly.[27] A few weeks later, the MUT cooperated with the Communist Party in organizing a series of meetings in favor of a constitutional assembly.[28] Other political moves by the MUT included telegrams sent to Vargas urging that he intervene on behalf of two Spanish underground leaders sentenced to death by the Franco regime, and others that demanded suppression of the fascist party, Acão Integralista.[29]

The MUT sent three delegates to the founding congress of the World Federation of Trade Unions in Paris in October 1945. These were Pedro de Carvalho Braga, leader of the electrical workers of Rio de Janeiro; Lindolfo Hill, leader of the construction workers of Minas Gerais; and Guillermo Tubbs, president of the São Paulo Textile Workers Federation.[30] The first two were later elected to the National Executive of the Communist Party.[31] Tubbs was a non-Communist and a member of the UDN.[32]

The tolerant attitude of the Vargas regime to the MUT is indicated by a story that appeared in the Communist paper *Tribuna Popular*. It recounted that in the process of a hearing on a dispute of the tobacco workers' *sindicato* of Rio de Janeiro in the Regional Labor Tribunal, the court allowed MUT representatives to use the microphone in the courtroom, for the purpose of demonstrating that the interests of the company itself would be served by a wage increase.[33]

The MUT continued in existence for about a year.

THE ROLE OF THE PARTIDO TRABALHISTA BRASILEIRO

As we have noted, the Vargas regime had organized the Partido Trabalhista Brasileiro (PTB) to rally Vargas's supporters among the working class. Michael Conniff argued that Getúlio Vargas had decided while the Estado Novo dictatorship was still completely in place "that he intended to remain in office after the war by creating a labor party." Conniff added, "To be sure, little mention of what came to be the Brazilian Labor Party . . . was made before the close of the war, but the direction of Vargas' policies was unmistakable."[34] I am inclined rather to believe that the establishment of the PTB was forced on Vargas once the Estado Novo had begun to unravel.

Getúlio Vargas himself was named honorary president of the PTB. Its effective head was José Segadas Viana, the director general of the Ministry of Labor. Although Segadas Viana told me that the PTB was organized by the ministry without previous approval of the President, Vargas did subsequently approve of its establishment. The avowed purpose of the party was to build up an organization that could combat the rapidly growing influence of the Communists.[35]

The PTB fulfilled its purpose. A year later, when I was studying the Brazilian labor movement, I found that the *sindicato* leadership, at least on the level of the local *sindicatos*, tended to be divided between Communists and PTB members. However, at that time, the affiliation of a *sindicato* leader with one or the other of those parties tended to a large extent to take the form of adherence to a particular political leader. Those who were Communists were *Prestistas*, followers of Luiz Carlos Prestes; those who were PTB members were *Getúlistas*, supporters of Getúlio Vargas.

The electoral law that Vargas decreed for the 1946 election was designed to enroll as many of the president's supporters as possible. John D. French noted:

To guarantee participation by working people in significant numbers, Vargas made voting obligatory for virtually all literate Brazilians . . . and established an ex-officio voter registration procedure designed to favor urban over rural areas. While most Brazilians had to individually register with the local electoral notary, this form of ex-officio group registration benefited all full-time or part-time employees of public offices, professional associations, and private, mixed or state businesses.

Professor French continued:

The appropriate company official was required to submit a list of employees to an electoral judge, who returned the required electoral
identification cards for distribution within the factory. Since the lists
submitted did not have the signature of the applicant, many illiterate
urban workers thus escaped disenfranchisement, despite the law's literacy provisions.[36]

During the interim between establishment of the PTB and the
overthrow of Vargas, the party specialized in holding mass meetings expressing adherence to Getúlio Vargas. Frequently, those
attending meetings would chant the slogan "Queremos Getúlio"
(We Want Getúlio). The PTB thus acquired the nickname of
"Queremistas."

During the election campaign, even after the ousting of Vargas, the Partido Trabalhista Brasileiro used Getúlio as its chief
selling point. He was nominated as candidate for Congress in the
Federal District and as head of the party's ticket in each state.[37]
Posters appeared with Vargas's picture on them and the slogan
"He said register and vote with the Brazilian Labor Party." Before
his ousting, Vargas made a speech to a PTB meeting in which he
urged that the workers "should defend themselves against attempts from extremist elements who want to absorb them," a jibe
clearly directed against the Communists.[38]

However, until the overthrow of Vargas, the Communists continued to urge that he continue in office, at least for some time.
They pushed the campaign for a constitutional assembly, arguing
that the contest for president "signifies nothing but simple change
of men in power," and that "people's representatives will give the
constitution the nation demands, as the surest road for following
the pacific road to democracy."[39] On one occasion, Luiz Carlos
Prestes said, "We insist that the campaign for a campaign for a
constituent assembly must proceed, but if within a reasonable
period of time, the Government does not meet the people's demands, the Communists will take the side of the people in the
electoral campaign."[40] Just which side "the side of the people"
was, Prestes did not specify.

Moisés Vinhas summed up the Communists' position in this
period, saying that they "decidedly supported Getúlio Vargas, going into the streets to fight for the constitutional assembly with
Getúlio, alongside the 'queremistas.' "[41]

OVERTHROW OF VARGAS AND THE 1945 ELECTION

In October 1945, events moved swiftly. On the third of the month, Vargas came out with endorsement of the idea of a constituent assembly.[42] A day or so later, Adolf A. Berle, Jr., the U.S. ambassador, made a speech in which he praised democracy, said that he and the American people were happy to see Vargas call elections, and made it clear that the United States favored the holding of the elections. It has been claimed that this speech was submitted to Vargas for comment before it was delivered.[43] But if that is so, it did not prevent a display of righteous indignation from Vargas at this "unwarranted interference" in Brazilian internal affairs.

Luiz Carlos Prestes also objected to Berle's speech: "We protest against the United States Ambassador's interference in Brazil's internal affairs. . . . We ourselves can solve our problems without any foreign intervention. . . . Berle's unfortunate words favor those who are seeking a coup, as in Argentina."[44]

Berle's speech no doubt strengthened the hand of the anti-Vargas groups, and matters were brought to a head during the last week of October, when Getúlio suddenly named his brother, Benjamin Vargas, as chief of Federal Police. The military men interpreted his appointment as meaning that Getúlio had decided to cancel the elections, and since they were committed to them, the army chiefs felt they had to move against the president. With the support of the two presidential candidates, General Eurico Dutra and Brigadier Eduardo Gomes, and of the minister of war, General Pedro Aurélio Góes Monteiro, Vargas was removed from the presidency, and as the constitution provided, the head of the Supreme Court was put in his place.

After a few days of uncertainty, the election campaign proceeded. A new candidate entered, when the Communists nominated Yeddo Fiuza, the former mayor of the city of Petrópolis and director of the Federal Highway Department, as their nominee, "not as a Communist candidate, but as a democratic candidate supported by the Communist Party," according to a Communist Party announcement.[45]

Although for several weeks after his overthrow Getúlio Vargas remained silent as to his preference in the presidential election, about a week before the poll he urged his supporters to back General Dutra. His support was largely responsible for Dutra's victory. The Communists were also an important element in Dutra's victory, by splitting the anti-Dutra forces with their nominee. Prestes had several times expressed preference for Dutra as against Gomes.[46]

The Communists did very well in the election, getting thirteen deputies and one senator, Luiz Carlos Prestes, who was elected from the Federal District. Their deputies were from the Federal District, São Paulo, Pernambuco, Bahia, and the state of Rio de Janeiro.[47] In the popular vote for president, the Communists came in second in São Paulo and Rio and received a majority in a number of smaller cities, including Santos, Natal, and Aracajú.[48]

The Labor Party also did well. It received thirty seats in the new constitutional assembly.[49] The party led the poll in Rio de Janeiro, where it got 110,000 votes, with the Communists second.[50]

ORGANIZED LABOR IN THE EARLY DUTRA ADMINISTRATION

The labor militancy that had characterized the last months of the Vargas regime continued during the provisional government that followed Vargas's ouster and the first year and a half of the Dutra administration, which took over in January 1946. Strikes were frequent. They included a national bank workers' walkout,[51] a public utility strike in Rio de Janeiro,[52] and a coal miners' strike in Rio Grande do Sul.[53]

In São Paulo in February and March 1946 there was a widespread strike movement that involved "at its height, 100,000 workers in the metropolitan São Paulo region."

However, the employers' groups, with growing support from the Dutra regime, strongly resisted the workers' militancy. John French, concerning the situation in São Paulo, the country's largest industrial area, wrote:

São Paulo's industrial employers, backed by the PSD in Rio and São Paulo, pursued a constantly repressive policy in an effort to demobolize the newly-militant postwar trade unionism. In the aftermath of the strikes of early 1946, they set out to purge their factories of union activists while encouraging police harassment of labor and the left, and government intervention in the trade unions. This resort to repression, however, intensified the workers' determination in 1946 and 1947 to guarantee their new-found rights and to bar a return to a past they had so thoroughly rejected.[54]

Professor French pointed out that in this period the leadership of the labor movement was divided into three different elements. These consisted, on the one hand, of the "labor Right," which generally controlled the higher echelon labor organizations, popularly referred to as *pelegos*; the Communists' "labor Left;"

and the "labor center," consisting of Vargas supporters in the rank and file and lower echelons of trade union leadership.

According to French:

Indeed the Brazilian labor movement that emerged from the Estado Novo was not in fact dominated by the so-called pelegos or labor right. The internal politics of postwar labor was marked by a complicated interplay between the minority labor right, the numerically dominant labor center, and a growing labor left represented by the Communist Party. The key to the left-center political complexion of the postwar labor movement lay precisely in the trajectory of this evolving if amorphous labor center.[55]

It is interesting to note that none of the three elements in the labor movement sought to free the trade unions from financial dependence on the government, that is, to abolish the *imposto sindical*. Manuel Lopes Coelho Filho, one of the principal Communist labor leaders of this period, explained to me that such a move would not be "wise," and that his group would certainly not advocate such a policy because it would make it virtually impossible for the *sindicatos* to operate.[56]

The only voice that came out with such a suggestion was *Vanguarda Socialista*, which several times pointed out the inconsistency of "trade union autonomy" and government subsidization of the *sindicatos*.[57] After the Vanguarda Socialista group merged with Esquerda Democrática to form the Partido Socialista do Brasil, that party's deputy, João Mangabeira, introduced a bill to reform the Estado Novo trade union setup that would, among other things, have eliminated the *imposto sindical*.[58] It never got out of committee.

NATIONAL LABOR CONGRESS

The high point of cooperation between what John French called the labor "center" and "Left" was the attempt in September 1946 to establish a central labor organization, an element that was not provided for in the Estado Novo legislation that still prevailed. The initiators of this move were the Movimento Unificador dos Trabalhadores, which previously organized a series of regional labor congresses.

The MUT finally issued a call for a national labor convention in Rio de Janeiro to be held August 20, 1946. However, soon after this call was issued, the Ministry of Labor called for a rival labor convention to meet on September 9. After several meetings between the MUT and government officials, an agreement was made for a joint congress. The agenda adopted for that meeting was practically the same as that which had been drawn up by the MUT.

In the preparation of the meeting, which was fixed for September 9, there was the fullest cooperation between the MUT organizing committee and the one set up by the ministry. It was decided that each *sindicato* or federation would have two delegates to the congress, one to be chosen by the organization's officers from among their own number, and one to be elected in a *sindicato* membership meeting. The election of both by the members was desired by the Communists, because they had more strength in the rank and file than among *sindicato* officials. The government put the leaders of all the federations then in existence in charge of actual arrangements for the congress, and this group worked closely with the MUT committee previously appointed for the purpose.[59] The MUT had in the meanwhile been officially outlawed by the government in May 1946.

The National Labor Congress met in Rio de Janeiro on September 9, 1946, and continued for about a week. There were, as might have been expected, three general tendencies in the congress: a pro-Communist group, a pro-Vargas group, and a progovernment element. In most matters, the first two worked together against the third.

The first sessions of the two-thousand-delegate meeting were exceedingly noisy, as everyone tried to speak at once. Manuel Coelho Filho, head of the metal workers' *sindicato* of Rio de Janeiro, was floor leader of the Communist element, and during the first session he and the progovernment figures who dominated the rostrum got along fairly well.

However, in the third plenary session of the congress, the congress's commission on constitution presented two alternative proposals. One was for the establishment of a Confederação Geral do Trabalho Brasileiro (Brazilian General Labor Confederation, or CGTB); the other was for the formation of a committee to undertake the fulfillment of the labor part of the structure established by the Estado Novo corporative system by organizing state and national federations and confederations as provided for in the Consolidação das Leis do Trabalho. The pro-CGTB idea was accepted in the commission on constitution by a 381–85 vote; the progovernment people voted against it. When this action was taken to the floor of the third plenary session, the delegates of the Federação dos Empregados no Comércio of São Paulo objected to the decision, asserting that the congress was being used for political purposes. When they were rebuffed, they walked out of the meeting, with several hundred other delegates following them.

These delegates then met in Niterói, across the bay from the federal capital, and asked the government to dissolve the congress because it was being used for political purposes. The Ministry of Labor obliged by officially dissolving the congress, but about eight hundred delegates continued to meet, ratified the formation of the Confederação Geral do Trabalho Brasileiro, and elected a provisional executive committee for the new organization. The group also voted to have the CGTB join the Confederación de Trabajadores de América Latina and the World Federation of Trade Unions.[60]

The CGTB continued to function openly for only a few months. However, during that period, it seemed to make very considerable progress. In March 1947 it launched in São Paulo a national campaign to enlist 200,000 new members in its affiliated *sindicatos*. However, shortly after the Supreme Electoral Tribunal in effect declared the Communist Party illegal, the CGTB was also outlawed on the grounds of "coincidence of orientation with the political line of the Communists."[61]

ORGANIZED LABOR IN THE LATTER PART OF THE DUTRA REGIME

The official "closing" of the CGTB congress marked an open split between the center and Left of the Brazilian labor movement, on the one hand, and the Dutra regime, on the other. The Ministry of Labor refused to give any kind of legal recognition to the CGTB. Rather it turned its attention to fostering the formation of the federations and confederations of workers provided for in the Estado Novo framework but never established under Vargas. The first of these national groups to be organized was the Confederação Nacional dos Trabalhadores no Comércio, organized in 1947 with state federations representing white-collar workers in São Paulo, Rio Grande do Sul, the Federal District, Pernambuco, and Minas Gerais. In the same year the Confederação Nacional dos Trabalhadores na Indústria, consisting of federations of workers in all types of manufacturing industries throughout the country was organized. At its first congress in August 1949 there were 541 delegates in attendance, one from each affiliated *sindicato*.

In 1948 two other national groups were established, the Federação Nacional de Estivadores, which included eighteen dock workers' *sindicatos*; and the Federação Nacional de Trabalhadores en Tranvias, which had trolley car workers' *sindicatos* from various states in its ranks. The Federação Nacional dos Trabalhadores em Turismo e Hospitalidade, which claimed 185,000 members and fifty-one affiliated *sindicatos*, was also established in 1948 to cover the workers in the hotel and tourist business, as well as in hospitals.[62] Subsequently, several other federations and confederations were organized.

Meanwhile, until the middle of 1947 the Communists continued to make marked progress, in both the electoral and trade union fields, in the latter still in more or less close cooperation with the labor leaders and rank and file who were loyal to the ex-President Getúlio Vargas. Their electoral progress was clear in the January 1947 elections for state legislatures, municipal councils, and some vacant seats in Congress. They elected forty-six deputies in fifteen states and got a majority in the city council of the Federal District, that is, the city of Rio de Janeiro. They also elected two additional members of the Federal Chamber of Deputies.[63]

The party ranks grew precipitously. By 1947 the party had about 200,000 members. Moisés Vinhas described the party's recruiting methods:

In São Paulo, they brought together hundreds of workers in sports clubs or other entities, generally on non-working days and presented an exposition of the policies of the Communists, followed by discussion. The discussion closed, they asked those who wished to join the PCB to remain in the room and the rest to leave. Sometimes, there remained hundreds of workers who would be divided into groups, according to the firms in which they worked. They then filled out their membership cards, being immediately organized into a cell and electing a secretariat, composed, generally of *sindicato* officials or people with leadership in the firm.[64]

The Communist national leadership in this period followed a cautious policy, seeking to prevent confrontation with the government. Within a few weeks of the fall of Vargas, Luiz Carlos Prestes had announced, "It is preferable, comrades, to pull in our belts to starve rather than to make strikes to create agitations— because agitations and disorders, in the historical epoch in which we are, can only serve fascism."

The Communist leadership stuck to that policy for a year and a half. Thus, soon after the January 1947 elections, when the party leaders in Recife decided to launch a campaign for general wage increases involving extensive strikes, the local leaders were called to Rio de Janeiro and told by Prestes to cancel all their plans for such walkouts.[65]

The Partido Trabalhista Brasileiro tended to lose considerable ground to the Communists in this period. This was due in part to the fact that it had been organized from the top down and included not only militant workers on the lower levels of the trade union structure, but also the *pelegos* who had managed the labor movement for the Vargas regime until 1945, and sought to continue to do so for the Dutra regime. They constituted much of the right wing of the PTB.

John D. French noted:

The PTB's cadre of leading unionists could have worked to consolidate getulista union supporters by operating within the broader current of postwar labor. Instead the labor right sought to pit the PTB and Getúlio's prestige against the majority of the union movement, including the centrist getúlistas. Nurtured under the noncompetitive conditions of the Estado Novo, this stratum of functionaries feared that the new ferment in labor would cost them their salaried positions. . . . In incorporating such rightist labor figures into their party's structure at the national and state level, the PTB weakened its own influence within the labor movement.[66]

In spite of their caution in the trade union field, the Communists could not prevent an ultimate showdown with the Dutra administration, which evidenced increasing hostility to the Partido Comunista. In May 1946, the government dismissed all government employees who were known to be Communists. In mid-April, the party's youth organization, the União de Juventude Comunista, was legally "suspended." Then the Dutra administration sued in the Supreme Electoral Court for the canceling of the legal registration of the Communist Party on the grounds that it was "antidemocratic," and parties of that nature could not function legally according to the new constitution. On May 1947, the court outlawed the PCB. Eight months later, Congress expelled from its membership all those who had been elected as Communists.[67]

The Dutra regime also moved strongly against the Communists in the labor movement. As we have noted, it outlawed the Confederação Geral dos Trabalhadores do Brasil. The Ministry of Labor also removed the leadership of 143 *sindicatos* throughout the country, out of a total of 944 after issuing Decree 23,046, which declared that *sindicatos* must keep "apart from all political and social movements."[68]

In some places the government "intervention" decimated the labor movement. John D. French noted:

One day after Decree 23,046, the *diretorios* of thirty-six São Paulo trade unions had already been ousted. Virtually the entire labor movement of the left-wing stronghold of Santos, sixteen unions in all, were intervened, as well as fourteen unions in the city of São Paulo, four more in the metropolitan region, and two in the interior of the state.[69]

However, the Communist Party was able to continue to function to a considerable degree. Moisés Vinhas noted that the party's daily newspaper in Rio Janeiro merely changed its name from *Tribuna Popular* to *Imprensa Popular*.[70] Probably more damaging to Communist influence in organized labor than government persecution was the party's reaction to being formally outlawed. In January 1948, it issued a manifesto demanding the resignation of President Dutra.

Vinhas noted:

One of the best areas to observe the process of movement to the left and loss of influence of the PCB was, undoubtedly, its working class and trade union activity. Adopting the slogan of "overthrowing the government," which it labeled one of "national betrayal," the Communists moved to stimulate all kinds of strike action, independent of time and place. They sought to gain control of *sindicato* executives at any price, and when they did not succeeded, sought a split. It is evident that such a position engendered resistance and created frictions of various kinds. Claiming that the existing trade union structure was tied to the Ministry of Labor, the Communists broke with it and undertook the construction of "parallel *sindicatos*." In truth those only succeeded in bringing together a small number of members, in their majority Communists. The successive failures of this policy brought disorganization to the working class base of the PCB, whether because its worker members were dismissed by the firms or because of the new sindicatos disappeared.[71]

As a result of the extremist and isolationist line adopted by the Communist Party after its outlawing, the party lost most of its membership. According to Moisés Vinhas, there were only 20,000 members by 1950, compared to the 200,000 people who had belonged in 1947.[72]

However, possible Communist influence in organized labor continued to preoccupy the Dutra government. As a consequence, in 1949 the Ministry of Labor postponed all further *sindicato* elections indefinitely.[73]

In spite of, or perhaps because of, the Dutra administration's hostility to organized labor, the trade union leadership to a considerable degree closed its ranks behind Getúlio Vargas's attempt to be reelected president of Brazil. He was the nominee of the Partido Trabalhista Brasileiro, and within the trade union movement his sympathizers formed the Frente Electoral Nacional Operário, to rally support for his candidacy.[74] Vargas was elected with a plurality among three candidates and finally after considerable controversy took office as constitutional president in January 1951.

THE LABOR MOVEMENT IN THE SECOND
VARGAS REGIME

With the return of Getúlio Vargas to the presidency, the situation of the labor movement markedly improved. The suspension of *sindicato* elections was ended, and in the next year and a half most of the country's sindicatos were returned to the hands of elected officers. The Ministry of Labor, under José Segadas Viana, who in 1945, as director general of the ministry had been largely responsible for the organization of the Partido Trabalhista Brasileiro, canceled the requirement that candidates for *sindicato* office present a statement of ideological "purity" from the police. Segadas Viana also ended the requirement that a Ministry of Labor official be present at all *sindicato* meetings.[75]

President Vargas also submitted to Congress a law permitting the labor confederations to join the International Confederation of Free Trade Unions (ICFTU) and its American regional organization, the Organización Regional Interamericana de Trabajadores (ORIT). Notably, however, this legislation did not provide that Brazilian *sindicatos* could join the so-called international trade secretariats, apparently because of fear that those under Communist control might join those similar organizations associated with the Communist-controlled World Federation of Trade Unions instead of those aligned with the ICFTU.[76]

One effect of these measures modifying government control over the *sindicatos* was a substantial increase in *sindicato* membership. Another result was a renewal of labor militancy. Moisés Vinhas noted, "In 1951 and 1952 there occurred various small strikes for wage increases or payment of back wages."[77]

One of these strikes was a weeklong walkout of the textile workers of Recife. It arose when the employers refused to pay wage increases decreed in a *dissidio coletivo* by the Regional Labor Court, arguing that they would not do so until their appeal of the regional court's decision to the Supreme Labor Court had been heard. After a week, the employers conceded the pay increase, and subsequently the *sindicato* won its appeal. However, as a result of the strike, the employers refused any longer to check off *sindicato* dues, arguing that a previous *sindicato*-management agreement by which they had been obliged to do so had been canceled by the strike. The result was that, whereas in 1952 some 19,000 workers paid *sindicato* dues, by 1956 the number had been reduced to 8,000.[78]

Another important strike in this period was that of the printing trades workers of Pôrto Alegre, which lasted twenty-nine days and was finally won by the *sindicato*. One interesting feature of this walkout was that the *sindicato* leaders used some of the *sin-*

dicato's income as a de facto strike fund, providing food and other necessities to the strikers and their families. Although this action was totally illegal according to the Consolidação das Leis do Trabalho, the *sindicato* and its leaders suffered no adverse consequences from their action.[79]

The high point in trade union militancy was reached in 1953 in two major walkouts. One was a near-general strike in São Paulo, which lasted twenty-nine days in March and April. The other was a general walkout of maritime workers in June.

Moisés Vinhas noted that the São Paulo walkout

> began in the Matarazzo textile factory . . . on the night of March 21. The workers demanded a 60 percent wage increase, stability in employment and measures against inflation. The employers offered 20 percent considered that it would not be possible to reach an accord with the *sindicato* and hardened their position. Vargas avoided becoming directly involved and left his Minister of Labor, Segadas Viana . . . in the line of fire. The Governor of São Paulo, Lucas Nogueira Garcez ended up serving as mediator. The movement involved about 300,000 workers and the majority of the fundamental branches of production at that time: metal workers, textiles, woodworkers, printing trades, glass workers, etc. Substantial aid was given both inside the factories and working class districts which mobilized in solidarity.[80]

Some *sindicatos* did not participate in the general strike. This was true of the construction workers, who during the walkout negotiated (without striking themselves) an agreement for a 24 percent wage increase with their employers.[81] In other cases, *sindicatos* joined the walkout considerably after it had started. This was the case of the Printing Trades Workers, who were out on strike for only sixteen days.[82]

The strike was marked by public demonstrations, parades, and a very large meeting in the Praça da Se, the city's central square, where there was a clash with the state police, in which army troops who were present refused to intervene. Strike committees were organized in the factories, and the general direction of the walkout was in the hands of an Interunion Unity Pact, consisting of leaders of the *sindicatos* involved, which pledged that no *sindicato* would make a separate settlement until there was an overall agreement with the employers.[83]

After several days, the strikers were offered a wage increase of 23 percent but turned that down. A bit later, the Metal Workers Union was offered by their employers a 32 percent increase if they would settle separately. However, the *sindicato* rejected this, in view of the strikers' agreement not to make individual settlements with the employers.[84]

The strike was finally settled after twenty-nine days. An assembly of strikers agreed to a 32 percent wage increase, the extension of this increase to all industrial categories, payment of workers for the days they had been on strike, freedom of all those arrested as a result of the strike, and guarantees against reprisals by the employers.[85]

The strike settlement was between the workers' *sindicatos* involved and the counterpart employers' *sindicatos*. At first, the textile employers refused to sign, but they finally agreed to put the matter to the regional labor court, which quickly decided that the agreement that had reached would be extended to the textile employers' group. That *sindicato* had agreed not to appeal the decision of the regional court.[86]

In part at least as a result of this strike, Jose Segadas Viana was removed by Vargas as minister of labor, and was replaced by João Goulart, the President of the Trabalhista Brasileiro. Goulart was a young man whose fazenda was next to that of Getúlio Vargas in Rio Grande do Sul. They had gotten to know one another very well when Vargas in the 1945–1950 period spent most of his time on his fazenda. In the election of 1950, Goulart had been chosen a federal deputy on the PTB ticket, and in 1951 Vargas had brought about his election as PTB president.[87]

João Goulart became minister of labor in June 1953, in the midst of the second major strike of the second Vargas administration, that of the maritime workers. The Maritime Federation was one of the country's strongest *sindicatos*. In 1953 as many as 70 percent of the seagoing workers were said to belong to the *sindicatos* of the federation. This was largely due to the fact that most of the member *sindicatos* had hiring halls, to which the employers went to get workers.[88]

The maritime strike, which involved all of the seagoing maritime crafts and was virtually universal throughout Brazil, was ostensibly over a series of economic demands. These include improvement of food on the ships, family allowances for the workers, and automatic wage increases in accordance with seniority.[89]

However, there were political factors in this walkout also. In part, at least, the strike was aimed at deposing João Baptista Almeida, the president of the National Maritime Federation. Joined against him were the Communists and the PTB trade unionists aligned with João Goulart. The reelection of Almeida, generally regarded as a *pelego*, had recently been contested and was in the courts at the time of the strike. The Communists and *Jangistas* (Goulart supporters) regarded the walkout in part at least as a demonstration against Almeida, who had opposed its being called.[90]

The General Strike Command was composed of fifteen people, three members from each *sindicato* involved. There was also a strike committee in each *sindicato*. At one point, the strike leaders not only were afraid of being arrested but also feared that the navy might mobilize the strikers as naval reservists. In case of reprisals against the strike leaders, successors to each had been secretly chosen.[91]

At one point the strike leaders were called to the Catete presidential palace to confer with President Vargas.[92] Finally, João Goulart, as minister of labor, resolved the walkout to the satisfaction of the strikers.

JOÃO GOULART AS MINISTER OF LABOR

João Goulart took over the Ministry of Labor with the promise to make sweeping changes in it. One of his first acts was to establish a labor-employer-ministry commission to look at the Fondo Sindical, the 20 percent of the *imposto sindical* that did not go to any of the trade union organizations, but remained in the ministry. It was scandal-ridden, and Goulart promised to see to it that his commission would "put an end to the scandals of the Fondo Sindical" and "punish those responsible for the diversion of the money of the worker."

He also promised to sweep out the sizable number of employees of the ministry who drew salaries without doing any work. He promised that "the hundreds of functionaries, men and women, will join their colleagues of the Ministry of Labor who daily justify themselves with work. . . . Otherwise they will be unemployed."

Goulart made several other promises. Although not himself pushing the matter, he promised that if the workers indicated an interest in establishing a central labor organization, he would cooperate with them in pushing such a measure through Congress. He also promised to work for a large increase in the minimum wage.[93] He did succeed in pushing through a minimum increase, although it was challenged in the courts.

Goulart also clearly had the objective of purging the higher echelons of the trade union movement, getting the removal of those *pelegos* who had dominated the federations and confederations since their establishment in the Dutra regime and supplanting them with people loyal to him. The only case in which he was successful in that objective was that of João Baptista Almeida, the head of the Maritime Federation.[94]

However, Goulart clearly put the fear of God into many of the old-time *pelegos*. Many, if not most, of them had never had much contact with the lower-ranking *sindicato* leaders, and had had even less with the *sindicato* rank and file. However, with the encouragement of United States Labor Attaché Irving Salert, some of these top-echelon officials began to travel widely around the country, trying to establish personal contacts with the local *sindicato* leaders, and to some degree with the rank and file.[95]

Goulart's activities aroused a great deal of resistance among the political opposition and within the military. Although many years later Getúlio Vargas's daughter told me that her father had not seen João Goulart as his political heir,[96] Goulart clearly saw himself in that capacity, and through the Ministry of Labor (as well as his presidency of the PTB) he certainly set out to establish himself as Vargas's successor as the political leader of the working class.

There is considerable evidence that even before Vargas' death, Goulart was widely regarded as Getúlio's heir-apparent. Jose Gomes Talarico, vice president of the Journalists' Federation and a leading PTB trade unionist, told me in July 1954 that there were by then only two political forces in the labor movement, the Communists and João Goulart, who had "supplanted" Vargas among the workers.[97]

Maria da Graça Dutra, vice president of the Journalists' Federation and one of the most important avowedly Communist trade unionists of that period, also saw Goulart as inheriting Getúlio Vargas's mantle. However, she saw Vargas, whose prestige among workers had fallen considerably, as using Goulart to indicate to the workers that his real desire was to help them, but that he was being blocked from doing so by the reactionaries.[98]

The mounting pressure on Vargas to remove Goulart finally succeeded in February 1954, when a group of colonels submitted a memo to the president demanding Goulart's dismissal. One story of how this came about was that Vargas was meeting with some of his close advisers to decide what to do about the colonels' memorandum. Pacing up and down, Vargas commented, "The Minister of War must go. He can not control his men." One of those present, who was an enemy of Jango (Goulart), then suggested that this would be a good time to clean house generally, and when asked by Vargas what he meant, the man said that it would be a good time to fire Goulart also. Vargas first asked, "What?" and then "Why?" and then said, "That is a good idea," and the decision was made.[99]

POLITICAL FORCES IN ORGANIZED LABOR IN THE SECOND VARGAS PERIOD

During the second Vargas administration there were clearly three "political" elements in the Brazilian organized labor movement. At the top of the trade union structure, heading the confederations and most of the federations, were the *pelegos*, who had been in charge since the Dutra period; contesting their apparent control on the labor movement were the Communists and the Partido Trabalhista Brasileiro elements, which were increasingly aligned with João Goulart.

The *pelegos*, although for the most part official members—and many of them officeholders—of the PTB—were in fact more or less creatures of the Ministry of Labor. Many of them had been *sindicato* officials since the days of the Estado Novo and had risen to control of the confederations and federations largely as a result of the support of the Ministry of Labor during the Dutra administration.

The position of the *pelego* leaders was to some degree strengthened by the fact that the existing confederations and some of the federations joined the International Confederation of Free Trade Unions and its Interamerican regional grouping, the ORIT.

Some boost to the prestige of the *pelegos* was given by the fact that the ORIT held its Second Regional Conference in Rio de Janeiro in December 1952. Greetings from Brazilian labor were delivered to the meeting by Luiz Augusto da França, treasurer of the Commercial Workers Confederation, described by the Rio de Janeiro newspaper *Correio da Manhã* as "a false leader who always supports all the ministers and all the presidents of the republic." Another *pelego*, Diocleciano de Holanda Cavalcanti, president of the Industrial Workers Confederation, served as presiding officer of the Congress.[100]

In 1952 the Communists abandoned, insofar as the labor movement was concerned, the isolationist position that they had adopted after the party was outlawed. In a trade union plenum they

determined that the Communists would return to the existing sindicatos, gather the demands of the workers, forge alliances with the forces that were active, especially the Petebistas [members of Partido Trabalhistas Brasileiro], and return to the struggle for unionization and for trade union unity. And only from correction of the line can one understand the successes that the Communists obtained, in the face of an economic crisis, in the leadership of the great strikes of the period.[101]

In their effort to reestablish trade union influence, the Communists kept alive the fiction of the CGTB, not as a central labor body, rather as a kind of general staff for the Communists in the labor movement. It was headed by Roberto Morena, an old-time Communist trade unionist and the only avowed Communist member of the Chamber of Deputies, elected on the ticket of the Partido Republicano Trabalhista, one of several splinters of the PTB.[102]

One of the most prominent Communist trade unionists of this period was Maria de Graça Dutra, a top official of the Journalists' Federation and labor editor of the Communist daily in Rio de Janeiro, *Imprensa Popular*. At one point, in June 1953, she gave me a list of "the most militant *sindicatos*" in Rio de Janeiro and São Paulo; militancy was presumably more or less synonymous with Communist control. In Rio, these were the Aeronautical Workers Union, the textile *sindicato*, the metal workers' *sindicato*, the journalists, the soft drink workers, the Union of Waiters and Sailors of the Merchant Marine, and the printing trades workers, headed by a founder of the CGTB. In São Paulo, Maria de Graça named the textile workers, the furniture workers, the graphic arts workers, the metal workers, the urban transport workers, and the glass workers.[103]

However, Communist influence in the *sindicatos* was not confined to Rio and São Paulo. Ronald Chilcote noted:

In Rio Grande do Sul Communist influence was maintained among dockworkers and railway workers. PCB labor leaders were active in the successful railway workers' strikes of June 1952 and May 1954. In Pernambuco, party strength lay in unions of spinners and weavers, urban transit employees, and dockworkers.[104]

On a national basis, the influence of the Communists was probably greatest in the Maritime Workers Federation. Armando Zanino Junior, one of the non-Communist leaders of the 1953 maritime strike, admitted to me a year later, "The Communist Party dominates the maritime workers."[105]

The Communists' relative success in organized labor in the second Vargas regime was undoubtedly due to several factors. One was the difficult economic situation, characterized by severe inflation. Another was the widespread disillusionment of the workers with Vargas during the period of his return to office, which was due to his apparent inability to handle the inflation and other problems. Finally, the dedication of the Communist militants was also undoubtedly of importance. One of the most significant *pelegos*, Luiz Augusto da França, the treasurer of the Confederation of Commercial Workers, admitted to me in June 1953 that the Communists were better disciplined than their opponents, and that at *sindicato* membership meetings they were often willing to stay all night in order to win their point.[106]

Another party that might have established a strong base in the organized labor movement but did not do so was the Socialist

Party. During the second Vargas period they won some influence in the labor movement, largely on the prestige of individual *sindicato* leaders. However, they were never able to present themselves clearly as a separate political force in the labor movement or in politics in general. They were torn between the competing attractions of Getúlio Vargas and the PTB, on the one hand, and the Communists, on the other. In the labor movement, they often collaborated with the Communists; in general politics they at one point seriously considered merging with the PTB.[107]

EXTENSION OF COLLECTIVE BARGAINING

During the second Vargas administration there was some expansion of the use of collective bargaining instead of the labor court system to resolve problems between the workers' *sindicatos* and employers. This was particularly the case in São Paulo and Rio de Janeiro. For instance, the printing trades workers of São Paulo reached an agreement with all of the employers in that industry in the city. However, the contract dealt only with wages, although by 1953 the *sindicato* was preparing to negotiate a contract covering a much wider range of issues.[108]

Similarly, in Rio de Janeiro there was an agreement between the chemical workers' *sindicato* and their employers. However, it, too, dealt only with wages.[109]

In 1953, Paulo Baete Neves, president of the Confederation of Commercial Workers, generalized about the collective contract situation in the country at that time. He noted that although there were "scattered" collective agreements in industry, there was none between commercial workers and their employers.[110]

Although there were relatively few collective contracts negotiated in this period, the *sindicatos'* attempts to handle grievances through collective bargaining were much more widespread. The union leaders sought to avoid taking grievances of individual workers to the lowest-level labor courts because those courts were overloaded with work, and as a result, getting cases before them took entirely too long. Instead, quite a few *sindicato* leaders tried to establish grievance procedures with the employers, through which problems of individual workers could be resolved.[111]

In at least one case that we encountered, that of the São Paulo Metal Workers' Union, a grievance procedure was provided for in the *sindicato's* collective agreement with the employers. In each factory there was a grievance committee recognized by the employer. If a grievance could not be negotiated successfully in a given plant, it was taken to the *sindicato*, which also sought to deal directly with the employer. According to the secretary general of that *sindicato*, about two-thirds of all grievances were being resolved in 1954 without recourse to the labor courts.[112]

Among the other *sindicatos* that dealt with grievances largely through a grievance procedure rather than through the labor courts were the Commercial Employees' Union of São Paulo, who reported that in 1953 only 20 of 5,000 grievances had ended up in the labor courts,[113] and the Electric Power Workers of São Paulo, who reported in 1954 that some 98 percent of all grievances were settled without recourse to the labor tribunals.[114]

In the São Paulo provincial city of Villa Americana, where 85 percent of the town's 9,000 textile workers belonged to the *sindicato*, the *sindicato* handled about 4,000 grievances. Only 6 cases were finally taken to the labor courts.[115]

In São Paulo, a few of the state federations participated in the negotiation of grievances and other matters. In the case of the Clothing Workers Federation, it joined ten member *sindicatos* in bargaining for wage increases and also handled the processing of grievances that its member *sindicato* had not been able to settle.[116] In the case of the Textile Workers' Federation, it from time to time intervened with employers, on both grievances and more general matters, in towns in which a *sindicato* did not yet exist.[117]

DEATH OF GETÚLIO AND WORKERS IN THE CAFE FILHO REGIME

In August 1954, the second government of Getúlio Vargas came to a sudden end. A crisis had arisen as a result of an attempt to assassinate the strongly anti-Vargas journalist Carlos Lacerda, which caused the death of an air force major who was accompanying Lacerda at the time. When the murder was traced to the head of the presidential bodyguard, the leaders of the armed forces demanded that Getúlio Vargas take an extended "vacation" until the end of his term. However, instead of doing so, President Vargas committed suicide, leaving a suicide note.

This event, and particularly the suicide note, was of great importance insofar as the organized labor movement was concerned. Whereas Getúlio's support among the workers had waned considerably during his second administration, his spectacular death, and particularly his last appeal to his supporters, had served suddenly to rehabilitate him in the eyes of a considerable part of the working class. It assured that for another decade Brazilian politics would continue to be divided sharply between pro-Vargas and anti-Vargas factions.

Vargas's successor was his vice president, João Cafe Filho. He had been chosen by Vargas as his running mate in 1950 as the result of an agreement with Governor Ademar de Barros of São Paulo. Cafe Filho was a major leader of de Barros's Social Progressive Party. However, he had been a longtime opponent of Getúlio Vargas and had been in exile during much of the Estado Novo period. Thus his succession to power meant the temporary implantation of a regime representing the anti-Vargas elements in national politics.

In a conversation with the author many years later, João Cafe Filho said that he had "assured the workers all of their rights and guarantees, in accord with the labor legislation, paying attention to the just and legitimate demands presented by the *sindicatos*. He did not restrict them in the exercise of any of their rights, nor did he permit the *sindicatos* to be used for political purposes." On August 24, 1954, Cafe Filho chose as minister of labor Senator Napoleão Alancastro Guimarães of the PTB and friend of Getúlio Vargas, whose funeral oration he gave, in a ringing discourse, on the Senate floor. Guimarães remained minister of labor until the end of Cafe Filho presidential period.[118] In spite of these protestations, however, there is little doubt that the organized workers generally regarded the Cafe Filho government as being unfriendly to the labor movement.

There were a few serious strikes during the Cafe Filho period. One of these took place in the mining and metallurgical complex surrounding the government's steel plant in Volta Redonda. In September 1955, when the Ministry of Labor refused to allow newly elected metal workers' *sindicato* officials to take office, the *sindicato* went out on strike. The situation became serious enough that the president sent in troops. However, no violence erupted, and the ministry finally allowed the elected *sindicato* officials to take up their posts.[119]

NOTES

1. *Allied Labor News*, New York, January 11, 1945.
2. *Daily Worker*, New York, January 8, 1945.
3. *Daily Worker*, March 25, 1945
4. John W. F. Dulles, *Brazilian Communism 1935–1945: Repression During World Upheaval*, University of Texas Press, Austin, 1983, page 208.
5. For unraveling of the Estado Novo, see ibid., pages 208–215.
6. United Press report, June 12, 1945
7. Dulles, op. cit., pages 210–214.
8. *Tiempo*, weekly newsmagazine, Mexico City, July 20, 1945.
9. *Tribuna Popular*, daily paper of Communist Party, Rio de Janeiro, June 8, 1945.

10. Interview with Luiz Carlos Prestes, secretary general of Brazilian Communist Party, in Rio de Janeiro, August 22, 1946.

11. *Allied Labor News*, June 21, 1945.

12. United Press Report, June 12, 1945.

13. Associated Press Report, August 17, 1945.

14. Interview with José Soares Sampaio, president of Sindicato dos Trabalhadores na Indústria do Fumo do Rio de Janeiro, in Rio de Janeiro, August 30, 1946.

15. Interview with José Francisco da Rocha, president of Sindicato dos Empregados no Comércio Hoteleiro e Similares do Rio de Janeiro, in Rio de Janeiro, August 27, 1946.

16. Interview with Manuel Lopes Coelho Filho, head of Metallurgical Workers Union of Rio de Janeiro, later secretary general of Confederação Geral do Trabalho Brasileiro, in Rio de Janeiro, August 29, 1946.

17. *New York Times*, May 28, 1945.

18. *Jornal de São Paulo*, May 1, 1945, page 1.

19. Interview with Orli Andrezzo, one of the editors of Communist newspaper *Hoje*, in São Paulo, August 3, 1946.

20. Ibid., and interview with Mario Pedrosa, editor of *Vanguarda Socialista*, in Rio de Janeiro, August 13, 1946.

21. Dulles, op. cit., page 269.

22. *Diário Carioca*, Rio de Janeiro, June 1, 1945.

23. *Allied Labor News*, August 16, 1946.

24. Quoted in Dulles, op. cit., page 210.

25. Ibid., page 209.

26. *Folha Carioca*, Rio de Janeiro, April 7, 1945.

27. *Daily Worker*, September 18, 1945.

28. *Daily Worker*, October 5, 1945.

29. *Daily Worker*, September 23, 1945.

30. Interview with Guillermo Tubbs, president of Federação dos Trabalhadores na Indústria de Fiação e Tecelagem of São Paulo, in São Paulo, August 20, 1946.

31. *A Clase Operária*, Communist Party newspaper, Rio de Janeiro, July 20, 1946.

32. Interview with Guillermo Tubbs, op. cit., August 20, 1946.

33. *Tribuna Popular*, May 20, 1945.

34. Michael L. Conniff, *Urban Politics in Brazil: The Rise of Populism 1925–1945*, University of Pittsburgh Press, Pittsburgh, 1981, page 168.

35. Interviews with José Segadas Viana, former director general of labor, in Rio de Janeiro, August 26, 1946, March 16, 1956.

36. John D. French, "Industrial Workers and the Birth of the Populist Republic in Brazil, 1934–1946," in *Latin American Perspectives*, Fall 1989, page 7.

37. *New York Times*, November 20, 1945.

38. *Daily Worker*, October 25, 1945.

39. Associated Press Report, August 17, 1945.

40. *Daily Worker*, October 27, 1945.

41. Moisés Vinhas, *O Partidão. A Luta por um Partido de Massas 1922–1974*, Editoria Hucitec, São Paulo, 1982, page 86.

42. *Daily Worker*, October 25, 1945.

43. Interview with Paul Van Orden Shaw, American newspaperman and teacher, in Rio de Janeiro, August 25, 1946.

44. *Daily Worker*, October 7, 1945 and October 8, 1945.

45. *New York Times*, November 25, 1945.

46. *New York Post*, December 7, 1945.

47. *El Popular*, newspaper of Confederación de Trabajadores de Mexico, Mexico City, January 7, 1946.

48. *El Popular*, January 27, 1946.

49. *New York Times, December 12, 1945.*

50. *Allied Labor News*, December 14, 1945 (article by Astrojildo Pereira).

51. *Vanguarda Socialista*, May 31, 1946.

52. Interview with Mario Pedrosa, op. cit., August 13, 1946.

53. French, 1989, op. cit., page 20.

54. John D. French, "Industrial Workers and the Origin of Populist Politics in the ABC Region of Greater São Paulo, Brazil, 1900–1950," Ph.D. dissertation, Yale University, 1985, page 266.

55. French, 1989, op. cit., pages 22–23.

56. Interview with Manuel Lopes Coelho Filho, op. cit., August 29, 1946.

57. *Vanguarda Socialista*, September 14, 1945, and February 8, 1956.

58. Interview with Arnaldo Sussekind, legal adviser of Confederação Nacional dos Trabalhadores Indústria of Brazil, in Havana, Cuba, September 10, 1949.

59. *Diário Oficial*, Rio de Janeiro, August 18, 1946.

60. *Tribuna Gaucha*, Communist paper in Rio Grande do Sul, September 28, 1946.

61. Vinhas, op. cit., page 94.

62. Interview with Arnaldo Sussekind, op. cit., September 10, 1949.

63. Vinhas, op. cit., page 88.

64. Ibid., page 90.

65. Ibid., page 91–92.

66. French, 1989, op. cit., page 19.

67. Ronald H. Chilcote, *The Brazilian Communist Party: Conflict and Integration 1922–1972*, Oxford University Press, New York, 1974, page 53.

68. French, 1985, op. cit., page 486; and Chilcote, op. cit., page 52.

69. French, 1985, op. cit., page 188.

70. Vinhas, op. cit., page 94.

71. Ibid., page 95.

72. Ibid., page 130.

73. Robert J. Alexander, *Labor Relations in Argentina, Brazil and Chile*, McGraw-Hill, New York, 1962, page 64.

74. Arturo Jaúregui, "The Labor Movement in Brazil Gains Strength," in *Inter American Labor Bulletin* of Inter American Regional Organization of Workers (ORIT), April 1951.

75. Interview with Irving Salert, U.S. Embassy labor attaché, in Rio de Janeiro, June 8, 1953.

76. Interview with Joviano de Araujo, Brazilian representative of International Confederation of Free Trade Unions and ORIT, in Rio de Janeiro, June 13, 1956.

77. Vinhas, op. cit., page 130.

78. Interview with Pedro Chavier de Paiva, president of Sindicato dos Trabalhadores na Indústria de Fiação e Tecelagem of Recife, in Recife, February 24, 1956.

79. Interview with Gabriel Marcelo Quintana, president of Sindicato dos Trabalhadores nas Indústrias Graphicas de Pôrto Alegre, in Pôrto Alegre, May 4, 1956.

80. Vinhas, op. cit., page 131.

81. Interview with Pedro Galardi Filho, president, Sindicatos dos Trabalhadores nas Indústrias de Construção Civil de São Paulo, in São Paulo, June 17, 1953.

82. Interview with Gervasio Eliseu Masckio, secretary of Sindicato dos Trabalhadores Graphicos de São Paulo, in São Paulo, June 17, 1953.

83. Vinhas, op. cit., pages 131–132.

84. Interview with Remo Forli, president of Sindicato dos Trabalhadores Metalúrgicos of São Paulo, in São Paulo, June 16, 1953.

85. Vinhas, op. cit., pages 131–132.

86. Interviews with Paulo Singer, member of Inter Union Strike Committee for Metal Workers Union, in São Paulo, June 18, 1953; and Antonio D'Agazio, head of office staff of Sindicatos dos Trabalhadores de Fiaçagem e Tecelagem, in São Paulo, June 17, 1953.

87. Robert J. Alexander, *The ABC Presidents: Conversations and Correspondence with the Presidents of Argentina, Brazil and Chile*, Praeger, Westport, 1992, page 154.

88. Interview with Manuel Bispo de Salles, secretary of Federação Marítima Nacional, in Rio de Janeiro, June 13, 1953; and José Gomes Talarico, a leader of Journalists Union, in Rio de Janeiro, June 9, 1953.

89. Interview with Comandante Armando Zanino Senior, a leader of 1953 maritime strike, in Rio de Janeiro, June 18, 1953.

90. Interviews with Irving Salert, op. cit., June 19, 1953; Joviano Araujo, op cit., June 20, 1953; João Baptista Almeida, president of Federação Marítima Nacional, in Rio de Janeiro, June 18, 1953; and Hilcar Leite, Socialist journalist, in Rio de Janeiro, June 19, 1953.

91. Interview with Comandante Armando Zanino Senior, op. cit., June 18, 1953.

92. Interview with Maria de Graça Dutra, secretary general of Federação Nacional de Jornalista, an editor of Communist daily *Imprensa Popular*, in Rio de Janeiro, June 10, 1953.

93. Yedo Mendonca. "Revolução Trabalhista," in *O Cruzeiro*, July 18, 1953, pages 86–88.

94. Interview with Joviano de Araujo, op. cit., July 1, 1954.

95. Interview with Irving Salert, op. cit., July 2, 1954.

96. Interview with Alzira Vargas de Amaral Peixoto, daughter of Getúlio Vargas, in Rio de Janeiro, January 10, 1966.

97. Interview with José Gomes Talarico, op. cit., July 6, 1954.

98. Interview with Maria de Graça Dutra, op. cit., July 3, 1954.

99. Interview with Irving Salert, op. cit., July 2, 1954.

100. *Correio da Manhã*, Rio de Janeiro, December 19, 1952.

101. Vinhas, op. cit., page 130.

102. Ibid., page 129; see also interview with Roberto Morena, longtime Communist labor leader, member of Chamber of Deputies, in Rio de Janeiro, June 10, 1953.

103. Interview with Maria da Graça Dutra, op. cit., June 10, 1953.

104. Chilcote, op. cit., page 61.

105. Interview with Armando Zanino Junior, a leader of Marine Officers' Union and of 1953 maritime strike, in Rio de Janeiro, July 1, 1954.

106. Interview with Luiz Augusto da França, treasurer of Confederação dos Trabalhadores de Comércio, in Rio de Janeiro, June 11, 1953.

107. Interview with Irving Salert, op. cit., June 8, 1953.

108. Interview with Gervasio Eliseu Masckio, op. cit., June 17, 1953.

109. Interview with José Ferreira Campello, president of Federação dos Trabalhadores nas Indústrias de Química e Farmácia do Estado do Rio y Distrito Federal, in Rio de Janeiro, July 6, 1954.

110. Interview with Paulo Baete Neves, president, Confederação Nacional dos Trabalhadores no Comércio, in Rio de Janeiro, June 9, 1953.

111. Interview with Vicente Orlando, president of Federação dos Trabalhadores na Construção Civil, in Rio de Janeiro, June 10, 1953.

112. Interview with Santo Rizzo, secretary general, São Paulo Metallurgical Workers Union, in São Paulo, July 5, 1954.

113. Interview with Nassim José, administrative secretary, Sindicato dos Empregados no Comércio de São Paulo, in São Paulo, July 6, 1954.

114. Interview with José Alonso García, president of Electrical Power Workers Union of São Paulo, in São Paulo, July 8, 1954.

115. Interview with Antonio Sgubin, president of Sindicato Têxtil Americano and secretary of Federation of Textile Workers of São Paulo, in São Paulo, July 8, 1954.

116. Interview with Luiz Fiuza Cardi, president of Federação dos Trabalhadores na Indústria of São Paulo, in São Paulo, July 7, 1954.

117. Interview with Arlindo Martins de Oliveira, grievance secretary of Textile Workers Federation of the state of São Paulo, in São Paulo, July 8, 1954.

118. Alexander, op. cit., pages 106–107.

119. Interview with Sr. Agostino, an editor of Communist newspaper *Gazetta Sindical*, in Rio de Janeiro, March 21, 1956.

4
Unionism in the Democratic Interregnum (1945–1964), Part II

In the elections of October 1955 the country's trade unionists undoubtedly supported the candidates of the two parties that had been established by Getúlio Vargas: Juscelino Kubitschek of the Partido Social Democrático, as nominee for president, and João (Jango) Goulart, head of the Partido Trabalhista Brasileiro, as vice president. Juscelino and Jango won a plurality, and although two coups by the leaders of the military in November 1955 were necessary to make it possible, Kubitschek and Goulart were inaugurated in late January 1956.

ORGANIZED LABOR IN THE KUBITSCHEK ADMINISTRATION

Two elements characterized the attitude of the Kubitschek administration toward the labor movement. One was the relaxation of controls over the *sindicatos*, and the other was refusal to make any fundamental legal changes in the labor relations system that had been established by the Estado Novo and had persisted thereafter.

These two approaches to the labor movement were in accord with the general philosophy and actions of President Juscelino Kubitschek. He presided over the most democratic regime that Brazil had had until that time. But he concentrated very heavily in his administration on the problems of economic development, rather than on social reform.[1]

One aspect of the democratic policy of the Kubitschek administration was its "semilegalization" of the Communist Party. In March 1958 charges against Luiz Carlos Prestes and other leaders of the party, which had been leveled against them during the Dutra years, were dismissed by the courts.[2]

Thereafter, as Moisés Vinhas wrote, the Communist Party

saw the light of day, from Luís Carlos Prestes and the Central Committee, to state, municipal and even district committees, they were established in their offices. Plenary sessions of the Central Committee and of many State Committees met in their headquarters. At the same time, the Communists succeeded in establishing the most varied social and party alliances for the elections of 1958, in which they participated on the slates of the PTB and other parties.[3]

Early in the Kubitschek administration Arnaldo Sussekind, head of the Planning Section of the Ministry of Labor and former legal adviser of the National Confederation of Industrial Workers (CNTI), noted that there was a general tendency of relaxation of government control over the *sindicatos*, although the government did not give up its legal right to intervene in them. However, Sussekind noted that the government's policy was one of non-intervention.[4]

The relaxation of controls over the labor movement was facilitated by a law that had been passed in December 1955 under the provisional government of the time that permitted *sindicatos* to hold elections and elected *sindicato* officials to take office without permission of the Ministry of Labor. It also permitted the reelection of *sindicato* officials, which had been forbidden in the past.[5] This ended the procedure whereby the ministry might hold up installation of *sindicato* officials for weeks or months, in situations of contested election results.[6]

At the beginning of the Kubitschek administration, the Ministry of Labor worked on a bill to be submitted to Congress that would have fundamentally altered the Estado Novo system. It would have set up machinery to encourage collective bargaining instead of the use of the labor courts; to further the establishment of works councils in each enterprise, with representatives of the employer and the *sindicato*, to deal with grievances, safety matters, social welfare, or anything else related to the role of the workers in the firm. Finally, the proposed legislation would have ended the anomaly by which the Constitution of 1946 authorized strikes but held that they should be regulated by law, pending which legislation, the Estado Novo legal prohibition of strikes continued.[7]

However, such legislation was never enacted during the Kubitschek regime. Although a bill to regulate the use of the strike, sponsored by a Socialist deputy, Aurélio Viana, passed the Chamber of Deputies, the Senate did not enact it.[8] The measure apparently received little or no support from the administration. More surprising was the fact that Luiz Carlos Prestes, in a press conference soon after coming out of hiding, when asked what he thought of Viana's bill, said that he thought it was "very radical."[9]

THE NATIONAL LABOR CONFEDERATIONS

Two of the national labor confederations provided for in the Estado Novo labor hierarchy to be organized were established during the Kubitschek administration. These were the Confederação Nacional dos Trabalhadores de Crédito (banks and other credit institutions), set up in 1959, and the Confederação Nacional dos Trabalhadores em Transportes Marítimas, Fluviais e Aereos, founded in June 1960. These joined the CNTI (industrial workers), which had been set up in October 1946; the Confederação Nacional dos Trabalhadores no Comércio (CNTC), organized in November 1946; and the Confederação Nacional dos Trabalhadores em Transportes Terrestres (CNTT), organized in 1953. The other two confederations called for by the Estado Novo, those of communications and publicity workers and of educational and cultural employees, were organized much later.[10]

Throughout the Kubitschek period there continued to exist the dichotomy between the leadership of the rank-and-file *sindicatos* and that of many of the federations and of the confederations. Increasingly, the leadership of the local *sindicatos* was really elected by the membership, whereas to a greater or lesser degree those heading the federations and confederations were *pelegos*, who were under the influence of the Ministry of Labor,.

Eva Maria da Graça Dutra, one of the principal avowedly Communist national trade union leaders and an officer of the Journalists Federation, claimed that the pelegos were "virtually extinct" by 1956, insofar as the local *sindicatos* were concerned. She estimated that not more than 10–20 percent of the local *sindicato* leaders could be so characterized. But, she added, the confederations were certainly still *pelego*-controlled.[11]

At about the same time, Luís Augusto de Castro Lisboa, president of the Bank Workers Union of Pôrto Alegre, claimed that there were virtually no *pelegos* left in Rio Grande do Sul. This was even true, he said, of the Pôrto Alegre Commercial Employees Union, which followed an "isolationist" policy and did not cooperate with the other *sindicatos* in the city.[12]

A few years later, in 1959, a leader at the confederation level made the same kind of claim to me. Heracy Wagner, secretary of the National Confederation of Workers of Industry, claimed that there were few "real" *pelegos*, that is, people who owed their posts to the Ministry of Labor and not to honest elections, left.[13]

However, Djalma A. Mariano, director of the Rio de Janeiro office of the International Confederation of Free Trade Unions and its regional group, ORIT, pointed out at about the same time that there were many federation and confederation leaders who held appointments as directors of the social security institutes and of other governmental agencies that were due to Partido Trabalhista Brasileiro patronage. Under these circumstances, they were subject to pressure from the Ministry of Labor, also controlled by the PTB, and could not publicly differ with the government policy.[14]

During the Kubitschek years, the confederations became more active than had previously been the case. Until then, these organizations, which had been set up largely at the instigation of the Ministry of Labor, had had little contact with the rank-and-file *sindicatos*, or in some cases even with the regional and national federations that were supposedly affiliated to them.

However, starting just before the Kubitschek period, Diocleciano de Holanda Cavalcanti, the longtime president of the CNTI, in large part because of the urging of U.S. Labor Attaché Irving Salert, a former official of the International Ladies Garment Workers Union, began to try to establish more or less continuous contacts with the affiliated federations and *sindicatos* in various parts of the country. He began to travel extensively to visit the federation headquarters, where he met with local *sindicato* leaders. The CNTI also established "delegations" in most of the states, to try to develop contacts on a continuing basis.[15]

At least some local *sindicato* leaders with whom I talked thought that the regional delegations of the CNTI were of use to the labor movement in their areas. For instance, an official of the Construction Workers Federation of Minas Gerais noted that the CNTI delegation there was particularly helping *sindicatos* in the state that were part of the CNTI but did not have a regional federation. It was run locally by a council composed of the presidents of all of the labor federations in the state affiliated with the CNTI.[16]

A leader of the Printing Trades Federation of Rio de Janeiro said in 1959 that since 1956 the delegation of the CNTI in Rio had established an advisory council that met regularly, dealing with problems such as lobbying for legislation on the right to strike, agitation against the high cost of living, as well as specific problems of individual *sindicatos* in the area. He said that this council was serving as a real intermediary between the local *sindicatos* and the confederation.[17]

At the beginning of his administration, President Kubitschek had a problem to deal with concerning the CNTI. Its president, Diocleciano de Holanda Cavalcanti, had been removed by the minister of labor in the interim government that was in power before Juscelino took office. Several of the federations belonging to the CNTI protested this move, wiring President Neuru Ramos that Cavalcanti had been elected, and it should be the workers' prerogative to decide whether he should continue.[18]

However, more significant was the pressure brought upon President-elect Kubitschek on his trip to the United States and Europe before taking office. The International Confederation of Free Trade Unions, to which the CNTI was affiliated, had alerted its member organizations, as had George Oldenbroek in Brussels; German trade union leaders also pressured him during his visit to that country.[19]

Perhaps as a consequence of this intervention by foreign labor leaders, a new election was soon held in the CNTI. Diocleciano de Holanda Cavalcanti was reelected by the federation leaders of the CNTI by a vote of twenty to nine.[20]

The reelection of Cavalcanti had been strongly opposed by the Communists. However, in 1959 he was reported to be increasingly collaborating with them, and particularly with Roberto Morena, the more or less official leader of the party in trade union affairs.[21] This change of position by Diocleciano undoubtedly reflected the growing influence of the Communists and their allies in the *sindicatos* and federations affiliated with the CNTI.

A new leadership had just taken over in the Commercial Workers Confederation before Kubitschek took office. It was headed by Fausto Cardoso, who was reported to be the most able, in terms of public relations, of the confederation presidents.[22] He told me in March 1956 that his confederation, which claimed to have as dues-paying members about 40 percent of the 1,300,000 commercial employees who paid the *imposto sindical*, was seeking to encourage activity in member *sindicatos* and was lobbying for basic changes in the Consolidação was Leis do Trabalho, particularly for the right to vote.[23] Cardoso was subsequently succeeded as president by Angel Parmiggiani, who was less active than his predecessor because of heart trouble.[24]

As president of the Land Transport Workers Confederation, Syndolfo Pequeno was widely regarded as the most corrupt of the confederation presidents. Serafino Romualdi, Latin American representative of the AFL-CIO and assistant secretary general of the ORIT, recounted an incident in which Pequeno, who, Romualdi said, was known to be a jewelry smuggler, at an ORIT congress offered Romualdi a "bargain" bracelet for his wife for $150. When Romualdi took it to a jeweler, he found that it was worth at most

$20 to $25 since the jewels in it were fakes; he told Pequeno that
he, Pequeno, had been swindled, whereupon the Brazilian gave
him back his $150. Romualdi added that it was not Pequeno who
had been swindled.[25]

In March 1956, the secretary of the Land Transport Confederation noted that the most important current activity of the
organization, were preparations for a conference with both worker
and employer groups to study the problem of productivity in the
Brazilian economy.[26]

The Credit Workers Confederation, from its inception in 1959,
was under Communist influence. The predecessor of the confederation, the Federação Bancária, had also been under Communist
leadership.[27]

THE FEDERATIONS

The federations, which were usually formed on a state level,
grouping together *sindicatos* in a particular branch of economic
activity, were in considerably closer contact with their member
sindicatos than were the confederations. Not infrequently, the
leadership of the federation was chosen from the leaders of the member *sindicatos*. However, there continued to be many local
sindicato leaders who complained about the ineffectiveness of the
federations with which the *sindicatos* were affiliated.

In conformity with the Estado Novo system that still prevailed,
the federations frequently provided legal assistance for *sindicatos*
that had to have dealings with the Ministry of Labor or the labor
courts.[28] In the state of São Paulo, such aid was reported to be of
particular importance to *sindicatos* in the interior of the state,
which had fewer financial resources than those in the capital
city.[29] The federations also sometimes worked with their member
sindicatos that were negotiating direct agreements with the employers, to avoid recourse to the labor tribunals.[30]

Some of the federations engaged in organizing activities. For
instance, early in 1956, the Clothing Workers Federation of São
Paulo was organizing a *sindicato* at the Bata shoe plant—
although the manager of the plant was characterized as "thinking
he was still in Czechoslovakia" and was resisting the organizing
efforts.[31]

The Paper Workers Federation of São Paulo was particularly
active in organizing new *sindicatos*. This federation had been established on the initiative of the paper workers *sindicato* of the
city of São Paulo, which had itself been instrumental in organizing the four other *sindicatos* necessary in order to form a
federation. Once established, that federation succeeded in orga-

nizing four other *sindicatos*, and in 1956 was reported to have brought into being three other "professional associations," the first step in establishing a legally recognized *sindicato*.

According to the president of the Paper Workers Federation, who had undertaken much of the organizing activity, he went to towns where there were paper mills, established contact with the workers in the plant, and organized a preliminary meeting, as which a "professional association" was formally launched. It then set about enlisting into in its ranks the two-thirds of the workers that were necessary to transform the association into a *sindicato*.[32]

Similar organizing activity was reported for the Metal Workers Federation of Rio Grande do Sul. Having nine *sindicatos* affiliated with it in mid–1956, it had recently organized three professional associations, the papers for which had been sent to Rio de Janeiro, to gain recognition as *sindicatos* by the Ministry of Labor.[33]

THE QUESTION OF A CENTRAL LABOR ORGANIZATION

Although there was considerable sentiment among labor leaders in favor of the establishment of a central labor organization, no definite steps were taken during the Kubitschek years to establish one. The nearest thing to such a group was a council composed of leaders of the confederations of industrial workers, commercial employees, and land transport workers, which met from time to time to discuss mutual problems. In telling me about this, Diocleciano Holanda de Cavalcanti, president of the Industrial Workers Confederation, stressed that that council could not be considered an illegal organization under the Consolidação das Leis do Trabalho, since it had no "formal structure," but rather was just three groups of trade union leaders getting together informally to discuss their mutual problems.[34]

In 1959, the secretary of the Commercial Employees Confederation also stressed that the coordination of activities in the confederation was "informal" and therefore was not illegal. At the same time, he claimed that sentiment for establishment of a central labor organization was stimulated principally by the Communists,[35] and that was hardly the case.

Although no central labor organization was formed, there was held in 1960 what was called the Third National Trade Union Congress. A substantial part of those attending went on record as favoring the organization of a central labor group.[36]

There also functioned a number of interunion groups on a municipal basis that were certainly not provided for in the Consolidação das Leis do Trabalho. One of these was the Comissão

Inter Sindical in São Paulo, which had originally been set up at the time of the general strike in that city in 1953 and continued to exist thereafter but by 1959 was reported to be "in decline."[37]

Another such municipal central labor group was the Conselho de Dirigentes Sindicais in Salvador, the capital of the state of Bahia, which had been organized some time before Kubitschek came to power. It met regularly every Thursday evening; among its reported activities were agitation against price increases of certain essential commodities, protest against Ministry of Labor interventions in some of the city's *sindicatos*, conducting of some classes for local *sindicato* leaders on such matters as how to keep *sindicatos'* financial records, as well as sponsoring of lectures on national problems such as the Brazilian petroleum situation.[38]

Certainly the most significant and long-lasting of these municipal labor groups was the Departmento Intersindical de Estatística e Estudos Socio-Econômicos of São Paulo. This was an organization of the *sindicatos* and federations of São Paulo established to conduct continuing cost-of-living surveys, in the city, as well as to undertake specific studies of the living and working conditions of the workers there. It was set up because of the observed unreliability of statistics published by the municipality of São Paulo. It was established in its first general assembly in December 1955 and began to operate in the following month.[39]

In 1959 there were thirty-seven *sindicatos* and federations affiliated with the department and contributing to its finances.[40] It was legalized by the state of São Paulo as a "public entity." Aside from its Directorate, the department had a Technical Consultative Council, which in 1955 included among its members three professors from the University of São Paulo, an economist from the state's Department of Agriculture, and an economist of the Bank of Brazil.[41]

Starting at the beginning of 1959, the department began publishing monthly cost-of-living figures, based on a family budget that calculated 45 percent for food, 30 percent for housing, 10 percent for clothing, and lesser amounts for health, furniture and utensils, transport, and other items. Each affiliated *sindicato* had a person responsible for distributing a questionnaire on prices, covering 160 items, and the staff of the department supplemented this with a control survey, sampling prices every other day.[42]

In addition to its continuing cost-of-living survey, the department carried out special studies, of which it had completed ten by early 1959. These included surveys of manpower in São Paulo, studies of unemployment in the city, and surveys of the supplies of key consumer goods in the city, including milk, beans, and meat.[43]

The work of the Departamento Intersindical, particularly its cost of living survey, gained a reputation for high reliability.

THE ICFTU-ORIT OFFICE

Throughout the Kubitschek period, there functioned in Rio de Janeiro an office of the International Confederation of Free Trade Unions (ICFTU), and the ICFTU's regional group, the ORIT. The ostensible reason for this was that the CNTI, the Commercial Workers Confederation, and the Land Transport Workers Confederation were affiliated with both the ICFTU and the ORIT.

We have noted that in December 1952 the Second Regional Conference of the ORIT had been held in Rio de Janeiro, and the Brazilian confederation leaders, particularly Diocleciano de Holanda Cavalcanti of the CNTI, had played leading roles in that session. A few months later, the ICFTU-ORIT office was opened in Rio.

Serafino Romualdi admitted in 1955 that the ORIT was in a peculiar position in Brazil, dealing with the heads of the confederations, who had little contact with the rank and file of the labor movement. However, he claimed that the ICFTU and ORIT had also built up a good deal of support among the secondary and tertiary leadership of the Brazilian *sindicatos*, which he hoped would pay off in wider support among the Brazilian labor movement for the still more or less formal connection with the ORIT and the ICFTU. However, he commented, it was hard to say to the confederation leaders, who attended all of the international conferences and sat on the boards of ORIT and the ICFTU, that it would be a good day for the Brazilian labor movement when they were ousted. But that was the truth, he added.[44]

The first person in charge of the ICFTU-ORIT office was Joviano de Araujo, until shortly before that the secretary of the National Maritime Federation. In the beginning, Araujo had extensive plans for propagating the ideas of the ICFTU and ORIT not only in the confederations, but also in the federations and rank-and-file *sindicatos*. He hoped to initiate with organizational efforts in areas where there were no *sindicatos*, particularly, he said, in rural areas.[45]

However, by 1956 it was clear that the work of the ICFTU-ORIT office was extremely modest. Joviano de Araujo himself admitted that the activities and influence of the office were quite limited, blaming this mainly on the lack of adequate financial resources.[46]

In the middle of 1956, Samuel Powell, a prominent Cuban labor leader, was asked by the ORIT to go to Rio de Janeiro to try to stimulate more activity by the ICFTU-ORIT office. He stayed for several months.[47] Perhaps as a result of Powell's visit, Joviano de Araujo was succeeded as head of the office by Djalma A. Mariano, who was considerably more active than his predecessor. By 1959 the monthly periodical of the office was coming out regularly, edited by two members of the Rio Printers Union, both Socialists. Mariano had in fact established a modest program for training labor leaders and had begun a series of visits to *sindicatos* in the interior to expound on the ideas and activities of the ICFTU and ORIT. He was also working more or less closely with anti-Communist leaders in some of the *sindicatos* controlled by the party.[48]

COLLECTIVE BARGAINING

As a consequence of the relaxation of government controls over organized labor during the Kubitschek regime, the use of collective bargaining instead of recourse to the labor courts continued to expand, particularly for the handling of individual workers' grievances. However, the situation continued to vary a great deal from one sector of the economy to another, and from one part of the country to another.

In Rio de Janeiro, the Metal Workers Union was able to maintain a system of shop stewards in the city's larger firms such as General Electric, Gillette, and Standard Electric. Almost all grievances in those cases were settled between the *sindicato* and the firm involved. Smaller employers, on the other hand, were more resistant to handling grievances directly. In 1956 these smaller firms were reported to be blocking the *sindicato's* proposal to negotiate a general collective agreement.[49] However, in 1959 the *sindicato* did succeed in negotiating a collective contract with the employers' sindicato, which covered not only wages, but a number of other items as well.[50]

In São Paulo, the Metal Workers Union also sought to handle grievances through direct negotiation. When a grievance arose, the *sindicato* asked the employer to send someone to the *sindicato* headquarters to discuss the matter. The *sindicato* was in 1956 establishing a system of shop stewards, usually choosing workers who had seniority (had worked in the enterprise for ten years) and therefore could not be dismissed easily by the employer. Not all of the employers would agree to handle matters directly with the *sindicato*, however.[51]

In the textile industry of São Paulo, the *sindicato* had since the early days of the second Vargas period sought to reach an agreement directly with the employers with regard to its annual demands for wage increases and other matters. It had been able to do so except in 1953 and 1954, when the labor courts made the decision, in both cases after strikes.[52]

The *sindicato* had a system of shop stewards in every plant, although these were not generally given official recognition by the employers. There were regular meetings of the shop stewards to report grievances to the *sindicato* officials. In most cases, the *sindicato* officers were able to settle grievances directly with the employers, either over the telephone or by a visit to a particular factory.[53]

In April 1956, I was able to observe the handling of two grievances in the headquarters of the São Paulo Textile Workers Union by Nivaldo Fonseca, the *sindicato's* second secretary. One involved a young worker who had been suspended from work for a day when he complained that it was demanded that he carry excessively heavy loads. Fonseca handled this over the telephone and came to an agreement with the employer that the young worker was willing to accept, that although he would lose his pay for the day he was suspended, he would not lose his pay for Sunday, as would be customary in such a case, and the employer agreed to see to it that the young man was not given assignments to handle excessive loads. When the young man then complained about "excessive discipline" in the plant, he was counseled by Fonseca to obey orders given to him, so that if he had a genuine complaint he could go into court with clean hands, so to speak.

The other case involved two women who had been laid off after working for their employer for nineteen months, whose employer was giving them dismissal pay appropriate to one year's employment, or at most a year and a half. Fonseca informed them that since they had been working for more than a year and a half, and the law provided only for cases of payment by the year, not the half year, they were entitled to dismissal pay for two years' employment; he told them to inform their employer of this and to inform him if the employer resisted.[54]

In the textile industry of the northeastern city of Recife, the local *sindicato* had considerable difficulty with the employers. In three large firms the *sindicato* had been able to have shop stewards and handled most individual worker complaints through a grievance procedure. However, some of the employers were very hostile to the *sindicato* and refused to deal with it. One employer was reported in 1956 to dismiss any worker who he found had joined the *sindicato*, although that action was completely illegal. As a consequence of the resistance of many employers, the *sindicato* still had to handle many grievances through the labor courts.[55]

In the Amazonian port city of Belem, where the labor movement was still very weak, even the key river transport workers' *sindicato* had serious problems with the unwillingness of many employers to work with the *sindicato*. Grievances were handled between the union president and the government's captain of the port, if they dealt with matters other than wages, but had to go to the labor courts if wages were involved, a condition about which the *sindicato* leaders were very unhappy. The *sindicato* president reported in 1956 that the previous captain of the port had been willing to deal with wage problems, using his power to prevent the employer from getting a new crew if the employer would not settle a grievance.[56]

The bank employees' *sindicatos* in different parts of the country had different results from attempts to bargain collectively. In Salvador, Bahia, although the bank workers' *sindicato* always tried to get an agreement with the employers, this was almost never possible so matters had to go to the Regional Labor Court.[57] In contrast, the bank workers' *sindicato* of Pôrto Alegre in Rio Grande do Sul was almost always able to negotiate an agreement with the employers' sindicato, and individual workers' complaints with most of the city's banks were handled through a grievance procedure.[58] Similarly, the bank workers' *sindicato* of Rio de Janeiro usually was able to get an agreement with the employers without recourse to the labor courts, in part at least because the banks themselves did not like to involve the government in their labor relations.[59]

The electric power workers' *sindicatos*, at least those of Rio de Janeiro and São Paulo, generally had amicable enough relations with the power company, The Light, that they were usually able to negotiate agreements on wages and other matters. Also, virtually all grievances were settled by direct negotiation.[60]

One of the more unusual collective bargaining situations was that of the Sindicato dos Arrumadores of Santos, covering all workers who handled coffee before it got to the docks, including those who sacked the coffee and those who hefted the sacks. The *sindicato* negotiated with the employers the wages for the work that its members did, according to the weight of the bag and its height off the floor when workers had to lift or fetch it. The agreed upon payments were then approved by the Commercial Association of Santos and were posted on bulletin boards in the workplace.[61]

Certainly one of the most comprehensive collective agreements entered into by a company's management and *sindicato* was that of the state-owned Volta Redonda steel works, which was signed in December 1959. It dealt not only with wage and salary increases, and other monetary issues, but also questions of hours of work, vacation time, a child care center, and health benefits.[62] An unusually high proportion of the employees of Volta Redonda—80 percent—belonged to the *sindicato*.[63]

Finally, at least two *sindicatos* dealt with employers on a national basis. One was the Sindicato Nacional dos Aeronautas, which covered all the flying crews of the commercial airlines. They usually were able to get a negotiated agreement on their demands, which were drawn up by a national assembly of the *sindicato*.[64]

The other union that bargained on a national level was the National Stevedores Federation, which took demands for wage increases to the National Maritime Council, which had representatives of the Ministry of Transport and Public Works, the employers' *sindicatos*, and the workers' federation. Negotiations took place in the council. This federation was virtually unique also because its member *sindicatos* operated hiring halls, where employers had to go to engage employees. As a consequence of this arrangement, almost all stevedores belonged to their *sindicatos*, since nonunion workers rarely were granted consideration by the *sindicato* hiring halls.[65]

UNIONS' SOCIAL SERVICES

In conformity with the trade union pattern of the Estado Novo, *sindicatos* continued to spend a large proportion of the funds they received from the imposto sindical, and sometimes even from *sindicato* dues, on social services for their members. The nature and extent and quality of those services varied a great deal from one *sindicato* to another.

One of the most extensive social service programs that we encountered was that of the Textile Workers Union of Recife. It had at the *sindicato* headquarters three general practice doctors at the disposal of *sindicato* members and their families. One was there every morning from Monday through Saturday, another every afternoon Monday through Friday, and the third every evening, Monday through Friday. There were also two nurses. A surgeon was available from time to time to do minor operations on the premises, as well as physicians who were specialists in women's diseases and childcare. The *sindicato* also had arrangements with other specialists whereby *sindicato* members could be attended to in the doctors' offices. The *sindicato* also employed a midwife. In addition to these medical services in the city of Recife, the *sindicato* maintained general clinics in three towns in the interior of the state to which the *sindicato*'s jurisdiction extended.

The *sindicato* also had a dentist on duty regularly, to do extractions and minor dental repair work, although more serious dental work the members had to have undertaken on their own. There was a pharmacy on the *sindicato* premises, which sold pharmaceutical products at wholesale prices.

The *sindicato* also employed four lawyers. Although they principally handled cases before the labor courts, they also were available for general consultation by members, although they usually would not go to court to defend a *sindicato* member.

The union maintained sewing and typing classes attended by about three hundred union members and their daughters. These were held not only in the Recife headquarters, but also in the three other towns covered by the *sindicato*. Finally, the sindicato had a small lending library, as well as a movie program, showing mainly "recreational and educational films.[66]

POLITICAL TENDENCIES IN ORGANIZED LABOR
DURING KUBITSCHEK PERIOD

There were several conflicting political tendencies within the organized labor movement during the Kubitschek administration. Kubitschek himself did not have any significant labor faction that was loyal to or oriented by him. Francisco Weffort explained the reasons for this:

Not only was his overture to the *sindicatos* too recent, but he had no political or trade union organization which would permit him to confront the inevitable competition of Goulart. . . . So Kubitschek seemed to be depending on the phenomenon of maturation, perhaps too slow for his objective, that is, the rise of a new tendency in the trade union movement that would be situated in the more modern sectors of industry, evidently those most favored by the results of his economic policy.[67]

One major influence in labor politics was certainly that of Vice President João Goulart. In negotiations leading up to the Kubitschek-Goulart ticket in the 1955 election, Kubitschek promised to have Goulart's PTB control the ministries of labor and agriculture, as well as the social security institutes. According to testimony of both Juscelino and Jango, Kubitschek kept his promise, although Juscelino noted that in the Ministry of Labor he had always appointed someone from the "more moderate" part of the PTB, meaning the part not under João Goulart's control.[68]

In and of itself, PTB control of the Ministry of Labor, and particularly of the social security institutes, gave Goulart very substantial patronage with which he favored, among others, labor leaders who were his political friends. But, in addition to that,

Goulart, as the presumed heir of Getúlio Vargas, enjoyed considerable labor support aside from the benefits of patronage.

At the outset of the Kubitschek administration João Goulart took a decidedly moderate stance. U.S. Labor Attaché Irving Salert noted that he was "using priests as his mouthpieces about increases in the minimum wage." Salert also said that Goulart was going out of his way to make it clear that he was not a Communist, but said that he did not want to conduct a campaign against the Communists in the labor movement, since that would lose him support.[69]

In May 1956, Vice President João Goulart visited the United States. Just before leaving on that trip he issued a statement:

I represent the Labor Party of Brazil, whose policy is clear and well defined against the extremists of the right, as well as those of the left. . . . We want better living and working conditions for the wage workers of Brazil because we know that this is the best way to fight Communism, which grows on the misery and suffering of the poor people.[70]

However, as time went on, Goulart came under increasing pressure from the PTB elements inside and outside the labor movement who were influenced by the strong current of more or less anti-Yankee nationalism that was widespread at the time. In 1959, I wrote Jay Lovestone of the AFL-CIO about this nationalism:

There is now a very widespread but virtually structureless 'nationalist' movement, especially powerful among intellectuals and labor people. However, this time I had the impression . . . that the Communists' role in this nationalistic movement is much less important now than it was four or five years ago.[71]

Nevertheless, the PTB nationalist trade union leaders were to a greater or lesser degree willing to work with the Communists. Probably in some cases they were in fact Communists disguised as Trabalhistas. This certainly aided the development of the Communists' strength in the labor movement, since undoubtedly a considerable majority of the *sindicato* leaders continued to be at least nominal members of the PTB.

During much of the Kubitschek period, the Communists gained or held control of very important *sindicatos*. These included the metal workers and textile workers of São Paulo. Communist control of the textile workers' *sindicato* was clear from the fact that the wall of the *sindicato*'s headquarters was decorated with an advertisement for the party's newspaper *Gazetta*

Sindical, as well as a picture given to the *sindicato* "by the workers of China."[72]

The party also largely dominated the metal workers' *sindicato* in Rio de Janeiro, where in 1959 its president, Benedito Cerqueira, belonged to the nationalist wing of the PTB; the editor of the *sindicato's* paper was a Socialist; and "some Communists" were on its executive.[73] The Communists were also very strong in the Rio de Janeiro textile *sindicato*. They controlled much of the labor movement in the port city of Santos. They had extensive influence among the bank employees in various parts of the country, and the new Bank Workers Confederation was, as we have noted, Communist-controlled from the outset.

Some indication of the Communists' influence in the labor movement was given in the party's new Central Committee, elected at its Fifth Congress in September 1960. Among the fifty-one full and alternate members were a textile unionist from Alagoas, a port worker from the state of São Paulo, a bank employees' leader from Minas Gerais, a journalist from Minas Gerais, Roberto Morena of the Rio de Janeiro construction workers, dock workers from the Federal District and the state of Rio de Janeiro, and a maritime worker from Rio de Janeiro.[74]

The Socialists continued to be of some, although secondary, influence in organized labor. The Socialist Party was the predominant group in the two airline workers' *sindicatos*, the Sindicato Nacional dos Aeronautas, covering flying personnel, and the Sindicato de Aerovias, composed of ground crews. Ivan Alkmin, vice president of the Sindicato Nacional de Aeronautas, himself a Socialist, claimed in 1959 that the party's trade union influence in the previous three years had been growing, with the return of Remo Forli, as head of the Metal Workers in São Paulo; the recent capture from the Communists of the Railroad Workers Union in Rio de Janeiro; and the defeat by the Socialist Bayard Boiteaux of a strong Communist bid to capture the Rio de Janeiro teachers' organization.[75]

However, the Socialists continued to suffer in the labor movement and elsewhere from the inability to distinguish themselves clearly from the Communists and the followers of the late Getúlio Vargas. The president of the São Paulo Textile Workers Union suggested in 1959 that the party suffered also from the fact that unlike the PTB, which had had Getúlio and in 1959 had João Goulart, and the Communists, who still had Luiz Carlos Prestes, the Socialists lacked a charismatic figure in a situation in which workers and other Brazilians were more often than not attracted by individual political leaders rather than by programs or ideologies.[76]

The quandary of the Socialists was well exemplified by Remo Forli, Socialist leader of the São Paulo Metal Workers Union. He had been president of the *sindicato* from 1953 to 1955 but was defeated by the Communists in the latter year. Two years later, he was the successful candidate of a ticket backed by both the Socialists and the Communists, and in 1959 this same joint list was the only one offered for election. Forli explained that he had accepted this joint Communist-Socialist ticket because he felt that it was better to hold office, even jointly with the Communists, than to let the Communists totally control the *sindicato*.[77]

The state of São Paulo presented a somewhat peculiar situation. Adhemar de Barros, who had been Getúlio Vargas's interventor (appointed governor) in the state for some years during the Estado Novo and in 1947 had been elected governor, even after leaving the governorship had considerable support among the workers. However, his Social Progressive Party did not apparently carry on much activity within the trade union, where the officials continued to be members of the Partido Trabalhista Brasileiro, the Communist Party, or, in some instances, the Socialist Party.[78]

A new political element began to appear in Brazilian organized labor during the Kubitschek period. This was the Catholics. What was by the 1950s the National Confederation of Workers Circles had been started in Rio Grande do Sul in 1932 by Father Ludwig Brentanno, S.J., mainly to proselytize the Christian gospel among workers. Even as late as the early 1950s the group had no involvement with the trade union movement.[79]

However, in 1955, the *círculos operários* (workers' circles) in Pôrto Alegre established a trade union leadership training program and in the first year had as many as five hundred workers who attended at least some of its classes. By 1956 they were offering classes in the philosophy of labor (using, interestingly enough, the book by the American onetime anarchist Frank Tannenbaum as the text) as well as others on Brazilian legislation and the function of trade union leaders.[80]

By 1959 the São Paulo Federation of Workers Circles also established a trade union leadership training school in the industrial city of Santo André.[81] Two years earlier the workers circles in Rio de Janeiro had established a full-fledged Workers Leaders School, which was one of their first extensive efforts to have such an institution. The emphasis was on training good trade union leaders, with the avowed hope of challenging the Communists in the labor movement. It ran two types of courses, one a basic one that met three nights a week, after which the best graduates were given the intensive thirty-day course, during which the workers' pay was provided by the Catholic University of Rio de Janeiro, which was collaborating with the Workers Circles, and where the classes were held.[82]

By the end of the Kubitschek regime, some of the graduates of the Workers Circles training institutions had begun to make their appearance in the lower ranks of the trade union leadership. They were to have considerable significance in the years that followed.

Ronald Chilcote has summed up the political situation inside the labor movement near the end of the Kubitschek administration:

Toward the end of Kubitschek's term a new leadership, in general anti-Communist and less concerned with nationalism than with wage demands, challenged the hegemony of PTB and Communist labor leaders. . . . The new leaders, known as "renovating" or "democratic," . . . promoted their cause at the third Congreso Sindical Nacional, held in Rio in 1960. Their program called for depoliticization of the labor movement, trade unionism based on collective contracts, and elimination of the labor tax.

Chilcote continued:

The Congress was attended also by a majority faction composed of a united front of nationalists and Communists who advocated the labor movement's political participation in the struggle for nationalism and for a Central Sindical Nacional. This current was labeled *pelegos vermelhos*, i.e., "red" labor leaders who cooperated with the Ministry of Labor. A third current called *pelegos amarelos* (elder "official" labor leaders), was dependent on labor funds and for political ties with the government. Because of ideological differences, the "official" leaders were unable to maintain their shaky alliance with the majority current, and eventually formed an anti-Communist organization known as the Movimento Sindical Democrático, which quickly established relations with the AFL-CIO supported Organización Regional Interamericana de Trabajadores (ORIT) and the International Confederation of Free Trade Unions.[83]

ORGANIZED LABOR IN THE SHORT JÂNIO QUADROS INTERREGNUM

In the election of 1960, the opposition candidate, the quixotic former governor of São Paulo, Jânio Quadros, was chosen to succeed President Juscelino Kubitschek. However, in the same election João Goulart was again chosen vice president, since there were two competing vice presidential nominees claiming to be the running mates of Jânio Quadros, Milton Campos of the União Democrática Nacional and Fernando Ferrari, named by a splinter group that broke away from the PTB.

Jânio Quadros remained in the presidency for only seven

months. In August 1961, he suddenly resigned, giving rise to a constitutional crisis when the three military ministers attempted to prevent Vice President João Goulart from assuming the presidency. Various explanations have been offered for Janio's resignation, but I am convinced that in effect he ran away from the job, rather than accepting any of the alternatives that might have made it possible for him to remain in the post and get through Congress at least some of the extensive programs of reform on which he had been elected.[84]

Before he took office, some trade union leaders were hopeful about Quadros's administration, particularly about his promises to clean up the corruption that was undoubtedly widespread. This was particularly the case with the São Paulo trade unionists.[85]

However, during his short period in power, President Quadros did not have time to alter to any significant degree the nature of Brazilian organized labor, even if he had wanted to do so. But Ronald Chilcote noted, "Under Quadros the Communist-nationalist coalition was weakened temporarily when control of the Labor Ministry was turned over to a Christian Democrat."[86]

THE NATURE OF THE GOULART REGIME

The resignation of President Jânio Quadros provoked a major crisis. The three ministers of the armed forces immediately announced that they would not recognize the ascension of Vice President João Goulart—who was at that moment in Beijing, China, heading an official trade delegation—to the presidency. However, this statement aroused widespread opposition, headed by Governor Leonel Brizola of Rio Grande do Sul (Goulart's brother-in-law), who was backed by General Machado Lopes, the commander of the Third Army, the country's largest, which was stationed in Rio Grande do Sul. Governor Mauro Borges of Goiás and Mayor Miguel Arais of Recife were among the other figures who pledged their support to Goulart. There were also a number of strikes by workers demanding that João Goulart be permitted to become president.[87]

The country was clearly faced with the possibility of a civil war. As a result, there was worked out a typically Brazilian compromise, whereby the constitution was amended to provide for a modified form of parliamentary government, limiting the president's power, under which João Goulart would be permitted to become president. On taking power, President Goulart named Tancredo Neves, a stalwart of the Partido Social Democrático in Minas Gerais, as his first prime minister. Some months later, the

PTB member Brochado da Rocha succeeded Neves, and subsequently he was succeeded by the Socialist Hermes Lima.[88]

During his first year, President Goulart devoted much of his attention to trying to regain full presidential powers. This he achieved when in January 1963 a referendum went overwhelmingly in favor of restoration of the presidential system.[89]

Goulart's first cabinet formed after regaining full presidential power was, as the Communist historian Moisés Vinhas noted, "a quite wide alignment of forces." However, as Vinhas also commented, Goulart's first major defeat occurred when the various left-wing forces vetoed the so-called Three Year Plan, drawn up by Santiago Dantas and Celso Furtado for that cabinet, which sought, among other objectives, to curb inflation by a "policy of controlled recession."[90]

After the dismissal of this cabinet, Goulart tended to veer to the Left, a direction that became definitive with the formation of his last cabinet in December 1963. As a consequence of this, Goulart was deserted politically by the middle classes and by March 1964 had definitively alienated the principal leaders of the armed forces.

Moisés Vinhas sketched the result of Goulart's policies:

One year after having obtained the massive support of the electorate for his government, João Goulart had already squandered the largest part of this support. . . . The economic crisis, the deterioration of the standard of living, subversive and destabilizing action of the bourgeoisie and of North American imperialism, which ably capitalized on the leftist accommodation, threw the middle classes into the arms of the right. . . . In this situation, what was weakness appeared to be strength, what was narrowing of the front and dangerous reduction of the social bases of support appeared as advance, purging and purification. In fact, it was the proletariat which became isolated. Against it was formed a "broad front." Before being beaten militarily, it had been defeated politically.[91]

In the first months of 1964 there seemed, from the point of view of Goulart and his various leftist supporters, to exist a "prerevolutionary situation." This was borne out by Leonidas Xausa, at the time a leader of the Christian Democratic Party and of the left-wing Catholic group Acão Popular in Rio Grande do Sul.

Xausa recounted two years later a conversation he had had in December 1963 with Paulo de Tarso, a national left-wing Christian Democratic leader and member of the Goulart government, in which Xausa tried to convince Paulo de Tarso that the Left and the Goulart regime were headed for disaster. However, Paulo de Tarso maintained that the armed forces were firmly under the control of the left-wing general Assis Brasil, and that in fact the government was trying to provoke a right-wing military coup attempt, so as to be able to crush it definitely. The national PDC leader also insisted that the labor movement, led by the CGT, would bring the economy of the country to a halt in the face of any movement against the government, and that the students, organized in the União Nacional de Estudantes, would provide the shock troops in the streets in the defense of the government. However, as Xausa commented, all of that was fantasy.[92]

Among others, the Communists shared this fantasy. Moisés Vinhas noted that "the Partido Comunista Brasileiro . . . did not escape the confusion and general radicalization which took hold of the democratic forces from the second semester of 1963."[93]

ORGANIZED LABOR DURING THE GOULART REGIME

During the Goulart period there was a rapid radicalization of the labor movement. A loose alliance of the Communists and "nationalists" of the PTB, Socialist Party, and left-wing Christian Democrats organized in a new party, Acão Popular, made very extensive gains. For the first time, they won control of three of the national labor confederations that had been dominated by the *pelegos*—the National Confederation of Industrial Workers, the National Confederation of Land Transport Workers, and the National Confederation of Maritime and Riverine Workers—as well as most of the federations affiliated with those groups.[94]

In the case of the Commercial Workers Confederation a deadlock developed, as ten federations supported a list of pro-Communist leaders and another ten opposing that list. At that point, the minister of labor "intervened" the confederation shortly before the coup against President Goulart.[95]

There is no doubt that the change in control of the confederations brought into office people who were more militant than their predecessors in trying to take advantage of the existing labor system to improve the position of their constituents. In 1962, Benedito Cerqueira, the new secretary of the CNTI, told me that the new administration of the confederation was exerting pressure to have the labor laws more strictly enforced and to this end had put in more militant unionists as workers' representatives on the Supreme Labor Tribunal. It was also pushing for simplification of the social security system, and for stricter compliance with existing social security laws. In addition, the CNTI leadership was pushing for a system of family wage for workers with large families. Finally, in the broader sociopolitical field, they were pushing for basic agrarian reform and banking reforms and other measures.[96]

The capture of the confederations greatly strengthened the patronage and political powers of the left-wing labor leaders, particularly after passage near the end of the Kubitschek government of a law reorganizing the social security institutions.

Kenneth Erickson outlined this new law and its significance:

This law assured labor leaders one-third of the seats on the governing councils of all social security agencies, thus providing them with a major lever to increase their political influence. Chairmanship of the councils now rotated among the three participant groups: labor, government, and employers. Prior to 1960, labor had no delegate on the executive bodies, and the chairman had always been a Ministry official or an appointed expert in social legislation.

Erickson went on:

This new law, therefore gave labor leaders a firm foothold in patronage, a major currency in Brazilian politics. The social security agencies employed nearly 100,000 of Brazil's 700,000 federal civil servants and disposed of a budget larger than that of any state except São Paulo. The autonomy of these councils offered protection against control from above, and their political use of the power of appointment, even in defiance of the president and labor minister has been documented in a case study of patronage.[97]

THE CGT AND OTHER INCIPIENT CENTRAL LABOR BODIES

Another characteristic of the labor movement during the Goulart presidency was the formation of a number of *sindicato* groups that were outside the Estado Novo labor structure. The most important of these was the Comando Geral dos Trabalhadores (General Labor Command [CGT]), which was originally established in mid–1962 as the General Strike Command, to organize and lead a general strike, but continued on a permanent basis as the CGT. Another group, the Comissão Permanente de Organizações Sindicais (Permanent Commission of Trade Union Organizations [CPOS]) had originally been established in Rio de Janeiro late in the Kubitschek regime. There were also the Pacto de Unidade e Acão (PUA), composed of maritime and railroad workers, and the Forum Sindical de Debates (FSD) in the port city of Santos.[98]

The organizers and leaders of these groups were "nationalists" and Communists. Moisés Vinhas noted:

Acting in these organizations alongside the PTBistas like Dante Pelacani, Clodsmith Riani, Benedito Cerqueira and others, were Communist trade union leaders and politicians with great prestige among the masses, such as Roberto Morena, Osvaldo Pacheco, Hercules Correa, Luís Tenório de Lima, João Massena de Melo, Paulo de Melo Bastos, Aluisio Palhano, Demostoclides Batista and others.[99]

INFLUENCE OF THE COMMUNISTS AND THEIR ALLIES

There is no doubt that a very considerable part of the labor movement in the Goulart period was controlled by the Communists and their allies, particularly left-wing members of the Partido Trabalhista Brasileiro and the Socialist Party. One Socialist trade union leader in Rio de Janeiro said in 1962 that the left-wing Trabalhistas were the dominant element in the metal workers, some of the port *sindicatos*, and the commercial employees; that the Socialists were strong in the airline workers, electric power employees, and some others; and that the Communists controlled the textile workers, woodworkers, and some of the port workers.[100]

The Communist historian Moisés Vinhas presented a more extensive picture of his party's influence in the labor movement during the Goulart years:

In São Paulo, it had decisive influence in the *sindicatos* of metal workers, textiles, chemicals, woodworkers, printing trades, glass workers, bakers, bank employees, journalists, railroad workers, among others. This influence was not limited to the capital of the State, but extended to Santos, where it dominated the sindicatos of the port workers, to the ABCD area where it controlled the metal workers, to Jundiai, textiles and metal workers, as well as to Campinas, Sorocaba and other municipalities.

Vinhas continued:

In Guanabara, the Communists were present in the sindicatos of maritime transport, stevedores, railroaders, metallurgy, textiles, bank employees, journalists, chauffeurs, public servants and others. In the State of Rio de Janeiro, they led the fields of railroad transport, shipyards, petroleum, metal workers and rural workers in the sugar mills. In Minas Gerais, the economy of which is quite decentralized, they were active in the industrial area of the periphery of Belo Horizonte, where there are metal, chemical and textile firms, and in the extraction of gold in Nova Lima, and mining. In Rio Grande do Sul their activities were concentrated among workers of the port of the capital, railroads, textiles, metallurgy, bank workers, journalists, public functionaries and in industries of the interior cities. In Pernambuco, in addition to the dockers, land transport, textile, bank workers and journalists, they were in the vanguard of the rural trade union movement.[101]

STRIKES DURING THE GOULART PERIOD

The Goulart period was marked by a wave of strikes. Moisés Vinhas noted, "During the years 1961 to 1963 there occurred around two hundred general strikes or sectoral general strikes, the majority for economic demands and a few, most significant, of political character." He pointed out the October 6, 1963, general strike of São Paulo, in which 700,000 workers in seventy-nine *sindicatos* and four federations of the CNTI participated, as the most significant of these walkouts.[102]

The opposition to President Goulart contended that this wave of strikes was political, and even revolutionary, in origin and intent. However, Kenneth Erickson argued that the situation was more complicated:

The success of strikes, measured by the extent of work stoppage, is not due to control of the workers by the leadership but rather to the impact of two other variables. The first is the immediate economic situation of the workers as reflected in the purchasing power of their wages. The other is the disposition of key military officers toward each strike.

Erickson continued:

Analysis of 17 major strikes and strike threats considered political between 1960 and 1964 demonstrates that these so-called political strikes were really economic in nature. . . . Nine of the ten which were moderately or very successful in terms of work stoppage occurred at moments which the economic situation was unfavorable to the workers. . . . In each of the six threats which did not result in work stoppages, key officers threatened to crush the workers if they took to the streets.[103]

However, it should be noted that many of the strikes that took place in the Goulart period involved workers employed by sectors of the economy controlled by the government. In these cases, the strikers were assured of receiving wages for the period in which they walked out, regardless of the outcome of the strike.

In some cases, local *sindicato* leaders sought to prevent their organizations from participating in strikes they deemed political. One such instance involved the Electric Power Workers Union of Campos in the state of Rio de Janeiro. The *sindicato* was on the verge of completing negotiations for a new agreement with the employer when some of the more radical *sindicato* members sought to call a strike against "the stalling of the company." The *sindicato's* president succeeded in thwarting this effort, and a satisfactory agreement was soon completed.[104]

There is no doubt that local officials of the Ministry of Labor frequently encouraged strikes. For instance, in the case of the railroad walkout in Espírito Santo state, the regional labor delegate spoke to a meeting of strikers and roundly denounced the railroad management.[105]

RURAL UNIONIZATION

An entirely new element on the Brazilian labor scene during the Goulart period was the rapid rise of a new rural labor movement. The idea of organization of rural workers was not entirely new. Indeed, one of the earliest laws dealing with organized labor was that of January 3, 1903, article 1 of which provided that "persons engaged in agriculture and rural industries of any kind may organize *sindicatos* for the study, support, and defense of their interests." However, the further provisions of that statute dealt principally with the establishment of cooperatives and made no mention of the possibility of rural workers' bargaining collectively with their employers or landlords.[106] This law was repealed by the Vargas regime in 1933. The Consolidação das Leis do Trabalho specifically exempted rural workers from most of its provisions.[107]

It was not until the 1950s that a serious effort began to unionize agricultural workers. The Communists, as early as 1954, established in São Paulo state the União dos Lavradores e Trabalhadores Agrícolas do Brasil (ULTAB). It was largely confined to that state and was quite limited in scope. Also, in 1955, a young lawyer in Pernambuco, Francisco Julião, had taken the leadership in organizing in that state "peasant leagues," which consisted not only of wageworkers, but also of sharecroppers and small landholders.[108] However, in neither of these cases did the organizers seek to establish their organizations as official sindicatos in conformity with existing labor legislation.

However, progressive elements within the Catholic Church were interested in establishing officially recognized *sindicatos*. After Pope João XXIII's encyclical *Mater e Magistra*, the Brazilian bishops endorsed the idea of unionization of rural workers and set about encouraging it. Each diocese or group of dioceses carried this out in its own way. In São Paulo, where the *círculos operários* had been very active among urban trade unionists, the church also undertook to organize rural *sindicatos*. In Paraná, Santa Catarina, Goiás, Pará, and Rio Grande do Sul, there was first organized a Frente Agrária (Agrarian Front), which then undertook to organize *sindicatos*.[109]

Dom Eugenio Salles, then bishop of Rio Grande do Norte, launched a movement to organize rural *sindicatos* in 1959.[110] By the end of the Goulart regime, Bishop Salles claimed to have between 50,000 and 75,000 workers in legally recognized *sindicatos* in Rio Grande do Norte.[111]

In 1961, a young parish priest, Padre Paulo Crespo of Pernambuco, called a meeting of fellow priests in Jaboatão, to discuss "the most effective way to meet the challenge of misery and political unrest in the state." The twenty-five priests in attendance agreed that the establishment of rural *sindicatos* would be most effective.[112]

The rural unionization movement spread rapidly in the northeastern states. In May 1962, a Congress of Rural Workers of the North and Northeast of Brazil met in Itabuna, Bahia, At the close of that meeting, it was announced that Minister of Labor André Franco Montouro had extended legal recognition to twenty-three rural *sindicatos*, five of them in Pernambuco. In the following month the first Federation of Rural Workers, in Pernambuco, also received legal recognition.[113]

In November 1963 a strike of sugar workers in Pernambuco lasted three days and closed down 90 percent of the sugar industry of the state. It was settled with the employers' promising to increase the minimum wage of sugar workers by 80 percent.

In the southernmost state, Rio Grande do Sul, the church claimed to have organized one hundred fifty *sindicatos*, with some 300,000 members. It was faced with the rival efforts of Governor Leonel Brizola, and *sindicatos* organized under his auspices were promptly legalized by the Ministry of Labor, whereas those established under Catholic auspices found the Ministry much slower about extending legal recognition.[114]

Competition among various political factions for control over the new rural *sindicatos* was intense. Cynthia Hewitt wrote concerning Pernambuco:

In the three years between the founding of the first sindicato and the revolution of April 1964, many factions struggled for control of the rural labor movement. The Labor Ministry of Goulart, the state government of Miguel Arraes, the Peasant Leagues of Francisco Julião, the Communist Party of Brazil, the Chinese Communists, a handful of Trotskyites, and the Catholic Church—all fought for the privilege of directing the organization of rural workers.[115]

An important element in this political struggle for control of the new rural worker *sindicatos* was a split in the ranks of the Catholic elements working in the field. The new left-wing Catholic group Acão Popular was very active in the rural unionization campaign and opposed the leadership of Padre Paulo Crespo and his colleague Padre Antonio Melo, who had launched the church's rural unionization program in Pernambuco. Acão Popular, unlike

Crespo and Melo, was quite willing to strike a deal with the Communists.

This issue came to a head at the congress held in Rio de Janeiro in December 1963, to establish a confederation of agricultural workers, which took the name Confederação Nacional dos Trabalhadores na Agricultura (CONTAG). There were twenty-seven rural workers' federations represented there, nine controlled by the Communists, five by Acão Popular, and nine by non-AP Catholic elements. The upshot was, as Ronald Chilcote related: "An agreement between the AP and the Communist leadership gave most of the top posts to Communists as Communists Lindolfo Silva, José Leandro Bezerra da Costa and Nestor Vera were elected respectively President, Second Vice President and Treasurer of the new confederation."[116] Manoel Gonsalvo Ferreira, a member of the AP and president of the original Pernambuco federation, was elected first vice president.[117] The new CONTAG was officially legalized by a presidential decree of January 31, 1964.[118]

Another important event involving the rural workers was the passage on March 2, 1963, of the so-called Statute of the Rural Worker. This had originally been introduced by a PTB congressman, Fernando Ferrari, in 1951. It provided for rural workers, like their urban counterparts, to have *carteiras profissionais*, that is, official work records; and to have a weekly rest day and some paid holidays. It also provided for extension of the imposto sindical to rural workers. In November of 1963, social security was also extended to rural workers.[119]

CONCLUSION

During the democratic interregnum from 1945 until 1964, the schema of labor relations and organized labor established in the Estado Novo was not fundamentally altered. The governmental control over organized labor that the Estado Novo had provided for continued to exist legally. Various administrations applied the Estado Novo rules with more or less leniency, but the basic framework persisted. Even in the Goulart period, when the labor movement seemed to be least under government control, the power of the new (and many not so new) labor leaders who emerged in those years depended to a very marked degree on their control of important government patronage, and on the weakness and incompetence of President João Goulart. Events that succeeded his overthrow were to demonstrate most clearly that the Estado Novo framework was still firmly in place.

NOTES

1. For a general view of the Kubitschek administration, see Robert J. Alexander, *Juscelino Kubitschek and the Development of Brazil*, Ohio University Monographs in International Studies, Athens, 1991.

2. Ronald H. Chilcote, *The Brazilian Communist Party: Conflict and Integration 1922–1972*, Oxford University Press, New York, 1974, page 70.

3. Moisés Vinhas, *O Partidão: A Luta por um Partido de Massas 1922–1974*, Editoria Hucitec, São Paulo, 1982, page 182.

4. Interview with Arnaldo Sussekind, head of Planning Section, Ministry of Labor, and former legal adviser of National Confederation of Industrial Workers, in Rio de Janeiro, April 5, 1956.

5. Interview with Irving Salert, U.S. Embassy labor attaché, in Rio de Janeiro, March 6, 1956.

6. Interview with Sr. Agostino, an editor of Communist newspaper *Gazetta Sindical*, in Rio de Janeiro, March 21, 1956.

7. Interview with Arnaldo Sussekind, op. cit., April 5, 1956.

8. Interview with Carlos Alberto Costa, executive secretary of Confederação Nacional dos Trabalhadores no Comércio, in Rio de Janeiro, August 24, 1959.

9. Interview with Jaime Wallace Nunes, Socialist leader in Sindicato de Chofers Autônomos of Rio de Janeiro, in Rio de Janeiro, August 21, 1959.

10. Interview with Djalma A. Mariano, director of Rio de Janeiro office of ICFTU-ORIT, in Rio de Janeiro, August 24, 1959; see also Chilcote, op. cit., page 149.

11. Interview with Maria da Graça Dutra, secretary general, Federação Nacional de Jornalistas, an editor of Communist daily *Imprensa Popular*, in Rio de Janeiro, March 21, 1956.

12. Interview with Luiz Augusto de Castro Lisboa, president of Sindicato dos Empregados em Establecimentos Bancários de Pôrto Alegre, in Pôrto Alegre, May 7, 1956.

13. Interview with Heracy Wagner, secretary of Confederação Nacional dos Trabalhadores na Indústria, in Rio de Janeiro, August 25, 1959.

14. Interview with Djalma A. Mariano, op. cit., August 24, 1959.

15. Interviews with Irving Salert, op. cit., March 9, 1956; and Diocleciano de Holanda Cavalcanti, president of Confederação dos Trabalhadores na Indústria, in Rio de Janeiro, March 9, 1956.

16. Interview with Jarbas Loureiro, administrative chief of Federação dos Trabalhadores de Construção Civil of Minas Gerais, in Belo Horizonte, March 28, 1956.

17. Interview with Walter Torres, treasurer of Sindicato dos Trabalhadores nas Indústrias Gráficas do Rio de Janeiro, in Rio de Janeiro, August 22, 1959.

18. Interview with Manoel Francisco da Silva, president of Federação dos Trabalhadores na Indústria de Alimentação, Secretary of CNTI, in Recife, February 22, 1956.

19. Interview with Irving Salert, op. cit., March 5, 1956.

20. Interview with Irving Salert, op. cit., March 9, 1956.

21. Interview with Djalma A. Mariano, op. cit., August 24, 1959.

22. Interview with Irving Salert, op. cit., March 9, 1956.

23. Interview with Fausto Cardoso, president of Confederação Nacional dos Trabalhadores no Comércio, in Rio de Janeiro, March 15, 1956.

24. Interview with Djalma A. Mariano, op. cit., August 24, 1959.

25. Interview with Serafino Romualdi, assistant secretary general, ORIT, in Washington, DC, December 29, 1955.

26. Interview with Sebastião Paiva, secretary of Confederaçao Nacional dos Trabalhadores no Transporte Terrestre, in Rio de Janeiro, March 16, 1956.

27. Interview with Djalma A. Mariano, op. cit., August 24, 1959.

28. Interview with Pasquale Damore, secretary of Federação dos Trabalhadores na Indústria de Vestuário, in São Paulo, April 18, 1956.

29. Interview with Nivaldo Fonseca, second secretary of Sindicato dos Trabalhadores na Indústria de Fiação e Tecelagem de São Paulo, in São Paulo, April 10, 1956.

30. Interview with Cherubim Mendes Coutinho, secretary of Federação dos Trabalhadores na Indústria de Vestuário do Estado de São Paulo, in São Paulo, August 26, 1959.

31. Interview with Pasquale Damore, op. cit., April 19, 1956.

32. Interview with Olavo Previatti, president of Federação dos Trabalhadores nas Indústrias do Papel, Papelão e Cortiças do Estado de São Paulo, in São Paulo, April 27, 1956.

33. Interview with Ramon Pereira, secretary of Federação dos Trabalhadores Metalúrgicos of Rio Grande so Sul, in Pôrto Alegre, May 3, 1956.

34. Interview with Diocleciano de Holanda Cavalcanti, op. cit., March 9, 1956.

35. Interview with Carlos Alberto Costa, op. cit., August 24, 1959.

36. Chilcote, op. cit., page 151.

37. Interview with Heitor Teodoro Mendes, president of Sindicato dos Trabalhadores nas Artefatos de Papel of São Paulo, August 27, 1959.

38. Interview with João Peixoto, vice president of Sindicato de Bancários of Bahia, in Salvador, March 3, 1956.

39. Interview with José Albertino R. Rodrigues, director of Departamento Intersindical de Estatística o Estudos Socio-Econômicos, in São Paulo, August 27, 1959.

40. "Relacão das Entidades Membros do Departamento Intersindical de Estatística e Estudos Socio-Econômicos," typed, n.d. (circa 1959).

41. "Departamento Intersindical de Estatística e Estudos Socio-Econômicos," typed, n.d. (circa 1959).

42. Interview with José Albertino R. Rodrigues, op. cit., August 27, 1959.

43. "Departmento Intersindical de Estatística e Estudos Socio-Econômicos," op. cit.

44. Interview with Serafino Romualdi, op. cit., December 29, 1955.

45. Interview with Joviano de Araujo, Brazilian representative of ICFTU-ORIT, former secretary of Federação Marítima Nacional, in Rio de Janeiro, June 13, 1953.

46. Ibid., March 7, 1956.

47. Interview with Serafino Romualdi, op. cit., July 30, 1956.

48. Interview with Djalma A. Mariano, op. cit., August 24, 1959.

49. Interview with Mario Matteo, secretary of Sindicato dos Trabalhadores na Indústria de Metal, Mecânica y Materiais Elétricos do Distrito Federal e Estado do Rio, in Rio de Janeiro, April 9, 1956.

50. Interview with Isaltino Pereira, editor of *Voz Metalúrgica*, organ of Metal Workers Federation of Federal District, in Rio de Janeiro, August 26, 1959.

51. Interview with Aldo Lombardi, secretary general of Sindicato dos Trabalhadores nas Indústrias Metalúrgicas, Mecânicas e de Material Elétrico de São Paulo, in São Paulo, April 17, 1967.

52. Interview with Julio Devichiatti, president of Sindicato dos Trabalhadores de Tecelagem e Fiação de São Paulo, in São Paulo, August 27, 1959.

53. Interview with Nivaldo Fonseca, op. cit., April 20 and 24, 1956.

54. Robert J. Alexander. "Observations on São Paulo Textile Union, April 24, 1956" (typed).

55. Interview with José Ribeiro, secretary of Sindicato dos Trabalhadores na Indústria de Fiação e Tecelagem of Recife, in Recife, February 24, 1956.

56. Interview with Bernardino da Costa e Silva, President of Sindicato dos Motoristas e Condutores em Transportes Fluviais no Estado de Pará, in Belem, February 13, 1956.

57. Interview with João Peixoto, op. cit., March 3, 1956.

58. Interview with Luiz Augusto de Castro Lisboa, op. cit., May 7, 1956.

59. Interviews with Sr. Gurgel, member of Diretorio of Sindicato de Empregados Bancários of the Federal District, in Rio de Janeiro, March 15, 1956; and Aurélio Lopes, functionary of Sindicato dos Empregados Bancários of the Federal District, Rio de Janeiro, March 15, 1956.

60. Interviews with José Carpintero Pinheiro, president of Sindicato dos Trabalhadores de Luz e Força of Rio de Janeiro, in Rio de Janeiro, March 23, 1956; and Francisco Patricio de Oliveira, lawyer of Sindicato dos Trabalhadores na Indústria de Energia Hidroelétrica de São Paulo, in São Paulo, April 14, 1956.

61. Interview with José Machado de Mello Sorbrinho, secretary general of Sindicatos dos Arrumadores de Santos, in Santos, April 25, 1956.

62. "Brazil—Volta Redonda Steel Workers—1959: Collective Agreement Entered into by the Metal, Mechanical and Electrical Industrial Workers' Union of Barra Mansa and the National Steel Company," typed manuscript, in English.

63. Interview with Luiz Antonio Leite, member of Conselho Fiscal of Sindicato Nacional dos Trabalhadores nas Indústrias Metais, Mecânicas, e Materiais Elétricos de Barra Mansa, in Volta Redonda, April 3, 1956.

64. Interview with Ivan Alkmin, vice president of Sindicato Nacional dos Aeronautas, in Rio de Janeiro, August 21, 1959.

65. Interviews with Domingos Brandão, first secretary of Sindicato dos Estivadores de Santos, in Santos, April 25, 1956; and Jaime Maceio, President of Sindicatos dos Estivadores da Bahia, in Salvador, March 1, 1956.

66. Interview with Pedro Chavier de Paiva, president of Sindicato dos Trabalhadores na Indústria de Fiação e Tecelagem of Recife, in Recife, February 24, 1956.

67. Francisco Weffort chapter in *Movimiento Obrero, Sindicatos y Poder en América Latina*, Editorial El Coloquio, Buenos Aires, 1975, page 138.

68. Robert J. Alexander, *The ABC Presidents: Conversations and Correspondence with the Presidents of Argentina, Brazil, and Chile*, Praeger, Westport, CT, 1992.

69. Interview with Irving Salert, op. cit., March 6, 1956.

70. Serafino Romualdi, *Presidents and Peons: Recollections of a Labor Ambassador in Latin America*, Funk and Wagnalls, New York, 1967, pages 279–280.

71. Letter of Robert J. Alexander to Jay Lovestone, September 26, 1959.

72. Robert J. Alexander. "Observations on the São Paulo Textile Union, April 24, 1956," op. cit.

73. Interview with Isaltino Pereira, op. cit., August 25, 1959.

74. Vinhas, op. cit., page 184.

75. Interview with Ivan Alkmin, op. cit., August 21, 1959.

76. Interview with Julio Devichiatti, op. cit., August 27, 1959.

77. Interview with Remo Forli, president of Sindicato dos Trabalhadores Metalúrgicos, in São Paulo, August 27, 1959.

78. Interview with José Gonçalves, president of Sindicato dos Operários nos Serviços Portuarios de Santos, in Santos, April 25, 1956.

79. Interview with Ludwig Brentano, S.J., national ecclesiastical adviser of Confederação Nacional de Círculos Operários, in Rio de Janeiro, March 12, 1956.

80. Interview with Isidoro Belmonte de Macedo, president of Círculos Operários Católicos Portoalegrande, in Pôrto Alegre, April 30, 1956.

81. Interview with Centino Laluce, secretary of public relations of Federação dos Círculos Operários do Estado de São Paulo, in São Paulo, August 28, 1959.

82. Interview with Antonio da Costa Carvalgo, S.J., assistant director of Escola de Lideres Operários, in Rio de Janeiro, August 25, 1959.

83. Chilcote, op. cit., pages 150–151.

84. See Robert J. Alexander, "The Rise and Fall of Jânio Quadros," 2 *Viertel Jahres Berichte*, Bonn, September 1973.

85. Interview with Dacyr Gatto, president of Federação dos Trabalhadores na Indústria de Vestuário de São Paulo, in São Paulo, September 26, 1959.

86. Chilcote, op. cit., page 151.

87. Vicente Barreto, "Carta de Rio de Janeiro: Brasil y Sus Problemas Concretos," Publication of Press Service of Congress for Cultural Freedom, November 2–9, 1963 (mimeographed).

88. Vinhas, op. cit., page 186.

89. Ibid., page 190.

90. Ibid., page 190; see also Kenneth Paul Erickson, *The Brazilian Corporative State and Working-Class Politics*, University of California Press, Berkeley, 1977, page 134.

91. Vinhas, op. cit., page 193.

92. Interview with Leonidas Xausa, former leader in Rio Grande do Sul of Christian Democratic Party and Acão Popular, in Pôrto Alegre, December 6, 1965.

93. Vinhas, op. cit., page 192.

94. Ibid., page 191.

95. Chilcote, op. cit., page 182.

96. Interview with Benedito Cerqueira, secretary of Confederação Nacional dos Trabalhadores na Indústria, in Rio de Janeiro, August 15, 1962.

97. Erickson, 1977, op. cit., page 62.

98. Chilcote, op. cit., page 153.

99. Vinhas, op. cit., page 191.

100. Interview with Jaime Wallace Nunes, op. cit., August 21, 1959.

101. Vinhas, op. cit., page 188.

102. Ibid., page 192; for discussion of this and other strikes of the period, see Erickson, 1977, op. cit., pages 97–150.

103. Kenneth Erickson, "Corporative Controls of Labor in Brazil," paper presented at 1971 Annual Meeting of American Political Science Association, page 10.

104. Interview with Juvenal Guerreiro Torres, president of Sindicato dos Trabalhadores nas Empresas Elétricas de Campos, R.J., in Campos, February 6, 1966.

105. Interview with Delveaux Sisenanda Marques, secretary of Junta Governativa da Federação dos Trabalhadores nas Indústrias de Espírito Santo, in Vitória, February 11, 1966.

106. J. V. Freitas Marcondes, *First Brazilian Legislation Relating to Rural Labor Unions*, University of Florida Press, Gainesville, 1962, pages 39–41.

107. Robert E. Price, *Rural Unionization in Brazil*, Land Tenure Center, University of Wisconsin, Madison, August 1965, page 7.

108. Chilcote, op. cit., page 157.

109. Interview with Adolfo Puggina, Partido Democrata Cristão member of Rio Grande do Sul state legislature, organizer of rural unions, in Pôrto Alegre, December 10, 1965.

110. Cynthia Naegele Hewitt, "An Introduction to the Rural Labor Movement of Pernambuco" (manuscript), page 11.

111. Interview with Padre Eugenio Salles, apostolic administrator of Archdiocese of Bahia, former bishop of Rio Grande do Norte, in Salvador, May 16, 1966.

112. Hewitt, op. cit., page 12.

113. Ibid., page 12.

114. Ibid., page 13.

115. Ibid., page 9.

116. Chilcote, op. cit., page 159.

117. Hewitt, op. cit., page 27.

118. *Diário Oficial*, February 5, 1964.

119. Hewitt, op. cit., page 31.

5
Unionism During the 1964–1985 Military Dictatorship

On March 31/April 1, 1964, President João Goulart was overthrown by a military insurrection. This uprising was supported immediately by the officers commanding the north and northeastern garrisons, as well as that in Rio de Janeiro, and after some hesitation by those in control of the armed forces in Rio Grande do Sul and São Paulo. It also had the support of key state governors, including those of São Paulo, Goías, and Guanabara (the city of Rio de Janeiro).

In the face of this insurrection, President Goulart first went to Brasilia, hoping to rally support there, but without success. He then flew to Pôrto Alegre, in Rio Grande do Sul, where he rejected the advice of his brother-in-law, Leonel Brizola, to attempt to mount armed resistance there and instead flew into exile in Uruguay, where he had a hacienda.

Attempts by his labor supporters to back him failed. The CGT leaders got on the radio while the military movement was under way and pledged their support to Goulart, but when they tried finally to call a general strike, they failed. The unionists who were opposed to the leftists stayed on their jobs, and the strike collapsed after only a few hours in Rio de Janeiro. Elsewhere, there was virtually no strike at all.[1]

THE NATURE OF THE MILITARY REGIME

With the overthrow of President Goulart, power was taken, temporarily, by a military junta consisting of the ministers of army, navy, and air force. On April 9, the Junta issued what it called an Institutional Act, justifying their coup: "The victorious revolution, as a constituent power, legitimizes itself. It deposed the former Government and has the capacity to constitute the new Government. It has the normative power inherent in the Constituent Power."

The Institutional Act provided that within two days Congress would elect a new president to fill out João Goulart's unexpired term. It also suspended for six months laws giving tenure to public employees and gave the three military ministers the right to suspend for up to ten years the "political rights" (to vote, hold public office, or speak or write about political matters) of any individual, as well as to remove from office any national, state, or municipal legislators.[2]

This was to prove to be only the first of five "institutional acts" enacted by the military regime. For so long as they continued in effect, they were regarded by the courts, including the Supreme Court, as constitutional amendments, albeit transitory ones.[3]

In pursuance of the First Institutional Act, Congress, ostensibly on the initiative of seven elected governors who had not been deposed by the new regime, elected General Humberto de Alençar Castelo Branco, chief of the Army General Staff, as the new president of Brazil.[4] Also, on the basis of the act, the military ministers deprived forty-one members of Congress of their posts and their civil rights. They also deprived of civil rights the former presidents Janio Quadros and João Goulart and a number of other people who did not hold public office.[5] Subsequently, Castelo Branco, assuming the right to *cassar*, that is, to ban people for ten years from all political activity, took this measure against the ex-president Juscelino Kubitschek, as well as several of the governors who had originally supported the "Revolution" of 1964.

President Castelo Branco was apparently sincere in his desire to restore an elected government at the end of his term in power. In the beginning, his administration concentrated particularly on trying to stem the rampant inflation and to produce certain economic and social changes. However, under pressure from the "hard-liners" among his military colleagues he made one compromise after another in the political field. Within only a few months of taking office, he submitted a bill to Congress extending his own term of office by one year.

Then in October 1965, when elections for many governorships were scheduled, although he insisted that they be held and that the opposition winners in Guanabara, Minas Gerais, and one or two other states be allowed to take office, he was faced with a showdown with the hard-liners. As a consequence, he enacted the Second Institutional Act, which dissolved all existing parties, and installed a biparty system, one supporting the government and the other the opposition; and added five new members to the Supreme Court, which had "too generously" been enforcing the habeas corpus provisions of the constitution, and provided for the indirect election (instead of popular vote) of the president by an electoral college consisting of the members of Congress and a number of people chosen by state legislatures. Also, shortly before leaving office, he enacted a very stringent "national security law," extending military courts' jurisdiction to many hitherto civilian cases.

The Castelo Branco regime established the pattern that was to be followed by all of the administrations during the military dictatorship. Key political decisions were the province of the leaders of the armed forces. However, economic and social policies were largely left in the hands of civilian technocrats, including economists, sociologists, and other social scientists. Also, at least until the administration of President Ernesto Geisel (1974–1979), both military men and technocrats worked very closely with representatives of organizations of industrialists, mercantile interests, and rural landlords.

Castelo Branco's successor was Marshal Artur Costa e Silva, the minister of the army. Under him there was at first certain relaxation of restrictions on civil liberties, and his minister of labor, Colonel Jarbas Passarinho, took a more tolerant attitude toward the labor movement than had characterized the Castelo Branco regime. But late in 1968, when Congress refused to remove the parliamentary immunity of a deputy who had displeased the hard-line military men, Costa e Silva adjourned Congress indefinitely, and enacted the Fifth Institutional Act. That document extended indefinitely the right to *cassar* dissidents and gave the president sweeping powers to enact legislation by decree.

Soon afterward, Costa e Silva fell mortally ill. He was succeeded by General Garristazú Médici, chosen by a poll among the generals and admirals and completely ignoring Costa e Silva's civilian vice president. The Médici regime was the most tyrannical of the military administrations. It was faced with attempts by the far Left to launch guerrilla activities and dealt ruthlessly with anyone involved in those efforts, but it also used "death squads" in the cities to murder opponents of various sorts, as well as some common criminals. It instituted strict pre-publication censorship of all news media. Symptomatic of the political situation was the Communist Party's decision in 1971 to have its leader, Luiz Carlos Prestes, go into exile, and to move the operations of its Central Committee abroad in 1973.[6]

Elections during the Médici period were totally rigged. Even the official opposition, the Brazilian Democratic Movement (MDB), found it exceedingly hard to function. Many new people were *cassado*, that is, deprived of their civil rights.

But the Médici period was also characterized by the so-called Brazilian miracle. The administration put major efforts into economic development, and for several years Brazil had one of the fastest growing gross national products in the world. However, as we shall see, the income generated by the "miracle" was exceedingly inequitably distributed.

General Médeci was succeeded by General Ernesto Geisel, who announced a policy of *distensao*, that is, "relaxation" of the dictatorship. Censorship was largely eliminated, the legal opposition had much more room to operate, and voting procedures were more honest, although when the opposition did very well in state and national elections, President Geisel did not hesitate to use his prerogative to *cassar* more opposition political leaders, so as to amend the results in at least one state, and to institute what came to be known as "bionic" senators, a certain number of members of the upper house who were in effect named by the president. Most importantly, however, shortly before leaving the presidency, General Geisel canceled Institutional Act 5, the military regime's most oppressive single piece of legislation.

President Geisel was faced with the first "oil crisis" of 1973. Because Brazil imported two-thirds of its petroleum, the Geisel government had to decide between cutting down drastically on its massive development program when oil prices went up 500 percent or continuing with development, while borrowing from international banks to finance imports that had to be paid for in foreign currency. Geisel chose the second alternative, laying the groundwork for the "foreign debt crisis" of the 1980s and 1990s.

However, although promising that his successor would not be chosen by the armed forces, Figueiredo refused to support a constitutional change calling for direct popular election of the president. The upshot was that the opposition decided to try to beat the military regime at its own game of indirect elections.

This effort of the opposition was helped by at least three conditions. First, the opposition parties had made substantial gains in congressional elections in 1982. Second, the government's own party, the Democratic Social Party (PDS), split on the direct elections issue. Finally, the PDS itself nominated a candidate who was not President Figueiredo's choice and was widely regarded as exceedingly corrupt.

The opposition put up the candidacies of Tancredo Neves, a longtime leader of the opposition MDB, for president, and José Sarney, a PDS dissident and president of the PSD until he broke with it, as vice president. In December 1984 this ticket won by a substantial majority in the electoral college.

However, shortly before he was to take office, Tancredo Neves became mortally ill, and José Sarney was inaugurated as acting president, and became constitutional president when Neves died a few days later. Under Sarney, a more or less democratic, and largely civilian, regime was finally reestablished.

PURGE OF THE LABOR MOVEMENT

With the overthrow of the Goulart regime, the succeeding military government carried out a massive purge of the organized labor movement. This not only involved the labor leaders who had been nationally prominent during the Goulart years, but reached down to the local *sindicato* level.

Among those who were *cassado* by the military junta even before the assumption of power by Marshal Castelo Branco was the PTB deputy Benedito Cerqueira, one of the major figures in the National Industrial Workers Confederation, who was also removed from the Chamber of Deputies.[7] Also on this same purge list were such national labor leaders as Clodsmith Rieni, Dante, Policani and Hercules Correia dos Reis, also of the CNTI, and the Communist stalwart Roberto Morena.[8]

Within the labor movement itself, the purge was widespread, with the removal of many elected *sindicato* leaders. Kenneth Erickson said that

the government intervened 67 percent of the confederations, 42 percent of the federations, and only 19 percent of the sindicatos. Bank and transport workers' organizations figured prominently in the political strikes between 1960 and 1965, and they were hit harder, proportionally, than those in other sectors. And, significantly, large unions suffered more than small ones: the ministry intervened in 70 percent of those sindicatos with 5,000 or more members; in 38 percent of those in 1,000 to 5,000 members, and in only 19 percent of those with fewer than 1,000 members. The military government simply decapitated the radical labor movement.[9]

The purge in the São Paulo labor movement was particularly extensive. According to the Labor Reporting Office of the U.S. Consulate-General in that city, the leaders of all the Communist-controlled *sindicatos* were removed, as well as some corrupt *sindicato* officials, and some *sindicatos* were intervened "by mistake." Most of the interventors named by government to take over these *sindicatos* were members of the *sindicatos* involved, or of closely related ones. This was in contrast, according to the U.S. official, to the situation in the Northeast, where many of the interventors were army officers.

By June 1965, the process of elections in the intervened *sindicatos* had begun. By October, twelve elections had been held in

São Paulo, and six of these were won by Communist-supported tickets. In the Metal Workers, there was a unity slate, in which a Catholic group, some independents, and the pro–Chinese Communists, and Socialist groups all participated; only the pro-Moscow Communists were not represented. Pro-Communist elements had lists in seven of the twelve *sindicatos* that had elections. In only two cases did the slate backed by the interventors win.[10]

One temporary casualty of the labor purge in São Paulo was the Interunion Research and Statistical Service, the Departmento Intersindical de Estatísticas e Estudios Socio-Econômicos (DIESE), which had been established in the mid–1950s. Two years passed before the DIESE could be reestablished and begin once more to collect data on the cost of living and other matters.[11]

The situation in the Rio de Janeiro labor movement was similar to that in São Paulo. As a result of the interventions in those *sindicatos*, virtually all of the sindicatos there lost members, and in some of those in which leftist influence had been particularly notable, such as the Metal Workers and Port Workers, the losses of membership were characterized as "dramatic." Only one *sindicato* in Rio, that of the radio workers, was reported to have increased its membership.[12]

The confederations still had their headquarters in Rio de Janeiro, in spite of the fact that the capital had been transferred to Brasilia. Four of the confederations were intervened, and when elections in them were finally held, nonleftist administrations were returned in all of them.

As happened in São Paulo, some of the *sindicatos* in Rio de Janeiro in which the Communists had been strong before the 1964 "Revolution" returned to Communist control when elections were finally held. One was the Metal Workers Union, where a pro-Communist slate defeated one composed of Socialists and Christian Democrats by a vote of two to one.[13]

Some right-wing elements were worried by the ability of the Communists and their allies to regain some strength in the labor movement. The newspaper *O Globo* reported in August 1965:

Trade union observers, who have been keeping track of the situation of trade unionism in Brazil, affirm that, within three years, all of the old trade union leaders going back to the period of Sr. João Goulart as Minister of Labor, will be directing, directly or indirectly, the second and third level trade unions, the federations and confederations, with the exception, perhaps, of those recently recognized by the Minister of Labor.[14]

Of course, nothing of the kind took place. The military regime sought to make sure that "subversive" elements would not again get control of the labor movement by limiting those who could hold *sindicato* office. In August and September 1965 the Ministry of Labor issued instructions governing *sindicato* elections. Reported the Rio de Janeiro daily *Correio da Manhã*:

It is obligatory that candidates in *sindicato* elections must present evidence that they enjoy political rights . . . accompanied by a certificate of political antecedents issued by the Department of Political and Social Order," that is, the political police. In defining those ineligible for *sindicato* office, the Ministry's August 1965 regulation provided that it included "those who have bad conduct, duly proven, which includes temporary or definitive loss of political rights.[15]

Another regulation of the ministry issued in August 1965 provided for tentative listing of people as candidates who had not been able to present the documentation on time. However, in such a case, the ministry could hold up for thirty days the installation of newly elected officials, after which, if the documents were still not on hand, the place of anyone who had not presented them would be taken by an alternative candidate. If there were no such alternatives available, the installation of new *sindicato* officers could be postponed more or less indefinitely.[16]

The situation of the *sindicatos* in some of the provincial towns and cities was particularly difficult. In the city of Campos in the state of Rio de Janeiro a number of *sindicatos* were intervened, and even one that was not, the Graphic Arts Workers Union, set up a Commission of Administration, which called new elections.[17]

In the sate of Espírito Santo, the three port workers' *sindicatos* and the bank clerks' *sindicato* in the state capital, Vitória, were all intervened. So was the state Federation of Industrial Workers, and several of its constituent *sindicatos*, one of which, the woodworkers, finally disappeared. The process of putting these organizations into the hands of elected leaders was not completed until early 1966.[18] In the state's principal railroad center, Cachoeiro do Itapemirim, the railroad workers' *sindicato* was intervened, although none of the other *sindicatos* in the city was.[19]

In Rio Grande do Sul, where the leftist forces in the labor movement had not been as strong during the Goulart period as in Rio, São Paulo, and some other states, there were, nonetheless, various interventions in *sindicatos* after the "Revolution." These included two metal workers' *sindicatos* in the interior of the state, the bank workers, the stevedores, and the light and telephone workers. Most had been restored to control of elected officers by the end of 1965, but in the case of the light and telephone workers, the state government was seeking to deny its right to exist, since the members' employer had been taken over by the state and so the workers, under the Estado Novo system, had no right to have legally recognized *sindicatos*.[20]

In the neighboring state of Santa Catarina, the intervened *sindicatos* included those of the metal workers in the city of Joinville, the construction workers' federation and its affiliated unions, as well as the coal miners' *sindicatos*. Although by late 1965 most *sindicatos* had been restored to elected leadership, this was not true of the construction workers' *sindicato*, which had been virtually closed down.[21]

In the state of Paraná, six of the *sindicatos* affiliated with the Federation of Industrial Workers were intervened, as well as the bank workers' *sindicatos* all over the state and some of the local commercial employees' *sindicatos*. Although by the end of 1965 most of these had been restored to an elected leadership, this was not the case in the bank workers' *sindicato* of Londrina, which virtually ceased to exist.[22]

Hostility toward the trade union movement in the early years of the military regime was particularly intense in the Northeast and in the Amazon Valley. For instance, in Pernambuco, the Sugar Workers Union suffered three successive removals of elected officers.[23]

In the case of the Bank Workers Union of Pernambuco, the interventor, who claimed to have been the only member of the pre–1964 leadership who had opposed Communist control of the *sindicato*, was several times called into the headquarters of the Fourth Army and lectured about being too militant in support of the *sindicato* members. Then, subsequent to the reestablishment of an elected leadership, many of the banks fired any workers who assumed office in the *sindicato*. At the same time, the government was claiming that the employees of the Bank of Brazil had no right to unionize, because of the government's partial ownership of the institution.[24]

In the northeastern state of Maranhão, the person who was head of both the Metal Workers Union of the capital city of São Luís and the state Federation of Industrial Workers was removed after the military coup. Perhaps because there was too much fear among other potential leaders, no one took over the *sindicato*. By April 1966 the time limit for holding new elections in the *sindicato* passed and both *sindicato* and federation were facing legal liquidation.[25]

In the state of Paraíba, sixteen of the eighteen *sindicatos* belonging to the Industrial Workers Federation were intervened, as were the bank clerks, port workers, and railroaders' organizations. By the middle of 1966 all of these had been restored to elected leadership.[26]

Finally, in Manaus, the Amazonian port town and capital of the state of Amazonas, all of the port workers' *sindicatos*, the bank clerks,' and the petroleum refinery workers' *sindicato* were among those that were intervened. Two of the city's smaller *sindicatos* suffered total extinction because of fear of the workers about participating in *sindicato* activities.[27]

The mere restoration of elected leadership did not assure *sindicatos* that they would have no further difficulties with the military government. Thus, for example, the Journalists Union of Guanabara suffered further intervention by the Ministry of Labor in October 1965,[28] and in the years that followed, many other *sindicato* organizations had the same experience.

In more general terms, one trade union leader in Campos told me early in 1966 that although the *sindicatos* could by then hold their meetings without previous permission of the police, at the least sign of what the authorities conceived to be "agitation," the police interfered with a *sindicato*'s activities. Furthermore, strikes were not permitted, even though the military regime had ostensibly passed a law authorizing strikes. Finally, the *sindicatos* had little to negotiate with either the government or employers, since the government itself was determining wage levels.[29]

Late in 1965, one observer from the U.S. Department of Labor commented to me that from what he could see of the situation of Brazilian labor at the time, organized labor had been largely deprived of its reason for existence. Government policy left little for the *sindicatos* to do.[30]

THE FATE OF THE RURAL UNIONS

A priori, one might have expected the military regime to have sought to wipe out completely the new branch of organized labor that had appeared during the period just before and particularly during the Goulart regime—the rural workers' movement. However, in that area, too, the dictatorship followed the policy adhered to with regard to urban organized labor, ruthlessly getting rid of the Communists and their allies and seeking to tame the rest of the rural *sindicato* movement.

The Agricultural Workers' Confederation (CONTAG) was one of the confederations that had been established under Communist leadership during the Goulart period that were, at least temporarily, totally liquidated.[31] In the northeastern state of Alagoas, the U.S. scholar Cynthia Hewitt found that virtually all of the rural *sindicatos* had been suppressed.[32]

The state of Pernambuco was the center of the traditional sugar industry, and the region in which the organization of agricultural workers received widest publicity during the Goulart period. There, after the 1964 coup the peasant leagues of Francisco Julião were suppressed by the new military regime. The legal rural *sindicatos* controlled by pro-Moscow Communist Party and other extremist groups were intervened. The Acão Popular member who was president of the Rural Workers Federation of the state resigned and as a result the federation was not intervened. Many of the Communist and other far leftist rural *sindicato* leaders were jailed or went into hiding. The only *sindicatos* that survived in the Pernambuco countryside were those organized by Fathers Paulo Crespo and Melo.

Many of the rural employers of Pernambuco took vengeance on their employees who had had the audacity to organize in defense of their interests. *Sindicato* leaders were dismissed and driven off the land. In spite of the fact that the collective agreement of 1963 was officially reconfirmed in 1964, many employers refused to adhere not only to the conditions established in the collective agreement, but even to the legal requirements such as that concerning the minimum wage.[33]

In the first phase of the "Revolution," the Catholic-led rural *sindicatos* of Pernambuco were divided between the elements led by the two priests, Padres Crespo and Melo. The former advocated a relatively militant confrontation with the employers who were refusing even to conform to the modest requirements of labor law, and even threatened to organize a general rural strike in the state. Padre Melo, on the other hand, sought to work more closely with the regional office of the Ministry of Labor.[34] This split was not healed for several years.

In general terms, the experiences of the rural *sindicatos* of Pernambuco were more or less similar to those of agricultural workers' organization in other parts of the country.

THE JUNE 1964 NATIONAL CONFERENCE OF TRADE UNION LEADERS

In the face of the widespread purge of the leaders who had dominated much of the labor movement during the Goulart period, the self-styled "democratic" trade union officials sought to capitalize on the situation for their own benefit. This was done at the National Conference of Trade Union Leaders, held on June 6–7, 1964.

This meeting was attended principally by representatives of *sindicatos*, federations, and confederations that had not been intervened by the military government. There were also present representatives of the AFL-CIO and the American Institute for Free Labor Development (Serafino Romualdi and William Doherty, respectively) and of the Inter American Regional Organization of Workers (ORIT) and several of the International Trade Secretariats, which some Brazilian *sindicatos* had joined before 1964.

There were wide-ranging discussions at this conference. The resolutions adopted stressed the need for substitution of collective bargaining for decisions of the labor courts, for "democratic elections" in the labor movement, and for enactment of a new Labor Code to take place of the Consolidation of Labor Laws, which code, it was said, would dramatically reduce government control over the labor movement. There was clearly a difference of opinion among the delegates as to whether the trade union tax (*imposto sindical*) should be continued.

The political orientation of the meeting was clear. Resolutions expressed support for the government of Marshal Castelo Branco. There were also considerable discussion and some resolutions stressing the important role that organized labor should assume in Brazil and throughout the hemisphere in the Alliance for Progress.

Apparently no permanent organization emerged from this conference.[35]

ALTERATIONS OF LABOR AND SOCIAL LEGISLATION

The military regime made significant changes in the country's labor and social legislation that had been enacted during the Estado Novo and subsequently. These alterations included not only matters dealing directly with the relations of workers and their employers, but also a fundamental alteration of the social security system.

An early move by the military government was ostensibly made to clear up the anomaly in the country's labor legislation with regard to the right to strike. Under the Estado Novo, that right did not exist. However, the Constitution of 1946 authorized strikes but provided that legislation concerning conditions under which strikes were legal was required. Since no such legislation was ever passed before 1964, the Estado Novo prohibition of legal strikes persisted.

The military regime enacted legislation in 1964 prohibiting political and solidarity strikes but authorized them for economic purposes. However, in fact, the labor courts interpreted this to mean that strikes would only be legal if they were intended to

force employers to obey labor laws or decisions of labor tribunals.[36]

During the first three military presidencies there was a drastic
decline in the number of strikes. For instance, in the case of São
Paulo in comparison with the 180 walkouts in 1961, 154 in 1962,
and 302 in 1963, there were only 25 in 1965, 15 in 1966, 12 in
1970, and none at all in 1971.[37]

During the short-lived administration of General Costa e Silva
there took place two important strikes, which presaged changes
in the nature and functioning of the labor movement that were to
a considerable degree going to transform it in the late 1970s and
the following decade. John Humphrey noted, "In April 1968 a
mass strike developed in Contagem, an industrial suburb on the
fringe of Belo Horizonte and in July of the same year there was a
further mass strike in Osasco, one of São Paulo's peripheral industrial zones."

Humphrey said of these walkouts:

Both strikes displayed two features that broke with the past practice of
the labor movement and foreshadowed its development in the seventies.
Firstly, they took place in the new industrial suburbs and large metal-
mechanical plants that had developed in the fifties and sixties. In Contagem and Osasco large and foreign-owned firms were much in evidence.
Although the new industrial suburbs had been expanding in the fifties,
they had not played a significant role in the working-class mobilizations
of the Populist period. . . . Secondly, the strikes were based on organization at the rank-and-file level, and they opposed the State instead of
relying on it. In Osasco, in particular, the movement was based on the
prior development of workers' committees in the major plants, and the
leadership of the Metalworkers Union was closely linked to them.

Humphrey concluded:

In the Populist period the mass strikes of 1953 and 1957 had been organized and channeled by the official trade union movement, and the
unions had looked to the State for a resolution of their grievances. After
1964 the unions faced a hostile State, and this forced them increasingly
to try and negotiate with the employers and openly oppose the State.[38]

However, while discouraging strikes, the military regime
sought to encourage membership in *sindicatos*. To this end, the
regime decreed that *sindicato* members would

enjoy preference in appointment to jobs in the civil service, ports, or
similar activities, if their source of employment fails; in credit from public
institutions for the purchase of their own home and for financing of vehi-
cles or tools for their trade; in purchasing or renting of certain properties

or apartments under public controls; and in scholarships for secondary education or vocational training for themselves or their children.

In spite of these preferences for *sindicato* members, other aspects of military government policy clearly discouraged *sindicato* membership. Kenneth Erickson noted:

Government promises to revitalize the sindicatos by expanding their social-service activities . . . had no positive effect upon membership rates by the early 1970s, probably because the same government was severely reducing workers' real wages and repressing any union activists who sought to mobilize workers in defense of their earnings.[39]

Among the changes in labor legislation most lamented by workers was the ending of the *estabilidade*, or tenure, the provision that workers employed by the same employer for ten years could not be dismissed except for grave offenses proved to a labor court. Employers had frequently sought to avoid the effects of this law by dismissing workers before they achieved tenure. The labor courts had decreed that dismissals at nine years were an attempt to evade the law, and so many employers had a policy of dismissing employees after seven and a half or eight years.[40] Nevertheless, *estabilidade* was widely regarded by the workers as a "conquest" of which they should not be deprived.

In 1966 President Castelo Branco submitted a bill to Congress to eliminate the tenure law. Congress did not want to pass such an unpopular measure and so allowed it to become law under a provision of the Second Institutional Act whereby bills declared "urgent" by the president automatically were enacted by Congress within certain time limits.

The new law established a Fundo de Garantia do Tempo de Serviço and ended tenure except for those workers already enjoying it (estimated by Kenneth Erickson at about 15 percent of all workers). The employers had to contribute the equivalent of 8 percent of their wage bill to an account for each worker in the Fundo, which the workers could withdraw "only in the event of their dismissal, retirement, or under other specified extraordinary circumstances."[41]

The end of tenure had several effects. For one, it made many workers more hesitant to express grievances against their employers. Erickson argued that the end of *estabilidade* had the general effect of lowering workers' wages.[42]

There was considerable worker dissatisfaction with the Fondo de Garantia do Tempo de Serviço. A major São Paulo labor leader told me in 1975 that the fund in fact only paid workers when a factory totally closed down, and that it took months for workers to collect, and when they did, they received only very small payments.[43]

Finally, the Castelo Branco government completely reorganized the social security system. That system had grown up over time and consisted by the early 1960s of six principal "institutes," covering industrial workers, commercial employees, transport workers, maritime and port workers, bank employees, and federal government employees. There were in addition "a number of smaller social security institutions generally known as *caixas*. Most of these deal with the employees of state and municipal governments. Others covered specials groups such as railroads, aviation and public utility workers."[44]

This diffused social security system had long been criticized, since each of the separate institutes and caixas had its own very substantial overhead. Also, there was considerable variation both in the contributions by workers enrolled and by the government to these institutions, as well as in the benefits received by workers enrolled in them.

In 1966, a new law replaced the existing social security institutions with a single National Social Welfare Institute (INPS). It was placed under the Ministry of Social Welfare instead of the Ministry of Labor, to which the previous social security institutions had been subordinate. Also, instead of control by a tripartite board with representatives of workers, employers, and government, which had characterized the institutes, the new INPS was controlled by a single director appointed by the government.[45]

THE WORKERS AND THE "BRAZILIAN MIRACLE"

There is no doubt that real wages of the workers of Brazil fell more or less dramatically during the twenty-one years of military dictatorship. Although during the administrations of General Médeci and General Geisel the Brazilian economy grew and developed rapidly, with major increases in industry, agriculture, and exports in particular, the country's workers benefited little from this expansion, and it was carried out in large degree at the cost of the nation's working class.

This situation occurred as a result of deliberate government policy, largely in the name of trying to curb inflation, which admittedly was threatening to get completely out of hand by the end of the Goulart administration. The Castelo Branco administration set out by establishing limits of wage increases in labor court dissidios colectivos and collective bargaining agreements. In the first few months, there were a fair number of cases in which employers agreed to pay their workers more than the government's guidelines provided for and labor courts did the same in *dissidios coletivos*.

As a consequence of this situation, new legislation passed in 1965

directed labor court judges to aim at reestablishing the average real wage over the 24 months immediately preceding the expiration of a labor contract, conditioned by the following factors: repercussions of the readjustments on the national economy and society; confirmation that the readjustment satisfies the basic necessities of the wage earner and his family; addition of the real loss of purchasing power between the time the case was begun and the date of the decision; and the need to correct distortions in the wage hierarchy within a given economic section to achieve social equity. Beginning in July 1966, judges were to add the productivity increase for the sector.[46]

Under this system by which wages were periodically to be raised to the average wage of the previous period, but not to the highest point of that period, and wage adjustments were only made every two years, real wages tended regularly to decline. This continued during the first three military administrations.

The government of President Geisel modified this system when it came to office. It provided for annual instead of biannual wage adjustments. It also for the first time had a deliberate policy of having wage increases above rises in the cost of living; as a result, according to Geisel's first minister of labor, wage increases of 43 percent were given in the first year, in contrast to the 19–20 percent that had been granted during the Médeci regime. The Geisel administration also raised the minimum wage by 41 percent, while forbidding that such increases used as a basis for the increase of rents and other prices. Finally, the Geisel administration decreed that employers could pay wage increases of more than the amount set by the government but could not pay less than the established minimum increase; if employers paid more, they could not pass on this additional wage increase to consumers.[47]

In 1975 the labor statistical service in São Paulo, the DIESE, published a survey of real wages in that city in the first years of military rule. It showed that these had dropped from an index number of 100 in 1964–1965 to 90 in 1965–1966, and reached a low point of 71 in 1973–1974, then improved in the following year to 78–79.[48]

In the latter part of the Geisel administration a new factor appeared, the revival of a relatively militant labor movement, first among the autoworkers of the vicinity of São Paulo, and then more widely. Then, in the Figueiredo administration occurred the foreign debt crisis that provoked the beginning of a state of inflation such as the country had never experienced before and that continued through the end of the 1980s.

LABOR POLICIES OF SUCCESSIVE MILITARY ADMINISTRATIONS

The administrations of all five military presidents shared the armed forces' visceral fear of the "subversive" potentialities of the organized labor movement. But there were measurable differences in the way in which they dealt with the trade unions.

We have already noted the extensive purge of labor membership at the beginning of the Castelo Branco government. However, by the end of that administration early in 1967, most *sindicatos* that had been intervened had been restored to an elected leadership, although the freedom of elections was severely limited. We have also traced the changes in labor and social legislation carried out by the first military president.

President Costa e Silva chose as his minister of labor Colonel Jarbas Passarinho, who as the governor of Pará appointed by Castelo Branco had gained a reputation as a "soft" rather than "hard" army officer. He made no important changes in government policy as minister, but opinion of trade union leaders concerning him and the policies he executed for the Costa e Silva regime varied. The president of the São Paulo Commercial Workers Federation considered him a "good" minister, and commented that he was a contradiction, that is, a liberal military man.[49] On the other hand, a teachers' *sindicato* leader from Rio Grande do Sul said that Passarinho was "the only politician able to get credit for doing things without really doing them."[50] The one-time president of the CNTI, and longtime *pelego* Diocleciano Holanda de Cavalcanti commented that Passarinho made extensive promises to improve the lot of the workers and their *sindicatos* on taking office but failed to fulfill them.[51]

A low point in the relations between the government and the labor movement was reached during the administration of General Médeci (1969–1974). The only labor leader who expressed to me any favorable opinion of that regime was Ary Campista, the most durable of the *pelegos*, who continued to hold high office in the National Confederation of Industrial Workers throughout the 1950s and 1960s. He expressed the opinion that although the workers' situation had not improved particularly, they had been given reason to hope because of the rapid expansion of the economy that was than under way and because of the "stability" that the regime had brought about; he said he was sure that the military government would soon provide a greater degree of political democracy.[52]

The fact was that the Médici regime removed from office a substantial number of the labor leaders whom it considered "subversive." Its wage policies were particularly designed to bring about the so-called Brazilian miracle to a considerable degree through driving down the real wages of the workers.

The U.S. labor attaché in this period characterized the Brazilian labor movement as being "emasculated." He said that the "good guys" were paid off by the regime, and those who did not toe to the line were sent back to be common workers. The labor movement, he concluded, was "powerless."[53]

The Médici administration banned all strikes. This ban was quite effective. Thus, although in 1965, under President Castelo Branco, there had been 302 walkouts, in 1970, under President Médeci, there were only 12, and in the following year there was none.[54]

Typical of most labor leaders' view of the Médici regime was that of Helcio Maghenzani, director of the Instituto Cultural do Trabalho, former leader of the Communications Workers Union of São Paulo, and ex-member of the Chamber of Deputies from 1963 to 1967. He commented that Julio Barata, Médici's minister of labor was very bad, strongly hostile to the *sindicatos*, and surrounded by a group of "armchair theorists," with no contact with the labor movement.[55]

The attitude of the government toward organized labor changed substantially during the first part of the administration of General Geisel (1974–1979). He chose as his minister of labor a former Christian Democrat, Arnaldo da Costa Prieto, who ended most of the *sindicato* interventions decreed by the previous regime reversed a ruling by the Médici government that workers in mixed government-private enterprises did not have the right to form *sindicatos*. As we have noted, he and President Geisel were considerably more liberal in their wage policies than their immediate predecessors had been. Also, both the president and the minister of labor were much more accessible to the *sindicato* leaders than had been the case under Médici.[56]

Events during the latter part of the Geisel administration, starting with massive autoworkers' strikes in São Paulo, began to change very extensively not only the relations between the government and organized labor, but the nature of the labor movement itself. This process continued through the last military presidency, that of General Figueiredo, and the restoration of civilian rule in 1985.

THE CONFEDERATIONS AND FEDERATIONS IN
THE MILITARY REGIME

The sectoral confederations continued to exist as the highest level of the legal trade union hierarchy throughout the twenty-one years of military rule. At least one new confederation was established.

The National Confederation of Industrial Workers (CNTI) was intervened by the Ministry of Labor right after Goulart's overthrow, as were twenty-one of its fifty-six federations. However, the other thirty-five federations were soon allowed to have new elections for CNTI officials.[57]

The new leadership of the CNTI was made up largely of men who had not previously held office in the Confederation, including federation leaders from São Paulo and Rio Grande do Sul.[58] Although in 1966 a Catholic group, which had the support of the Communists, challenged the new CNTI leadership, it received the backing of only eight federations, against forty that backed the incumbents.[59]

For the next decade the group that took over the CNTI leadership in 1964 continued to control it. However, they tended periodically to redistribute the leadership posts among themselves.[60]

The most durable of the CNTI leaders was Ary Campista, who had been in the leadership of the confederation since the 1950s. When Rudor Blum, the president of the CNTI, was named to the Supreme Labor Tribunal (DST), Campista insisted that Blum resign as president, to be succeeded by Ary Campista in that position. But when he himself was named to the DST, he insisted that there was no incompatibility between the two posts and continued for some time as president of the CNTI.[61]

At one point during the Médeci administration Ary Campista picked a quarrel with the two international organizations to which the CNTI was affiliated, the International Confederation of Free Trade Unions and ORIT, as well as with the American Institute for Free Labor Development (AIFLD). He withdrew the CNTI from the ICFTU and ORIT and broke off relations with the AIFLD. However, by 1975 he had changed his position once again and was on the board of directors of the AIFLD's training school in São Paulo, the Instituto Cultural do Trabalho.[62]

Although the CNTI was not in the ICFTU for a number of years, some of its federations belonged to the International Trade Secretariats associated with the ICFTU. This was the case with the Metal Workers Federation of São Paulo, and the Chemical Workers Federation of São Paulo.[63]

The National Commercial Workers Confederation (CNTC) had been intervened by the Ministry of Labor shortly before the fall of Goulart. After the coup, those of its federations that had been controlled by the Communists and their allies were also intervened, and the upshot was that the Confederação was returned to safely non-Communist leadership and remained so throughout the military regime. The political orientation of at least key CNTC leaders was revealed in my conversation with the 1975 executive secretary, in which he opined that the system of leaving it to the generals to choose presidents of the republic needed to continue for a considerable period because of the "ignorance" of the citizenry; that Ruy Brito, former head of the Bank Workers Confederation who had been removed by the Médeci regime, had been "foolish" to alienate the government; and that the atomic energy agreement of the military regime with West Germany that had been denounced by the opposition and by virtually all of Brazil's atomic scientists was fine.[64]

The National Bank Workers Confederation was the one that gave the military regime most trouble during the early years of the dictatorship. During the period before 1964, when that confederation had been controlled by the Communists and their allies, the principal opposition within the bank workers had been that of Catholic workers affiliated with the Confederação Brasileira dos Trabalhadores Cristões (CBTC). It was that group that came to power within the confederation after the intervention. It was led by Ruy Brito de Oliveira Pedrosa, known popularly as Ruy Brito.

Ruy Brito carried out a policy of militantly supporting the interests of the bank workers and their local *sindicatos*. He protested against the wage, social security, and other policies of the Médeci administration. When the Ministry of Labor removed the leadership of the bank workers' *sindicato* of Guanabara on the grounds that they were Communists, he also protested vigorously, claiming that most of them belonged to the CBTC.

In 1972 the Médeci administration removed the leadership of the confederation and banned Ruy Brito from running for reelection.[65] When elections were again finally held in the confederation, in 1975 under the Geisel administration, there was only one list of candidates, headed by Wilson Moura. Brito did not run, not wishing to cause "trouble" for the organization, according to Moura,[66] who was described by an official the of the National Commercial Workers Confederation as being "like a good Mineiro [resident of Minas Gerais], very cautious."[67]

Ruy Brito was perhaps an exception among the new Catholic trade union leaders associated with the Confederação Brasileira dos Trabalhadores Cristões in the militancy that he demonstrated. Howard Wiarda noted:

The support of Catholic leaders of the 1964 coup and the subsequent activities of the CBTC in aiding the new military regime provoked a split in the ranks of the Catholic labor movement and ushered in a period of crisis. . . . Some CBTC leaders felt that the coup would be beneficial to them; the anticipated purge of the CGT, they reasoned, would leave the field wide open to Catholic leaders. They therefore reported many Communists (and some who were not Communists) to the government; while the *Círculos* themselves, especially in Rio de Janeiro and São Paulo, played a role in nominating government "interventors" whose duty it was to "clean up" labor union leadership. For these activities, the CBTC, though reaping some short-term advantages, lost much of its support among the workers.[68]

During the military regime the Confederação Nacional dos Trabalhadores na Agricultura (CONTAG), which had been founded only a few months before the overthrow of the Goulart regime, became the largest of the national labor confederations. It consisted not only of rural wage workers, but also of sharecroppers and small landholders. By 1975 the confederation claimed 2,000 *sindicatos* and 4 million members.[69] However, on a state level there was only one federation in each state, in contrast to most of the other confederations, which had several different federations in each state.[70] The military government encouraged the spread of rural *sindicatos*, principally as a means of extending social services to agricultural workers.[71]

The CONTAG worked for different objectives, depending on the kind of workers involved. There was no possibility of getting collective agreements with landowners for their wage-earning members, and so CONTAG concentrated on seeking to force employers to pay the legal minimum wage and obey legal provisions on social security, vacations, and other matters. In the case of sharecroppers, the confederation and its subordinate organizations sought to get legal contracts with the landowners and to limit the share of the crop the sharecroppers had to give to the landlords to a legal range of 10–30 percent instead of the 50 percent that was widespread. Similarly for cash renters, the sindicatos of the confederation sought to limit the amount of rent demanded from them and to establish the right of renters to renew their rental contracts. Finally, they sought to use whatever influence they might have to induce official banks to make loans to their small landholder members.

One of the main concerns of CONTAG in the military period was to effect expansion of social security to rural workers. By 1975 they had succeeded in getting legal provisions for retirement pay at one-half of the legal minimum wage, widows' pensions, disability benefits, and workmen's compensation.

The health benefits program of social security had not been generally extended to the rural workers, although there did exist a fund for Social Insurance (FUNRURAL). CONTAG had representatives on national, state, and local boards of FUNRURAL, whose local *sindicatos* reached agreements in many cases to help finance the *sindicatos'* medical, dental, and other programs, on which the CONTAG spent a large part of its time and financial resources.

Consistently, the CONTAG gave formal support to the idea of an agrarian reform, that is, land redistribution. The Costa e Silva administration in 1968 had passed a very limited agrarian reform law, but in spite of CONTAG's frequent lobbying of the government, by 1975 no administration had put that law into execution.[72]

The CONTAG published a periodical, *O Trabalhador Rural*. It also published and tried to distribute labor laws dealing with rural workers enacted by the military regime, as well as positions that CONTAG itself took on various issues. It likewise carried on a number of regional radio programs.[73]

The Confederation of Land Transport Workers had perhaps been the most *pelego*-dominated confederation before the 1964 coup. There was a change in leadership in the period after the "Revolution." The Médeci government made a concession to it, allowing those railroad workers employed by companies owned by the government to choose whether to be regarded as private employees or as government workers who would not be legally entitled to form a *sindicato*. Some 80 percent of the workers involved opted to be regarded as being privately employed.

This confederation joined the International Confederation of Free Trade Unions and the ORIT. It also affiliated with the International Transport Workers Federation (ITF), an international trade secretariat.[74]

The Confederação Nacional dos Trabalhadores nas Comunicações was one of the more recently formed labor confederations. By the early 1970s, it claimed to have 102,000 members, with approximately 78 percent of all the workers in the categories within its jurisdiction belonging to its affiliated *sindicatos*, a claim that seems highly unlikely. It was particularly strong among telephone and telegraph workers but had smaller membership in newspapers, radio, and television.[75] At least one of the federations in this confederation was affiliated with the Postal Telephone and Telegraph International, an ICFTU-allied International Trade Secretariat.[76]

A new confederation established during the military regime was the Confederação Nacional dos Trabalhadores em Estabelecimentos de Educação e Cultura, established in 1966, which included teachers in private schools, as well as artists, sports professionals, horse racing employees, and people employed in science and technology research organizations. It did not include public education employees, who as government workers were not eligible for membership in *sindicatos*. It was established in 1966 and by 1975 claimed to have eighty-nine *sindicatos* in six federations, and between 150,000 and 200,000 members. It had not affiliated with any international labor group.[77]

COLLECTIVE BARGAINING OR LACK OF IT IN THE MILITARY PERIOD

During the first three military administrations—Castelo Branco, Costa e Silva, and Médeci—the negotiation of collective agreements by the *sindicatos* with their employers was exceedingly difficult. Since in the previous periods such agreements had centered principally on wages and related issues, and the military governments took into their own hands the determination of wage levels, with little or no consultation with the *sindicatos*, there was not much left for the *sindicatos* to negotiate.[78]

However, a few *sindicatos* were apparently able to get some fringe benefits through negotiation with their employers. For example, the Commercial Employees Union of Rio de Janeiro reported early in the Geisel administration that it had been able to obtain increased vacations and reduction of working hours from forty-eight to forty-four through negotiations with the city's department stores.[79]

The Costa e Silva administration did enact a proviso that encouraged *sindicatos* to try to deal with grievances in direct negotiations with employers before going to the labor courts.[80] In subsequent discussion with various labor leaders, some of them told me that they had grievance procedures that were able to handle most of the workers' complaints without recourse to the labor courts. However, how general this capacity was is hard to say.

THE AMERICAN INSTITUTE FOR FREE LABOR DEVELOPMENT

A significant role was played in Brazilian organized labor during the military period and subsequent years by the American Institute for Free Labor Development (AIFLD). The AIFLD was run by the American Federation of Labor/Congress of International Organization.

In Brazil, as elsewhere, the AIFLD had two basic programs. The first was that of labor education, carried out by training courses for *sindicato* leaders in the country and in a "graduate school" in the vicinity of Washington, D.C. The second program was that of "social projects," helping Brazilian *sindicatos* to organize and finance such programs as cooperatives, housing projects, and local credit institutions for *sindicato* members.

The AIFLD had begun to operate in Brazil in 1963. For its labor education program it took over a preexisting organization, the Instituto Cultural do Trabalho (ICT). Within Brazil, it operated on two levels. In various cities throughout the country, it conducted relatively short courses for local labor leaders. These were on two levels, rather rudimentary sessions on basic elements of trade unionism under existing conditions, known as Trade Union Orientation Courses, and somewhat more advanced ones. Figures for the period 1969–1975 show that attendance at these courses ranged from about 2,000 to 5,000 people a year.

Students from these courses were then selected by their local *sindicato* and federations and the confederations with which they were affiliated for much more extensive sessions at the ICT headquarters in São Paulo. The São Paulo courses had about twenty-five students each and lasted eight to nine weeks. Four such courses were run each year.

The materials covered in the ICT courses in São Paulo were very wide ranging. They included organization and structure of Brazilian unionism; history of the Brazilian and international labor movements; fundamentals of Brazilian social law; procedures to conduct meetings; individual labor contracts; Communist, Socialist, and capitalist ideologies; public speaking; social security; trade union elections; labor economics; collective bargaining; and the labor court system, among other subjects.

Instructors in these courses included faculty members of the local universities, trade union leaders, and people from appropriate government institutions. The university people were paid nominal amounts.

The costs of housing and administering the program were borne by the AIFLD through the Instituto Cultural do Trabalho. However, by the middle 1970s, the *sindicatos* whose members were at the São Paulo school usually paid their transportation costs. The ICT also paid small stipends to the families of those attending the courses in São Paulo.

A few of the graduates of the ICT headquarters school were sent by the AIFLD to attend the courses it ran in the vicinity of Washington, D.C.

The objectives of the ICT training were, according to its long-term director Helcio Maghenzani (a leader of the São Paulo Communications Workers Union), both long-range and short-range.

On the one hand, they wanted to prepare their students to be in a position to take advantage of the inevitable relaxation of government control over the *sindicatos* and the advent of widespread collective bargaining. They sought particularly to train people who could, when the time came, confront the Communists, who, Maghenzani said, had their own labor education programs. The second objective was to make their students as capable of getting as much as possible for their *sindicato* members under the existing labor-management setup.[81]

By March 1989, some 72,000 people had taken part in regional classes of the ICT, and 4,893 had taken the course in ICT headquarters in São Paulo. Lawrence Doherty, by then the Brazilian director of the AIFLD, was sure that the long-run objective of the Institute's training program in Brazil had been successful. A majority of the leadership of the second largest of the new central labor groups, the CGT, were graduates of the Instituto Cultural do Trabalho, and a considerable number of leaders of the rival labor group, the CUT, had also had ICT training.[82]

In the beginning of AIFLD's operations in Brazil it concentrated much of its "social projects" activity in the Northeast, particularly in connection with the new rural *sindicatos* there. It established three Rural Labor Centers in different parts of the state of Pernambuco, where different *sindicatos* had their headquarters and a wide variety of activities were centered. Educational programs ranging from basic literacy to the elements of trade unionism to some agricultural subjects were established. A full-time nurse was employed in each of the centers, as well as less frequent doctors' services.[83]

The operations of the AIFLD in Brazil aroused considerable opposition from a variety of quarters. Understandably, the Communists and their friends in and out of the labor movement had nothing but antipathy for the AIFLD. However, it also aroused the hostility of some elements of the military regime. Julio Barata, the minister of labor under President Médeci, was openly hostile and on various occasions threatened to close down AIFLD operations, although he never in fact did so. Barata was opposed to the Brazilian labor movement's having any foreign contacts or affiliations.[84]

There were also doubts about the program among some Agency for International Development (AID) and diplomatic people. Both the AID and the U.S. Embassy in Brazil had doubts about the social projects work of the AIFLD, with the result that AID insisted that each individual social project be approved by the AID Washington headquarters, instead of the AIFLD Washington office.

There was also in the middle 1970s criticism from AID and the U.S. Embassy of the Rio de Janeiro central office of AIFLD in

Brazil. Its task was both to coordinate the social projects and educational activities and to serve as a link between the United States labor movement and that of Brazil. Américo Ramos, the longtime country director, had developed a very wide acquaintance with Brazilian labor leaders at all levels. In 1974, the embassy made the decision to have the Rio office closed within two years.[85]

John Crimmins, the U.S. ambassador in the middle 1970s, had considerable reservations about AIFLD's operations in the country. He did not think that the AIFLD's long-range objective of training Brazilian labor leaders for the day when the military regime would relax its control of organized labor and permit both free trade unionism and collective bargaining was very practical, because he did not foresee any such relaxation. In the second place, at a time when AID operations in Brazil were on the way to being eliminated, he found it hard to defend the idea that the AIFLD operation, financed by AID, should continue to operate. Finally, he feared that the operations of AIFLD had the effect of making the U.S. labor movement and the U.S. government appear to be collaborating too closely with an oppressive regime.[86]

In the summer of 1975 I was one-half of a two-person team to study the operation of AIFLD throughout Latin America for the Agency for International Development. Brazil was one of the countries that I was charged with looking at at first hand. Although recognizing all of the arguments of Ambassador Crimmins, I concluded that the usefulness of the AIFLD operations in Brazil, in terms of acquainting relatively large numbers of labor leaders with the nature of free trade unionism and collective bargaining and at the same time helping them to learn how to make the best use of the extremely limited opportunities for leadership provided under the existing labor law and military rule, and perhaps at the same time offering some protection from being treated even more harshly than they were, justified its continuance. That is what we recommended in our report.

NOTES

1. Interviews with Herbert Baker, U.S. Embassy labor attaché, in Rio de Janeiro, August 5, 1965; Jack Liebof, consul and labor reporting officer of U.S. Consulate General of São Paulo, in São Paulo, October 7, 1965; Rudor Blum, secretary of international relations, Confederação Nacional dos Trabalhadores na Indústria, in Rio de Janeiro, August 10, 1965; for a general view of 1964 "revolution," see Mario Víctor, *5 Anos que Abalaram o Brasil*, Editoria Civilização Brasileira, Rio de Janeiro, 1965, pages 515–561, and Nelson Werneck Sodre, *História Militar do Brasil*, Editoria Civilização Brasileira, Rio de Janeiro, 1965, pages 389–

410.

2. Víctor, op. cit., pages 546–548.

3. Interview with Evandro Lins, member of Brazilian Supreme Court, in Brasília, March 17, 1966.

4. Víctor, op. cit., pages 562–563.

5. Ibid., pages 548–550.

6. Moisés Vinhas, *O Partidão: A Luta por um Partido de Massas 1922–1974*, Editoria Hucitec, São Paulo, 1982, page 248.

7. Víctor, op. cit., page 548.

8. Ibid., page 550.

9. Kenneth Paul Erickson, *The Brazilian Corporative State and Working-Class Politics*, University of California Press, Berkeley, 1977, pages 157–158.

10. Interview with Jack Liebof, op. cit., October 7, 1965.

11. Interview with Joaquim dos Santos Andrade, president, Sindicato dos Trabalhadores Metalúrgicos of São Paulo, in New Brunswick, NJ, April 28, 1968.

12. Interview with José Benedicto de Assis, president, Sindicato dos Trabalhadores em Empresas de Radiodifusão do Rio de Janeiro and of Federação Nacional dos Trabalhadores em Empresas de Radio o Televisão, in Rio de Janeiro, October 27, 1965.

13. Interview with Herbert Baker, op. cit., in Rio de Janeiro, December 27, 1965, and interview with Olavo Previatti, President, Federação dos Trabalhadores nas Indústrias do Papel, Papelão e Cortiças do Estado de São Paulo, in Rio de Janeiro, May 27, 1966.

14. *O Globo*, Rio de Janeiro, August 23, 1965.

15. *Correio da Manhã*, Rio de Janeiro, August 22, 1965, page 20

16. *Correio da Manhã*, September 12, 1965, page 9.

17. Interview with Hermes Manlaes, president, Sindicato dos Trabalhadores na Indústria Gráfica of Campos, R.J., in Campos, February 6, 1966.

18. Interview with Delveaux Sisenanda Marques, secretary of Junta Governativa of Federação dos Trabalhadores nas Indústrias de Espírito Santo, in Vitória, February 11, 1966.

19. Interview with Valentin Miranda, delegate of Sindicato Nacional dos Trabalhadores Ferroviarios in Cachoeiro do Itapemirim, Espírito Santo, February 9, 1966.

20. Interview with Heitor Nunes Fraga, adviser to delegation of Confederação Nacional dos Trabalhadores na Indústria of Pôrto Alegre, in Pôrto Alegre, December 10, 1965.

21. Interview with Paschoal F. da Costa, president, Federação dos Trabalhadores na Indústria of Santa Catarina, in Florianópolis, December 6, 1965.

22. Interviews with Marina Martima, secretary of Federação dos Trabalhadores nas Indústrias of Santa Caterina, in Curitiba, December 1, 1965, and Valmyr Rafael dos Santos, president, Sindicato dos Empregados no Comércio of Londrina, in Londrina, November 29, 1965.

23. Interview with Jaime Gouvea da Fonseca, president, Sindicato dos Trabalhadores na Indústria do Açucar do Estado de Pernambuco, in Recife, August 5, 1975.

24. Interview with Josef Hirschley, executive secretary of Sindicato dos

Empregados em Estabelecimentos Bancários de Pernambuco, in Recife, May 4, 1966.

25. Interview with José de Patrocinio Freitas, president, Sindicato dos Operários de Fiação e Tecelagem do São Luís de Maranhão, in São Luís, April 15, 1966.

26. Interview with Pedro Ribeiro, member of Executive Committee of Federação dos Trabalhadores na Indústria de Paraíba, in João Pessoa, April 29, 1966.

27. Interview with José Ferreira Lima, vice president, Federação dos Trabalhadores na Indústria de Amazonas, in Manaus, February 28, 1966.

28. *Correio de Manhã*, October 13, 1965.

29. Interview with Juvenal Guerreiro Torres, president, Sindicato dos Trabalhadores nas Empresas Elétricas of Campos, R.J., in Campos, February 6, 1966.

30. Interview with Tom Powers, official of U.S. Department of Labor, in Rio de Janeiro, December 27, 1965.

31. Interview with Herbert Baker, op. cit., August 5, 1965.

32. Interview with Cynthia Hewitt, Columbia University graduate student, studying Brazilian rural unions, in Rio de Janeiro, September 1, 1965.

33. Cynthia Naegele Hewitt, "An Introduction to the Rural Labor Movement of Pernambuco" (manuscript) pages 35–38; see also "Contrato Coletivo de Trabalho, na Lavoura Canaveira de Pernambuco," in Recife, November 1964.

34. Hewitt manuscript, op. cit., pages 38–44.

35. *Conferencia Nacional de Diregentes Sindicais Pela Defesa da Democracia e Bem-estar do Trabalhador, Rio de Janeiro, GB-6/7 de Junho de 1964*, Rio de Janeiro, n.d. (circa 1964).

36. Erickson, op. cit., pages 158–159.

37. Ibid., page 159.

38. John Humphrey, *Capitalist Control and Workers' Struggle in the Brazilian Auto Industry*, Princeton University Press, Princeton, 1982, page 25.

39. Erickson, op. cit., page 160.

40. Robert J. Alexander, *Labor Relations in Argentina, Brazil and Chile*, McGraw-Hill, New York, 1962, pages 121–122.

41. Erickson, op. cit., page 166.

42. Ibid., pages 166–167.

43. Interview with Abreu Egydio dos Santos, president, Federação dos Trabalhadores nas Indústrias Metalúrgicas, Mecânicas e Materiais Elétricos do Estado de São Paulo, in São Paulo, July 30, 1975.

44. Alexander, op. cit., page 99.

45. Erickson, op. cit., page 159.

46 . Ibid., page 161.

47. Interview with Arnaldo da Costa Prieto, minister of labor, in Brasília, August 7, 1975.

48. Departamento Intersindical de Estatística e Estudos Socio-Econômicos: "10 Anos de Política Semanal," São Paulo, August 26, 1975 (mimeographed).

49. Interview with Antonio Ferreira Magaldi, president of DNTD, in

São Paulo, July 30, 1975.

50. Interview with Raquel Sfair, secretary, Teachers Union of state of Rio Grande do Sul, in New Brunswick, NJ, September 12, 1968.

51. Interview with Diocleciano de Holanda Cavalcanti, ex-president of Confederação Nacional dos Trabalhadores na Indústria, in Rio de Janeiro, June 1, 1968.

52. Interview with Ary Campista, secretary general of Confederação Nacional dos Trabalhadores na Indústria, in Rio de Janeiro, June 11, 1971.

53. Interview with John Omans, U.S. Embassy labor attaché, in Rio de Janeiro, June 11, 1971 and June 8, 1972.

54. Robert Wesson and David V. Fleischer, *Brazil in Transition*, Praeger Publishers, New York, 1983, page 36.

55. Interview with Helcio Maghenzani, secretary general and Director, Instituto Cultural do Trabalho, in São Paulo, July 30, 1975.

56. Interviews with Arnaldo da Costa Prieto, op. cit., August 7, 1975, and Wilson Moura, president of Junta da Intervenção of Confederação Nacional dos Trabalhadores de Crédito, in Brasília, August 7, 1975.

57. Interview with Herbert Baker, op. cit., August 5, 1965.

58. Interview with Rudor Blum, op. cit., August 10, 1965.

59. Interview with Olavo Previatti, op. cit., May 27, 1966.

60. Ibid., May 27, 1966, and interviews with Diocleciano de Holanda Cavalcanti, op. cit., June 1, 1958, and Helcio Maghenzani, op. cit., July 30, 1975.

61. Interview with Helcio Maghenzani, op. cit., July 30, 1975.

62. Ibid., July 30, 1975, and interviews with Ary Campista, op. cit., June 11, 1971, and José Calixto Ramos, vice president, Confederação Nacional dos Trabalhadores na Indústria, in Brasília, August 7, 1975.

63. Interviews with Abreu Egydio dos Santos, op. cit., July 30, 1975; José Calixto Ramos, op. cit., August 7, 1975.

64. Interview with Hilton Silva Araujo, executive secretary, Confederação Nacional dos Trabalhadores nas Empresas de Crédito, in Rio de Janeiro, June 2, 1972.

65. Interview with Ruy Brito de Oliveira Pedrosa, president, Confederação Nacional dos Trabalhadores nas Empresas de Crédito, in Rio de Janeiro, June 2, 1972.

66. Interview with Wilson Moura, op. cit., August 7, 1975.

67. Interview with Hilton Silva Araujo, op. cit., August 7, 1975.

68. Howard J. Wiarda, *The Brazilian Catholic Labor Movement: The Dilemmas of National Development*, Labor Relations and Research Center, University of Massachusetts, Amherst, 1969, page 19.

69. Interview with José Francisco da Silva, president, Confederação Nacional dos Trabalhadores Agrícolas, in Brasília, August 8, 1975.

70. Interview with Américo Ramos, country program director in Brazil of American Institute for Free Labor Development, in Washington, DC, June 30, 1975.

71. Interview with José Francisco da Silva, op. cit., August 9, 1975, and Rui Campos, official of Federação dos Trabalhadores na Agricultura do Estado de Paraná, in New Brunswick, NJ, November 3, 1978.

72. Interview with José Francisco da Silva, op. cit., August 9, 1975.

73. Interview with Antonio Dias, communications adviser, Confedera-

ção Nacional dos Trabalhadores em Transportes Terrestres, in Brasília, August 6, 1975.

74. Interview with João Airton dos Santos, president, Confederação Nacional dos Trabalhadores em Transportes Terrestres, in Brasília, August 6, 1975.

75. Interview with Alceu Portocarrero, president, Confederação Nacional dos Trabalhadores nas Comunicações, in Rio de Janeiro, June 11, 1971.

76. Interview with José Benedicto de Assis, president, Sindicato dos Trabalhadores em Empresas de Radiodifusão do Rio de Janeiro and of Federação Nacional dos Trabalhadores em Empresas de Rádio e Televisão, in Rio de Janeiro, October 27, 1965.

77. Interview with Paulo José da Silva, president, Confederação Nacional dos Trabalhadores em Establecimentos de Educação e Cultura, in Brasília, August 8, 1975.

78. Interview with Hermes Manlaes, op. cit., February 6, 1966.

79. Interview with Luisanto de Mata Rama, president, Sindicato dos Comerciários de Rio de Janeiro, in Rio de Janeiro, August 1, 1975.

80. Interview with Herbert Baker, op. cit., May 31, 1968.

81. Interview with Helcio Maghenzani, op. cit., July 29, 1975.

82. Interview with Lawrence Doherty, director of Brazilian Branch of American Institute for Free Labor Development, in São Paulo, January 30, 1990.

83. Interviews with Arthur López, head of American Institute for Free Labor Development in Pernambuco, in Recife, May 2, 1966, and Harold Jorgenson, agrarian reform expert of American Institute for Free Labor Development, in Recife, May 2, 1966.

84. Interview with James Shea, labor attaché, U.S. Embassy, Brasília, July 28, 1975.

85. Interview with Américo Ramos, op. cit., August 1, 1975.

86. Interview with John Crimmins, U.S. ambassador to Brazil, in Brasilia, August 9, 1975.

6

Organized Labor and the Restoration of Democracy

President José Sarney took office early in 1985, the first civilian president in twenty-one years. Although he was never regarded by the old opponents of the military regime as their real presidential choice, important changes did take place during his administration. The Estado Novo system of labor relations was modified in important ways. Real political freedom existed—one seventy-year-old Communist Party Central Committee member telling me in 1990 that the Sarney regime was the most democratic one, insofar as his party was concerned, that he could remember.[1] A new constitutional assembly met for a year and a half during the Sarney regime.

However, Sarney failed in at least two regards. When he sought to have agrarian reform enacted he met not only opposition in Congress, but also armed resistance from landowners in the countryside. He also failed in his numerous efforts to deal with the country's economic crisis—the foreign debt problem and the massive inflation.

Finally, at the end of 1989, the first popular presidential election in almost thirty years was held. In the runoff phase of this contest, the two candidates were Fernando Color de Melo, an until recently obscure northeastern politician who was the candidate of the Right, and Luiz Inácio da Silva, head of the new Partido dos Trabalhadores, which had arisen as the result of a new kind of labor movement that had appeared in the latter part of the Geisel administration. Color won this contest—but what happened to him is beyond the purview of this volume.

THE RISE OF THE "NEW UNIONISM"

In the late 1970s there appeared, rather suddenly, a "new unionism," also sometimes referred to as "authentic unionism." This reflected in part the modest liberalization of the political system under President Geisel. In view of where the new unionism originated, it also owed much to the growth of heavy industry, particularly of the automobile industry, from the Kubitschek administration onward.

The center of the new unionism was the Metal Workers Union of São Bernardo, in the southern environs of São Paulo. Starting in the early 1970s, that *sindicato* was taken over by a group of leaders who tended to concentrate on establishing connections with the rank and file of the workers in the auto factories and trying to establish direct bargaining relations between the *sindicato* and the management of the automobile plants.

By the late 1970s, the president of the São Bernardo Metal Workers Union was Luiz Inácio da Silva, popularly known by his nickname, Lula. A native of the Northeast, who had moved with his mother and siblings to the São Paulo area as a child, he had taken a course to become a skilled metal lather in the government-employer training program SENAI and subsequently worked in several different metallurgical plants in the industries around São Paulo.

In 1969, Lula first entered the leadership of the São Bernardo Metal Workers Union, as an alternate member of its executive. By 1975 he was elected president; for a year he was overshadowed by his predecessor, who remained the *sindicato's* secretary general. However, by 1976 Lula was in full control of the *sindicato*. In 1978 he was reelected without opposition for a three-year term. He was thus the undisputed leader of the organization when the new unionism emerged in 1978.[2]

The way in which the events of May 1978 developed was not planned by the *sindicato* leadership. However, throughout 1977 the *sindicato* had carried out an intensive propaganda campaign for *reposição*, that is, reestablishment of the real wage level that had been lost in the early 1970s.

In 1978, the São Bernardo Metal Workers Union demanded of the automobile firms a 20 percent wage increase beyond the amount that had been granted by the Regional Labor Court in its annual *dissidio coletivo*, as well as recognition of *sindicato* representatives in each factory. But negotiations stalled.

Then on May 12, the workers in the toolroom of the Saab-Scania plant laid down their implements. They were soon joined by most of the plant's other workers, and within a few days, sit down strikes had also developed in the Ford, Mercedes, and

Chrysler plants in São Bernardo. Although the Volkswagen management sought to resist, when a settlement granting the workers an 11 percent increase was finally reached, the Volkswagen workers were included.

In this conflict, the Geisel government adopted a hands-off attitude. However, the government did not have this attitude in 1979, when a renewal of the conflict in São Bernardo took place when the São Bernardo *sindicato* refused to accept the terms of the *dissidio coletivo* worked out by the Federation of Metal Workers of the state of São Paulo for the annual settlement.

The March 1979 walkout was not a sit-down strike, as in 1978. Pickets were put around the various plants, and mass demonstrations were organized on various occasions. The government then cracked down, intervening the São Bernardo Metal Workers Union and removing its leadership. However, this action did not break the strike. Again, the *sindicato* gained some of what it had sought, and the *sindicato* leaders were restored to office.

The third chapter in the emergence of the new unionism in São Bernardo took place in April 1980. When strikes once again swept the industrial suburbs of São Paulo, particularly São Bernardo, the government of President Figueiredo not only once again removed the officers of the São Bernardo Metal Workers Union, but a couple of days later arrested Lula and several other leaders of the *sindicato*. However, those actions did not break the strike, which was converted into a demand for the release of the *sindicato* leaders, and drew wide support from the general public, and particularly from the Catholic Church in São Paulo. With the support of Cardinal Evaristo Arns, a liturgical service in support of the jailed unionists was held in São Paulo cathedral, and "basic centers" (local catechismal and social action groups) of the church rallied in support of the strikers, with food, money, and other contributions.

After thirty-one days, Lula and the other *sindicato* leaders were released from jail. This time, they were *cassado*, that is, forbidden to hold *sindicato* offices. However, in spite of this, Lula supporters were overwhelmingly returned to office when new elections were finally held in the São Paulo Metal Workers Union.[3]

Although the initiative for launching the new unionism was by the São Bernardo *sindicato*, the phenomenon was by no means limited to that city or even that region of São Paulo. It spread quickly. John Humphrey noted with regard to the 1978 strikes:

In the first four months of the strike movement it is estimated that 280,000 workers in over 250 firms stopped work, and that the number of workers affected directly or indirectly by the wage settlements resulting from these stoppages exceeded one million. . . . From the dynamic industries and the industrial centers the strike movement spread. There were strikes in the schools, hospitals, banks, and other public service sectors as the grievances of more than a decade were unleashed.[4]

In September 1978, the São Bernardo *sindicato* leadership took their case to a national congress of the National Confederation of Industrial Workers. Although they were outvoted there, the São Bernardo *sindicato* and others allied with it issued the "Letter of the Authentic Leaders," which was signed by leaders of the metalworkers' *sindicato* of São Bernardo, Santos, and José Monlevade (Minas Gerais); the Tanker Drivers of Campinas; the Bank Workers of Pôrto Alegre; the Gas and Electricity Union of Rio de Janeiro; "and a number of others." According to Humphrey:

They were united in their opposition to the dominant current in the official union structure and in their support of a broad program which included democratization (and as a series of specific movement toward it—a Constituent Assembly, amnesty for political prisoners, free elections), a more just economic strategy, freedom for unions and workers, and a reform of labor legislation.[5]

The leaders of the "authentic" *sindicato* group began to propagandize their position in the general labor movement. They not only visited many *sindicatos* around the country, but also began to become involved in specific labor conflicts in *sindicatos* other than their own.[6]

As had been the case in 1978, the March 1979 strike in São Bernardo was followed by many walkouts elsewhere in the country. In the five months after the accession to power of President Figueiredo in March 1979 there were reportedly eighty-three "major" strikes. According to Humphrey, in some areas the strike movement took the form of "mass local strikes, with different groups of workers going on strike at the same time." Many of these walkouts "showed a degree of determination and discipline that indicated the presence of stable organization. Such organization was not confined to the workers in the dynamic industries."[7]

The "authentic unionism" thus represented more than a new kind of challenge to the country's employers. It also defied the labor relations structure that had been largely intact since the Estado Novo, and had been particularly heavily enforced during the first years of the military regime. At the same time, it had political overtones that were a challenge to the military government itself.

Roque Aparecido da Silva noted the long-run importance of the strikes of the late 1970s, which constituted a change in the concept of the strike in the understanding of society. The right to strike had never been fully recognized in Brazil and the paralyzation of work was always considered a disorderly act provoked by subversive agitators. Daily acquaintance with the strike, beginning at the end of the decade brought society, public opinion, the means of mass communication, the parties, the government, and even the armed forces to consider it a normal occurrence, which didn't present any danger.[8]

THE GROWTH AND ACTIVITY OF THE RURAL LABOR MOVEMENT

Other major changes affecting organized labor in the late 1970s and continuing through the next decade were the expansion and increasing militancy of the rural labor movement. This occurred in large degree because of earlier policies of the military regime.

As we have seen, with the inception of the military dictatorship in 1964, it moved ruthlessly to attack the organizations of agricultural workers and peasants that had appeared during the Goulart administration. It destroyed the "peasant leagues" whose principal leader had been Francisco Julião, and they never revived. It also drastically purged the legal *sindicatos* of agrarian workers and at first even drove a number of them out of existence.

However, for a variety of reasons,[9] the leaders of the military regime chose not to destroy the legal rural labor movement. Rather, during the two decades of armed forces rule the number of rural *sindicatos* skyrocketed. Whereas at the end of 1963 there were only 266 legally constituted agricultural workers' *sindicatos*, there were 2,144 in 1980. By the 1980s, the Confederação Nacional dos Trabalhadores na Agricultura (CONTAG), the confederation of rural *sindicatos*, was the largest of all the confederations established in conformity with the Consolidação das Leis do Trabalho, the trade union structure originally established during Getúlio Vargas's Estado Novo.[10] In 1985, CONTAG had 9.4 million members in 2,732 *sindicatos*.[11]

Of course, during most of the military regime, the agricultural workers' *sindicatos*, like those of the urban workers, were made insofar as possible to conform to the model established during the Estado Novo. Their principal functions were those of social welfare. They, like their urban counterparts, received the proceeds of the *imposto sindical*, and they spent the greater part of this income in providing medical and dental care, some educational services, and legal help in dealing with the labor court system. They were not expected, or for many years permitted, to engage in collective bargaining with the landlords, their employers.

Substantial economic changes during the military regime also had a major impact on the rural workers. Successive armed forces presidents strongly supported the technological modernization of agriculture. This was particularly noticeable in those areas (São Paulo and the Northeast) where sugar production was located but was characteristic of the country as a whole. This process meant a large degree of substitution of capital (agricultural machinery, etc.,) for large masses of labor, working under a variety of arrangements—sharecropping, renting, permission to use some of the landlord's land in return for their work, and so on. By the end of the military period, a much larger percentage of the rural workers depended on money wages for their subsistence than had two decades earlier. Also a large proportion of them lived in nearby towns, rather than on the plantations where they worked.

These socioeconomic changes were the background for what began to happen with the relaxation of the military regime in the late 1970s. Undoubtedly, the rise of the new unionism in urban areas of the state of São Paulo and elsewhere had its impact in rural sectors all over the country. The *sindicatos* belonging to CONTAG began to demand to be recognized by the landlord-employers for the purpose of collective bargaining. Perhaps the most striking example of this was a general strike called in the sugar producing areas of Pernambuco in 1979 by the state federation of CONTAG. It ended with a general recognition of the CONTAG *sindicatos* in the state and the signing of a collective agreement between the state federation and the principal state organization of sugar-producing landlords. Virtually every year thereafter in the 1980s there was an annual areawide strike in Pernambuco, with the negotiation of a new collective agreement.

The growth of a climate of collective bargaining in rural areas forming in the late 1970s was by no means entirely peaceful. Although owners of large and more highly mechanized landholdings, where the price of labor as a percentage of the cost of production was considerably lower than it had been two decades before, were frequently more able and more willing to negotiate with *sindicatos* over, and often concede, higher wages and other labor costs than they had previously been, this was not universally the case. Smaller, less mechanized, and less prosperous landowners (some of whom by the 1980s were former tenants or sharecroppers) were much more resistant to collective bargaining. If Pernambuco is any indication, there was considerable violence by landlord-employers who were resisting the unionization of their workers, although such violence apparently did not, during the 1980s at least, threaten the rural collective bargaining system as a whole.[12]

Thus, from the late 1970s on, the legal rural workers' *sindicatos* had a twofold set of activities—collective bargaining as well as social welfare work. They became particularly the spokesmen for and representatives of the more or less permanently employed rural wage earners. This resulted in a none-too-subtle but obvious change in CONTAG and its affiliates from what they had been like in the early 1960s to what they became two decades later.

Insofar as their collective bargaining activities were concerned, the CONTAG *sindicatos* were principally concerned with issues of wages, hours, and working conditions. Although CONTAG still had among its stated goals a massive redistribution of land ownership—an agrarian reform—this was no larger its major preoccupation, as it had been in the rural workers' movement of the Goulart period. The last major struggle of CONTAG to try on a national basis to bring about an agrarian reform occurred at the constitutional convention of 1988, where the supporters of agrarian reform were defeated and the convention adopted procedures for redistribution of land that made it considerably more difficult than it had been during the military dictatorship.

As a consequence of this situation, there grew up by the late 1980s a number of other organizations, most notably the Movimento dos Trabalhadores Rurais Sem Terra, made up of landless rural workers who did not have steady (if any) employment on the landholdings whose owners engaged in collective bargaining with the *sindicatos* belonging to CONTAG. By 1990 these groups had become major challengers of CONTAG and its affiliates.

THE PARTIDO DOS TRABALHADORES

A direct result of the emergence of the new unionism was the establishment of a new element in national politics, the Partido dos Trabalhadores (Workers Party or PT). It differed fundamentally from the older Partido Trabalhista Brasileiro, which had been established in 1945 through the agency of the Ministry of Labor and the existing Estado Novo trade union hierarchy. The formation of the PT was a grass roots movement, originating with the new unionism current in organized labor and drawing into its fold a group of intellectuals as well as a fringe of politicians from the old party of opposition to the military regime, the Movimento Democrático Brasileiro (MDB), and various Marxist groups that hoped to profit from the new party.

Rachel Meneguello noted that after 1978 three tendencies within the Brazilian labor movement were more or less clearly definable. The first she calls "the trade union oppositions," which she says "included Catholic militants and the remainders of small groups of the left. Their activity since the end of the 1960s was devoted to establishment of extra-official trade union organizations based on factory committees."[13]

The second group, which called itself "trade union unity" (*unidade sindical*), was the largest element; it

had as its basic line of action avoiding rupture with the *trade union establishment* maintained through a certain alliance with the Partido Comunista Brasileiro. The leaders of this tendency, aligned with the orthodox Marxist left, remained in the old party of the opposition, MDB, when in 1979 it was rechristened the PMDB [Partido do Movimento Democrático Brasileiro]. (emphasis in the original).

The third element was the "new trade unionism." Meneguello noted, "The new trade unionism and a good part of the trade union opposition moved towards establishment of the PT in 1979."

The idea of launching a new working-class party apparently originated with Luiz Inácio da Silva (Lula), who first proposed the idea in a press interview on July 15, 1978.[14] By 1980, banned from further direct participation in trade union administration, Lula threw himself into the work of bringing into existence the new party.

Although many, if not most, of the trade union leaders associated with the new unionism supported the idea of establishing the PT, Lula did not confine the planning of the new party to labor leaders. He also conferred extensively with a group of intellectuals and some of the more progressive leaders of the opposition party, the MDB.

There had grown up during the dictatorship a number of economic and social research organizations, particularly in São Paulo, which served as a refuge for professors and others who had been expelled from the universities during the military regime. Among those drawn from such organizations who participated in planning the establishment of the new party were Francisco Weffort, José Álvaro Moisés, Roque Aparecido da Silva, Fábio Munhoz, Francisco de Oliveira, and Paul Singer.[15]

The first provisional meeting of the Partido dos Trabalhadores took place in São Paulo in August 1979. At that point, only two MDB deputies had agreed to join the new party, Edison Khair of Rio de Janeiro and Antonio Carlos de Oliveira of Mato Grosso do Sur. However, after a split in the PMDB in São Paulo in 1980, the deputies Geraldo Siqueira, who had particular strength among the students; Irma Passoni, who was closely associated with the new Catholic Church organizations; and Sérgio Santos, Marco Aurélio Ribeiro, João Batista Breda, Eduardo Suplicy, and Airton

Soares also joined the Partido dos Trabalhadores. The last three of these became the leaders of the party's bloc in the Chamber of Deputies.[16]

Two leading political figures who were active in the original planning for the new party did not become members of it. These were the sociologist and PMDB leader in São Paulo, Fernando Henrique Cardoso, and Almino Afonso, who before 1964 had been a leader of the left-wing of the Christian Democratic Party and had only recently returned from exile.[17]

As the Partido dos Trabalhadores emerged after 1979, there were four principal sources from which it drew support and leadership. The first consisted of the "new" or "authentic" trade unionists. Their principal spokesman, Lula, continued to be the party's principal public spokesman, and *sindicatos* associated with this segment of organized labor established the first of the new central labor organizations that appeared in the 1980s, the Central Única dos Trabalhadores, which had a close association with the PT.

Another key element in the Partido dos Trabalhadores was the Catholic Church. Starting in the late 1960s, the church began to organize a great variety of "mass" organizations, including "basic religious communities," peasant groups, and rank and file organizations in the slums (*favelas*), to pressure the government to get pieces of land for the peasants, sewer systems for a neighborhood, and a housing project for a *favela*. They also taught grass roots democracy and mass participation in public affairs by common citizens.[18]

One Dominican brother, Frei Betto, who was particularly close to Lula, claimed that although church organs had estimated in 1975 there were 40,000 of these "mass communities," there were less than a decade later about 80,000. They encompassed about two million members.[19]

These Catholic basic communities had been of key importance in rallying public support for the strikes of 1978, 1979, and 1980. They also became a major recruiting ground for both leadership and rank and file membership in the Partido dos Trabalhadores.

Another element that entered into the formation of the PT were people who had been student leaders in the early years of the military regime, some of whom had attempted unsuccessfully to organize guerrilla groups during the Medici administration. Many of these people were jailed, were exiled, or went into the underground. However, by the early 1980s an important segment of them joined in forming and giving leadership to the PT.

The fourth element in the new party consisted of older intellectuals who had been active in the earlier democratic period and were from various political backgrounds. Many of these people were attracted by Lula and the labor movement from which he came.[20]

The preexisting Marxist-Leninist groups took different attitudes toward the Partido dos Trabalhadores. The three principal Stalinist parties, the pro-Soviet Partido Comunista Brasileiro, the originally pro-Chinese Partido Comunista do Brasil, and the ex-guerrilla group MR-8 were strongly opposed to the PT. They led elements in the labor movement that were opposed to the new unionism. The three principal Trotskyist groups, on the other hand, tried to a greater or lesser degree to penetrate and work within the new party.[21]

The PT remained a minority party throughout the 1980s. By the beginning of 1990, it had sixteen members of the Chamber of Deputies, but no senators. It had forty state legislators; thirty-six mayors, particularly in São Paulo (including the state capital); and 1,000 municipal councilors throughout the republic.[22]

In the first popular election of the president in almost thirty years, the Partido dos Trabalhadores ran Luiz Inácio da Silva (Lula) as its nominee. He finished second in the first round of the presidential election, when he was supported only by the PT, the Partido Comunista do Brasil, and the small Partido Socialista Brasileiro. In the runoff election, most of the other parties that had had nominees in the first round threw their support to Lula. However, he again came in second to the right-wing candidate, Fernando Collor de Melo.

In preparation for the 1989 campaign, the PT organized a seminar to prepare a rounded political, social, and economic program for the party. It was attended by over two hundred people, including many of the country's leading economists, sociologists, and other intellectuals.[23]

A number of factors undoubtedly contributed to the defeat of Lula in 1989. One was the continuing strength in the northeastern states, where Collor did particularly well, of the traditional political machines of the so-called colonels, who, understandably, were strongly opposed to the PT nominee. Another factor undoubtedly was the fact that the PT administrations that had governed many of the more important cities in the year just previous to the election had not been particularly successful, hampered as they were by straitened financial circumstances and the still on-going strong influence of the federal government in the states and municipalities, particularly in financial matters.

PT officials claimed that the media tended to be biased against Lula. They likewise admitted that in a face-to-face television debate with Collor, Lula had not been at his best.[24]

Finally, an important element working against the Partido dos Trabalhadores in the 1989 election was undoubtedly the split that had developed during the 1980s in the labor movement, between the new or authentic unionists and their bureaucratic and ideological adversaries.

THE CENTRAL ÚNICA DOS TRABALHADORES

One of the most important results of the emergence of the new unionism was the establishment of central labor organizations. As we have noted, there had been several attempts to set up such groups in the past. The anarchist-controlled Confederação Operaria Brasileira had had a sporadic existence from 1906 until the Revolution of 1930; the Communists had had the Confederação Geral do Trabalho Brasileiro in the late 1920s and after the end of the Estado Novo had joined a short-lived effort to revive it.

In the 1980s an effort was first made to set up a single national central labor group. However, political differences, and disagreements over the relationship of the labor movement with lingering Estado Novo labor-management structure, soon led to the splintering of this effort. By 1990 there were, in fact, at least five different central labor groups.

The initiative for formation of a new central labor organization arose from Luiz Inácio da Silva, who issued an invitation to *sindicatos* throughout the country to meet with that object in view. Although the minister of labor "forbade" the meeting, it took place anyway in Praia Grande, São Paulo, in August 1981, with some 5,000 delegates representing 900 organizations reported as being present. That meeting issued a call for a further meeting the following year to establish a Central Única dos Trabalhadores (CUT). However, the intense concentration on the political campaign of 1982, the first free election of members of Congress and state governors and legislators since the 1964 coup, made it advisable to postpone the second meeting for another year.[25]

Sindicatos of varied political tendencies participated in the 1981 meeting, which was called the Conferencia Nacional das Classes Trabalhadores (CONCLAT). These included not only those influenced by the new unionism, but many of the more conservative-led organizations as well as those controlled by various political factions.

However, differences soon arose within the Comissão Nacional Pro-CUT, which had been set up by the 1981 CONCLAT meeting, between the new or authentic unionists led by Lula and aligned with the new Partido dos Trabalhadores and the other two groups. Those not aligned with the PT demanded that the congress to establish the CUT be further postponed. Although it was put off from June to August 1983, the trade unionists following the lead of Lula held the founding congress of the Central Única dos Trabalhadores in São Bernardo in the latter month, with 5,059 delegates, representing some 900 *sindicato* organizations throughout the country. More conservative and pro-Communist *sindicato* leaders met in November 1983 to form the first central labor group competing with the CUT.[26]

A year after its foundation, the CUT held what it called its First National Congress in São Bernardo. There were reported to be 937 *sindicatos* and other groups represented by 5,222 delegates. Of these, 1,600 delegates represented agricultural workers' *sindicatos*, 1,000 *sindicatos* in basic industry. They were from all of the country's twenty-four states and the Federal District and claimed to represent three million workers. It was noted that the largest representation was from São Paulo, Rio de Janeiro, and Rio Grande do Sul.

Much of the attention of this congress was taken up with the presidential election scheduled for the end of the year, assessing the failure to achieve direct election of the president and deciding to have nothing to do with the major parties' plans to try to defeat the military regime in the indirect election. There were also many resolutions dealing with matters of international labor solidarity.[27]

A third congress of the CUT met in September 1988. There were 6,244 delegates representing 1,154 "trade union entities."[28] This congress modified the statutes of the organization, providing that only *sindicatos* or "oppositions" within *sindicatos* not affiliated with the CUT could belong.

The statutes of the CUT, as modified in the 1988 congress, constituted a very interesting document. It particularly stressed the independence of the labor movement. Its Article 3 proclaimed that the CUT "defends the organization of the workers with total independence vis-à-vis the State and autonomy with relation to the political parties and must decide freely the forms of organization and material support." The succeeding article pledged the organization "to struggle to overcome the existing corporative trade union structure, developing all the efforts for the establishment of its trade union organization based on trade union freedom and autonomy."

Among the evidence of its rejection of the Estado Novo trade union structure was the fact that the CUT had no room in its pattern of organization for most of the confederations organized in conformity with the structure. In their place, it provided for what it called "vertical organizations," the key element of which consisted of "departments" for branches of economic activity.

Article 10 of the CUT statutes provided:

The attributions of the national, interstate and/or state departments are: I. to undertake to implement the policy and plan of struggle of the Central; II. to define a specific plan of struggle for their branch of activity; III. to agree on specific national, interstate or state agreements for their branch of activity, on the basis of the agreements of the Central; IV. to motivate, develop, encourage and coordinate trade union oppositions and other organizational forms of the CUT, in the trade union basis of their branch, where the *sindicato* is not affiliated with the Central; V. to develop tactics for policy action to confront the official trade union structure, in accordance with the reality of each region and each branch of activity, to fortify the CUT and dismantle the official corporative structure.[29]

In spite of its general repudiation of the old confederations and establishment of CUT organizations to take their place, the CUT did accept the affiliation of one of the existing confederations. This was the Confederação Nacional dos Trabalhadores da Educação. It was the last of the confederations provided for in the Estado Novo framework to be established, founded in 1966 and legally recognized in the following year. At that time, it covered only teachers in private schools, since those in government schools were not permitted to have legally recognized *sindicatos*. By 1975, it had eighty-nine *sindicatos*.[30]

In 1988 a new leadership took over the confederation. It decided to expand its jurisdiction, to include not only teachers but also supervisors and other workers in the educational field. It also decided to affiliate with the CUT.

By 1990, the Confederação Nacional dos Trabalhadores da Educação included not only workers in private schools, but also those in public institutions, since the new constitution permitted government employees to unionize. The confederation had affiliated *sindicatos* in fifteen states. The *sindicato* in Rio de Janeiro had the highest percentage of education workers as members, 16,000 out of 24,000. The educational *sindicatos* were very active in collective bargaining, particularly over wages and salaries.[31]

The CUT statutes sought to make the organization and its affiliates as democratic as possible. To this end, they provided that proportional representation prevail in elections within the organization, except that where there were just two lists of candidates, the minority one had to get at least 30 percent of the vote to gain representation, and if there were three or more lists, only those that got at least 10 percent of the vote would elect anyone.

The statutes provided for financing of the CUT by its affiliated *sindicatos*. Each affiliate was to contribute 5 percent of "its gross annual receipts" to the Central Única dos Trabalhadores. It was the duty of the state organizations of the CUT to collect this money from the *sindicatos* in their respective states, and the contribution of each *sindicato* would be allocated on the basis of 40 percent staying with the state CUT organizations, 25 percent going to the national CUT, 25 percent to the regional CUT organization, and 10 percent to the department of the CUT with which the individual *sindicato* was affiliated.

The statutes defined the CUT as

a trade union mass organization of the highest level, of a class character, autonomous and democratic, whose bases are the commitment to the defense of the immediate and historic interests of the working class, the struggle for better conditions of life and work, and dedication to the process of transformation of Brazilian society in the direction of democracy and socialism.[32]

The statutes of the CUT did not commit the organization to having any overt association with the Partido dos Trabalhadores; however, most CUT leaders belonged to the PT. The head of the CUT in the Federal District (Brasília) explained early in 1990 that the Partido Democrático Trabalhista of Leonel Brizola had some influence in the CUT, the Partido Comunista Brasileiro controlled a few of its affiliated *sindicatos*, the pro-Albanian Partido Comunista do Brasil controlled the bank workers' *sindicato* of Rio de Janeiro, a CUT affiliate, and at least four groups of Trotskyists also had "some influence" in the CUT. However, he added that "most CUT leaders" wanted the organization to be independent of any political party.[33]

A leader of the São Paulo state organization of the CUT confirmed that most of the CUT leaders belonged to the PT, as did she, but insisted that the CUT members were "first of all, unionists." She said that within the CUT there were several political tendencies, of which the one headed by Lula and known as *articulação* (unity faction), was in the majority. However, both Communist parties, as well as the Trotskyists, and progressive Catholic elements also had more or less influence in the organization.[34]

The CUT had a program for leadership training, working with the Instituto Cajamar for this purpose. Although the American Institute for Free Labor Development and the Instituto Cultural do Trabalho sought to get the CUT to use their long-established facilities for labor training, the CUT rejected these overtures.[35]

The CUT was very active in the 1989 presidential election campaign. The founder, Luiz Inácio da Silva, was one of the principal candidates, coming in second in the first round of the election and finally losing to Fernando Collor de Melo in the second.

It was clear that the CUT and its affiliated *sindicatos* supported the candidacy of Lula. One of its *sindicatos*, that of the teachers of the Federal District, published a special issue of its periodical, *Quadro Negro*, before the first round of the election analyzing in detail each of the ten candidates. For those who had been members of the Constituent Assembly, it had charts showing how they had voted on issues crucial to labor. It was clear that they preferred Lula, but they also spoke in more or less friendly terms of Leonel Brizola, and of Roberto Freire, the candidate of the PCB, who had "voted correctly" on all issues in the assembly.[36]

In the second round, the National Directorate of the CUT officially endorsed Lula. In its statement to that effect, it said, "The national directorate of CUT will develop, together with the directorates of the regional State CUTs and the *sindicatos*, an ample mobilization indicating to the workers and the people in general to vote for Lula's candidacy."[37]

By 1990 the Central Única dos Trabalhadores was undoubtedly the largest and most militant of Brazil's central labor organizations.

THE CUT, THE EMPLOYERS, AND COLLECTIVE BARGAINING

The new unionism that culminated in the formation of the CUT had as one of its basic premises the freeing of the labor movement and of labor relations in general from control of the state. In striving for this, the new unionists had the surprising concurrence of a substantial part of the employing class.

Roque Aparecido da Silva sketched this community of interest between the CUT unionists and many employers:

The leaders of the *new unionism* came together on the basis of strongly criticizing the intervention of the State in trade union life assured by the old legislation, raising as one of its banners free negotiation between the forces of capital and of labor without interference of agents of the state. In this they had the concordance of the employer representatives of the most dynamic sector of the economy, who also sought to overcome the intervention of he State, exacerbated during the military government. . . . The opposition to the authoritarianism of the military governments motivated the employers and workers to autonomously seek an understanding in the field of labor relations. This process was the mutual recognition between actors with opposing interests that for the survival of both they needed to reach certain level of understanding in their daily relations so that the productive system and the society could continue functioning.[38]

Difficulties in finding such a basis of agreement were present on both sides. The employers were not accustomed to collective bargaining, and many at first resisted it. But, also, to make collective bargaining feasible, the *sindicatos* had to be different from those that were traditional in Brazil. As Roque Aparecido da Silva wrote:

To successfully undertake negotiation, the *sindicato* had to be representative and have a great capacity for mobilization and pressure. Particularly in our milieu in which the employer was not accustomed to that type of relationship, and as a result had great difficulty in negotiations. An indication of this was that the majority of the strikes had as their first objective forcing the employer to begin negotiations.

However, in spite of these difficulties, both sides became accustomed to collective bargaining, which spread beyond discussions merely of wages "to include the most diverse issues relative to relations between capital and labor." This not only made obsolete the old trade union structure and functioning, but also "emphasized the primary need for reorganization of the working class."[39]

THE CGT AND ITS SPLINTERS

The CUT did not by any means have within its ranks all of organized labor. Many of the *sindicatos* controlled by more conservative or moderate *sindicato* leaders or opposed to the apparent domination of the CUT by the Partido dos Trabalhadores did not take part in the foundation of the CUT. Neither did most *sindicatos* controlled by the three Communist Parties—Partido Comunista Brasileiro, Partido Comunista do Brasil, and MR-8.

Almost three months after the establishment of the CUT there met, in November 1983, what was called the First National Congress of the Working Class, in Praia Grande in São Paulo, which founded the Coordenação Nacional da Classe Trabalhadora (National Coordination of the Working Class), or CONCLAT. There were reportedly in this congress 4,234 delegates claiming to represent 1,243 trade union groups.

During the next two and a half years, CONCLAT had a wide variety of different activities. The magazine *CGT* summarized these:

CONCLAT had an effective participation in the campaign for direct elections . . . and later had meetings with the then candidate of the opposition to the presidency of the Republic, Tancredo Neves, and later, with President José Sarney. . . . It participated in various wage campaigns throughout the country, organized such events as the "National Day of Support for Agrarian Reform" . . . and organized the First National

Congress of the Working Woman in January 1986 that had the participation of about 4 thousand delegates of the countryside and city.

During those years, too, "CONCLAT expanded, organizing in an ample and united way in practically all of the States of the Country." It had two plenary sessions of its Executive.[40]

Finally, in March 1986 the CONCLAT held what it called the Second National Congress of the Working Class, where it was converted into the Central Geral dos Trabalhadores (CGT). It was claimed that the 5,546 delegates at that congress represented 1,341 "trade union entities."[41]

The 1986 congress was pictured as "reconstructing the CGT," that is, reestablishing the provisional central labor group originally established in the Goulart period that had been dissolved in 1964 by the military regime.[42]

Like the CUT, the CGT proclaimed its opposition to the Estado Novo framework, calling for an end "to the restrictions of Chapter V of the CLT [Consolidação das Leis do Trabalho] and of its fascist structure imposed by the dictator Getúlio Vargas."[43] However, unlike the CUT, the CGT did not call for the end of the trade union tax (by then labeled the *contribuição sindical*), but merely "the return of the part of the *contribuição sindical* today unjustly retained by the Ministry of Labor, to the trade union bodies."[44]

In one other way the CGT was less clearly in favor of the abolition of the Estado Novo structure than was its rival. Although its statutes called for the "creation of the National Departments of the CGT, of provisional character," these were clearly not the sectoral groupings provided for in the CUT. Four are named in the statutes: departments of the Working Woman, the Retired Workers, Workers in State Enterprises, and Public Servants.[45] Furthermore, five of the old confederations were represented at the CGT congress, and there was provision in the statutes for the confederations to be represented in the National Council of the organization.[46]

The CGT was clearly formed and headed in its first years by a coalition of disparate elements. The first president of the organization was Joaquim dos Santos Andrade, head of the Metal Workers Union of the city of São Paulo. He had held that post since 1969, being regularly reelected every three years. On his reelection in 1975, he had said that he "knew perfectly well that the *sindicato* should not have a social welfare character, that that is not the attribute of a *sindicato*."[47] He had been national coordinator of the CONCLAT and had issued the call for the meeting that established the CUT.[48]

In spite of a long struggle against the Communists in his own *sindicato*, Joaquim dos Santos Andrade was classified by Lawrence Doherty, the local representative of the American Institute for Free Labor Development, as being one of the CGT leaders who, although not Communists, were willing to work with them within the CGT. Others in this category were José Francisco da Silva, president of the rural workers' organization of the CONTAG, and vice president of the CGT, and Mario Monte, head of the São Paulo printers' *sindicato* and member of the National Fiscal Council of the CGT.

Among the CGT leaders who were associated with one or another of the Communist groups, were Sérgio Barroso, first secretary of the CGT; Francisco Fraga de Souza, member of the National CGT Executive; Roberto Guerra, second secretary of the CGT; and Arnaldo Gonçalves, president of the Metal Workers Union of Santos and second treasurer of the CGT as well as Brazilian representative of the World Federation of Trade Unions. The rest of the CGT National Executive were classified by Doherty as "anti-Communist democrats."[49]

In 1989, the internal conflicts within the CGT led to a splintering of the organization. The first group to leave consisted of *sindicatos* under the influence of the pro-Albanian Partido Comunista do Brasil, which had established their own organization, the Corrente Sindical Clasista (CSC), which had held its first congress in February 1980.[50] In a meeting of its National Council, the CSC agreed to seek affiliation with the CUT.[51]

More serious splits took place as a result of the Second Congress of the CGT in April 1989. There was a showdown between those who wanted to remove representatives of the other two Communist parties, the PCB and MR-8, from the leadership of the organization and the supporters of those parties and other CGT leaders who were collaborating with them.

Those opposed to continuing Communist influence in the CGT leadership presented a list of candidates for the new National Executive of the organization that did not have a single member of any of the Communist parties. It was headed by Antonio Rogerio Magri, head of the electrical workers of São Paulo. They offered the outgoing president, Joaquim dos Santos Andrade, the position of secretary general, but he refused it. He finally walked out of the congress, followed by some of the delegates from São Paulo, Rio Grande do Sul, Amazonas, Paraná, and Rio de Janeiro. After these people left, the Magri ticket was elected by the majority of the delegates who remained.[52]

There was considerable violence during this CGT Second Congress, which Magri attributed to members of MR-8. Magri's opponents claimed that he had paid the way to the congress of many of the delegates who supported him, which he admitted. They also accused him of receiving money for this from "an American *sindicato*," which he denied.[53]

The delegates to the CGT Second Congress voted to change the name of the organization from Central Geral dos Trabalhadores to Confederação Geral dos Trabalhadores. The retiring president, Joaquim dos Santos Andrade, and his followers, some 300 of the 3,500 delegates, soon called their own version of the CGT congress, attended by some 400 delegates. They announced the reestablishment of the Central Geral dos Trabalhadores, and there ensued a legal battle over the use of the initials CGT. A further split occurred when Antonio Pereira Magaldi, vice president of the National Confederation of Commercial Workers, took the lead in establishing the União Sindical Independente, the most conservative and smallest of the central labor bodies.[54]

The Confederação Geral dos Trabalhadores applied for admission to the International Confederation of Free Trade Unions and its American regional organization, the ORIT. The confederations that had belonged to the ICFTU and ORIT had by then withdrawn from the international organizations.[55]

The Confederação Geral dos Trabalhadores mounted its own program for leadership training. In organizing this, it worked with the Instituto Cultural do Trabalho, the organization that was still associated with the American Institute for Free Labor Development.[56]

The position of the Confederação Geral dos Trabalhadores in the presidential election of 1989 was very different from that of the CUT. After the purge of the Communists from leadership, the CGT directing bodies included members of the Partido de Social Democracia Brasileiro, the Partido Democrático Trabalhista, and the PMDB, and even a few from the Partido dos Trabalhadores.[57] Thus, there was a certain difficulty in working out a common position for the election.

The first National Plenum of the reorganized CGT took place in September 1989. Among its other decisions was that to submit to each of the presidential candidates an open letter, asking his position on a number of questions including suspensions of payments on the foreign debt, agrarian reform, and general participation of *sindicato* representatives in negotiations on issues of foreign policy that directly affected workers.[58]

The CGT remained neutral during the first round of the presidential election. However, in the second round, the CGT leadership endorsed Fernando Collor de Melo, the opponent of Luiz Inácio da Silva, the founder of the CUT. The CGT of the state of Pernambuco, however, endorsed Lula and suffered no negative consequences from the national CGT for taking that position.[59]

Those who walked out of the Second Congress of the CGT subsequently held their own congress, as we have noted, under the name of the Central Geral dos Trabalhadores. However, Joaquim dos Santos Andrade was unhappy with that organization and "dedicated himself to agitating, together with discontented sectors of the two CGTs and some unionists, the formation of a new central body, which was founded in 1991, with the name Fuerza Sindical (FS).[60]

In the early 1990s, the FS was the second most important central labor organization in Brazil, "because of its capacity to intervene politically." However, Antonio Carlos Granado noted, "the extent of its influence in the trade union movement is low." It had about one-third of the Brazilian organized metal workers in its ranks; the other two-thirds was in the CUT. It also had "a good representation of *sindicatos* in the food industry, textiles and commerce."[61]

Meanwhile, the Central General de Trabalhadores was reduced to "the trade union center with the least important of the four existing ones." By the early 1980s it had only twenty *sindicatos* affiliated with it, and as Antonio Carlos Granado wrote, "It is a transmission belt for the MR-8." [62]

THE REMNANTS OF THE ESTADO NOVO

During the 1980s, much of the Estado Novo framework of labor-management relations that had stood for almost half a century was swept aside. However, at least two of its components remained to some degree intact by 1990. These were the confederations established under the Estado Novo system and the old *imposto sindical*, rechristened the *contribuição sindical* (the deduction from every worker of one day's pay a year to finance various parts of the *sindicato* structure).

Much of the transformation of the status of the Brazilian labor movement was confirmed in the constitutional assembly that met in 1987 and 1988. A report of the United States Consulate in São Paulo commented on this process:

The rights text, as approved by the Assembly in final version (August 1988) reconfirmed victories labor had won at earlier stages in the drafting process. These included a workweek reduction from 48 to 44 hours, double pay (up from 25 percent) for overtime, vacation pay one-third more than normal, 120 days of paid pregnancy leave (in lieu of 90), and paternity leave (an innovation). Over strong objections from business, the Assembly approved a "six-hour day for work taking place in uninterrupted shifts, except (where changed) by collective bargaining." The Assembly also approved no less controversial language regarding unions' unrestricted right to strike, at the same time extending (in limited form) that right to government workers.[63]

One of the most important victories of the labor movement in the constitutional assembly was the freeing of *sindicatos* from the requirement of approval of the Ministry of Labor of their functioning. The new constitution provided for freedom of organization and specified only that *sindicatos* should register with "an appropriate government organization." However, it did not specify what that organization was. As a consequence, new sindicatos, which were being formed in considerable numbers in 1989 and 1990, were in many cases just recording their existence with equivalents of notaries public (*cartorios*). The Ministry of Labor had stopped keeping track of statistics of new *sindicatos*.[64]

The report of the U.S. Consulate in São Paulo recorded the effectiveness of the lobby of organized labor at the constitutional assembly:

Labor's accumulating legislative successes were not the product of reason alone. With strategy developed and coordinated out of labor's Brasília lobby headquarters (DIAP), the unions mounted a nationwide information network that kept worker-constituents informed as to how their elected representatives were doing. Assemblymen returning to their home constituencies encountered trade unionist praise when they voted favorably on worker rights issues and criticism when they opposed. Those running in national municipal elections (held November 15, 1988) were particularly aware of the voting "scorecards" DIAP compiled and published ("Who Was Who in the Constituent Assembly"). The wage bill passed by Congress in December recognized the role of the DIAP and DIEESE, assuring both organizations an advisory role in the "Permanent Commission on Minimum Wage" created to implement the legislation's readjustment requirements.[65]

However, in spite of the changes in the Estado Novo system during the 1980s, the new constitution did not do away with the Estado Novo federations and confederations. We have noted the newest of these, the Educational Workers Confederation, affiliated with the Central Única dos Trabalhadores. In fact, the four vice presidents of the CGT after 1989 were the heads of the confederations of industrial workers, land transport workers, credit employees, and workers in communications and publicity.[66] In spite of this, many of the rank-and-file *sindicatos* ostensibly belonging to those confederations were in fact members of the CUT.[67]

The policy of the CGT was to try to absorb the old confederations. After the reorganization of the CGT in its Second Congress in 1989, it set about establishing separate sections covering workers in different parts of the economy, along the lines that the CUT had earlier adopted. The CGT policy was to "invite" the old confederations to become part of these new CGT sections. However, if the old confederations refused to do so, CGT leaders felt, they would be left with virtually no membership.[68]

One new confederation that was not provided for in the Consolidação das Leis do Trabalho of the Estado Novo was established in the 1980s, the Metal Workers Confederation. Leadership in setting up this group was assumed by Jorge Noman Neto, president of the Federation of Metal Workers of Minas Gerais. He hoped that with the establishment of this confederation it might be possible to carry out collective bargaining in the metallurgical sector on a national basis.[69]

The organization of the Metal Workers Confederation was the result of resolution of the Eleventh National Congress of Metal Workers late in 1983.[70] For some time, the metal workers had maintained a Professional Department of Metal Workers, with its headquarters in Belo Horizonte. It had published an official periodical, as well as a series of pamphlets on metal workers' problems, such as *Risks of Professional Diseases of the Metallurgical Sector*, all of them edited by Jorge Noman Neto.[71]

Opinion in the labor movement remained divided over the continuation of the *contribuição sindical*. Although the National Executive of the CUT, in its introduction to the CUT statutes, proclaimed that "the trade union legislation imposed fifty years ago is absolutely inoperative," there was no specific repudiation of the *contribuição sindical*. However, the only confederation affiliated with the CUT, the Education Workers, refused to accept the part of the *contribuição sindical* to which it was still entitled under the law.[72]

The most spectacular attack on the *contribuição sindical* was made by Antonio Rogerio Magri, at the time president of the Electrical Workers Union of São Paulo and later head of the CGT, who went to court in March 1989 to demand that the employers in his industry not deduct the *contribuição sindical* from the electrical workers' wages.[73] Although his demand was apparently upheld, the CGT Congress in April refused to support Magri's position, urging that the *contribuição sindical* be continued, advocating merely that the 20 percent of the *contribuição sindical* that went to the government be turned over to the *sindicatos*.[74]

The new constitution did maintain the trade union tax, because of the strong support not only of the employers, who sought insofar as possible to maintain the *sindicatos* as social welfare organizations rather than "class struggle" groups, but of the Confederação Geral dos Trabalhadores. The 1989 constitution also retained the Estado Novo provision that legal *sindicatos* be organized on the basis of municipalities rather than of firms or industries, as well as the right of the labor courts to intervene in collective bargaining conflicts.[75]

By 1990, the *contribuição sindical* was principally of importance to the federations and confederations remaining from the Estado Novo labor system, for which it provided almost all of their financing. In the rank-and-file *sindicatos*, on the other hand, dues increasingly were the major source of income.[76]

THE NATIONAL DIEESE

An important development in the Brazilian labor movement during the latter part of the 1970s and the 1980s was the expansion of the Departmento Intersindical Estudos Econômicos Socio-Estatísticos (DIEESE). As we noted earlier, this organization was established in 1955 in São Paulo, principally to collect statistics on the cost of living and to do special studies for the *sindicatos* of São Paulo. Although it had difficulties in pursuing its work for a while after the coup of 1964, it soon recovered and expanded its activities.

In the 1970s the DIEESE assumed national proportions. It established its first regional office in Rio Grande do Sul. By 1990 it had such branches in fifteen states and had 180 functionaries, the largest group of whom were in São Paulo.

On a national level, the DIEESE was governed by a national directorate composed of ninety-eight members, from the *sindicatos* affiliated with it, elected for three-year terms, with one-third renewed each year. Similarly, in states in which it had branches, those were renewed annually by assemblies of representatives of the *sindicatos* affiliated with it.

As it had since its establishment, DIEESE continued to maintain a detailed cost-of-living index for São Paulo—to do so elsewhere was too expensive. The São Paulo index research kept track on a monthly basis of 50,000 prices of 320 products. In addition, it kept indices of prices on a monthly basis of 12 or 13 basic food products in thirteen state capitals, and other specialized studies.

Individual affiliates of DIEESE called upon the organization for help in their collective bargaining by providing detailed analyses of the balance sheets of firms with whom the *sindicatos* were dealing as well as general material on the state of the particular sector of the economy. Then, if the *sindicato* involved requested it, the DIEESE sent one of its experts to join the sindicato leaders in their negotiations.

The Departamento also carried on various other activities. It published a monthly bulletin that was sent to its affiliates and contained statistics, information on recently negotiated collective agreements, and specialized articles. In 1984 it also established a Trade Union School, to train educational directors for individual *sindicatos*. It also organized trade union seminars on collective bargaining, trade union administration, new technologies, and other subjects.

The organizations affiliated with DIEESE included local *sindicatos*, federations, confederations, as well as both the Central Única dos Trabalhadores and the Confederação Geral dos Trabalhadores. All factions of organized labor supported the Departamento, as a result of the excellent reputation for accuracy of its studies.[77]

COLLECTIVE BARGAINING AND STRIKES IN THE 1980s

The decade of the 1980s was marked by a great deal of labor conflict. This was the result of several factors. Among them were the relaxation of the military dictatorship in the first years of the decade and the establishment of a civilian regime in 1985. Another factor was the decay of the Estado Novo system, and with it a rapid growth of the membership of the *sindicatos*, and a vast increase in their sense of power, and therefore in their militancy.

Another element in the upsurge of organized labor in the 1980s was the condition that throughout the decade the country was in the grip of massive inflation. The government of President Figueiredo tried to deal with this, on the advice of the International Monetary Fund, with orthodox measures of government budget balancing and "liberalization" of the economy. The Sarney government launched "plans" to deal with the inflation, starting with the Cruzado Plan in 1986–1987, which sought to freeze wages and prices. After a short spate of success, that plan failed, and on at least two later occasions, the Sarney government launched other "plans" to deal with the problem. But when my wife and I were in Brazil just before the end of the Sarney administration, prices were rising at the rate of 50 percent a month.

Collective bargaining became widespread during the 1980s. One U.S. observer commented in 1990 that a few years before, both sides in a labor dispute would be more likely to laugh at the proposals of the other than to negotiate on the basis of them. Then a strike might occur, and a labor tribunal would enter the situation and decree a settlement. But by 1990 there was a generally more honest process of negotiation, and there were relatively few recourses to the labor courts.[78]

The status of grievance procedure was still in flux by 1990. The CUT and the CGT both favored a system of shop stewards and a recognized grievance procedure in which they would participate. In fact, the CUT had sent a mission to Milan, Italy, to try to see how the Italian *sindicatos* dealt with this problem. However, as one CUT official noted, there were *sindicato* representatives on each of the country's juntas of conciliation and arbitration, as well as on the regional labor courts and the Superior Labor Court, and these people were resisting the idea of eliminating those institutions, although their importance had certainly shrunk drastically.[79]

In some cases, the labor courts modified their traditional role, established under the Estado Novo system. They assumed the position of conciliators, seeking to induce *sindicatos* and employers to reach agreement, rather than just issuing a decree (*dissidio coletivo*) to "settle" a labor-management dispute.

There were innumerable strikes during the 1980s, which included three general strikes supported by both the CUT and the CGT to protest the economic policies of the Sarney regime.

The strike wave broke out while the military regime was still in power. The Metal Workers Union of São Bernardo was in the vanguard, as had become customary. As a consequence, President Figueiredo's Ministry of Labor again removed the *sindicato's* leadership in 1983.[80]

One U.S. Trotskyist source summed up the Brazilian strike situation in 1984:

The steelworkers launched "operation go-slow" in the ABC district. They occupied and camped out at factories in São José dos Campos, São Andre, São Bernardo and other areas. They won a big victory in Volta Redonda and carried out numerous struggles throughout the country. Teachers and university employees waged a national and unified strike for more than two months, and first and second grade teachers went on strike and took to the streets. . . . Bank workers, mechanics, oil workers and other categories of workers launched important struggles throughout Brazil.[81]

In 1985, 653 strikes were recorded, involving five million workers. These walkouts spread all over the country and "confronted different types of reaction by the employers."[82] The strike situation had not been significantly modified two years later. A Sarney government price stabilization policy and system of determining wage rises established in 1987, and known as the URP, provoked a wide strike reaction, when in April the government suspended wage increases for government workers. The U.S. Consulate in São Paulo reported:

Excluding walkouts related to the URP's suspension, strikes logged by DIEESE in April 1988 involved approximately 180,000 workers and 5.8 million lost man-hours. Including URP-related strikes, both these figures doubled. A two-day national protest by federal government employees helped swell May's figures to 2 million strikers and 49 million lost man-hours. The numbers receded somewhat in June and July.[83]

The strikes of the 1980s involved two important groups that previously had played a more or less passive role in the labor movement until then, the government employees and the agricultural workers.

Under the constitution in effect until 1988 government employees and those of many government firms were not legally allowed to join *sindicatos* or engage in strikes. However, this prohibition did not prevent these workers from taking part in the strike wave of the 1980s. As early as July and August 1984 there was a strike of the professors of the country's universities,[84] which was the longest strike in the country's history according to the São Paulo newspaper *Folha de São Paulo*.[85] In 1985 there was another university strike as well as walkouts of doctors employed by the city and state of São Paulo, state functionaries in Rio Grande do Sul, and federal employees in Rio de Janeiro, as well as numerous teachers' strikes in various parts of the country.[86] In May 1986 there was a strike on the Central do Brasil railway.[87] In July 1986 there was a walkout of the employees of the social security system.[88]

The newsweekly *Veja* gave figures indicating the growing importance of strikes among workers employed by the government and its enterprises in the mid-1980s. It said that whereas in 1983, the workers of the "public sector" provided 13 percent of the strikers, and in 1984 some 8 percent, and 12 percent the following year, in 1986 they constituted 68 percent of the workers on strike.[89]

Agricultural workers also became considerably more militant in the 1980s. This was particularly the case of those in the state of São Paulo, where as early as May 1984 there was a widespread strike of rural wageworkers. A Rio de Janeiro newspaper noted that these walkouts indicated an important change in the strategy of CONTAG:

This change, although not applied in the whole country, represents a shift of 180 degrees for CONTAG, which centered its activity on the question of land ownership by the worker and saw in the rural wageworker (or boia-fria) "a species of lost daughter," as the economist José Graziano da Silva observed. It was as early as 1979 that trade union work among the boais-frias in São Paulo was intensified, observed the president of the Federação dos Trabalhadores na Agricultura do Estado de São Paulo (Fetaesp), Roberto Heriguti.[90]

The heterogeneous nature of the rural *sindicatos*—made up of small landholders and tenants as well as agricultural wage earners—drew the attention of the CUT, which proposed the idea of organizing the rural wage workers and the landholders and tenants in separate organizations, since there was often a conflict of interest between the wage workers and the other two groups. However, no step in this direction had been taken by 1990.[91]

Collective bargaining on the employers' side changed substantially during the 1980s. This was perhaps most dramatically demonstrated in São Paulo, where a branch (Group 14) of the Federation of Industries of São Paulo bargained with the state's metal workers' *sindicatos*.[92]

The Sarney government tried insofar as possible not to interfere in the *sindicatos*, or even in strikes. Sarney had as his minister of labor Almiro Pazzianotto, who had been the lawyer of the Metal Workers Union of São Bernardo during the strikes of the 1970s.[93]

However, in at least two instances, there was government intervention. The U.S. Consulate in São Paulo described one of these cases, a sit-down strike in the Volta Redonda steel plant in November 1988: "Volta Redonda workers struck and occupied their plant. The government opted to dislodge the strikers and sent in troops who, in a confrontation November 9, fired tear gas, then live ammunition. Three strikers were killed, dozens wounded."[94]

In the next year, in May 1989, it was the state of São Paulo that intervened when the workers of São Bernardo staged a forty-eight-hour sit-down strike. Supporters of the walkout, parading 20,000 strong, were attacked by state police. The police finally withdrew when the workers refused to be intimidated, even after the police had opened fire on them.[95]

SUMMARY AND CONCLUSION

By 1990 there were about 11,000 trade union organizations in the country, from confederations to local *sindicatos*. About 3,000 of these belonged to some central labor group.[96]

For the first time since it had been established half a century before, the Estado Novo was to a large degree dismantled in the 1980s. This was due in large degree to the rise of the new unionism, starting with the autoworkers' strikes of 1978 and thereafter. It was also due, at least indirectly, to the democratization of the Brazilian regime, and to the massive industrialization, particularly the growth of heavy industry during the 1950s and the military regime.

De facto at first, then de jure in the new constitution of 1988, the right to strike was restored, and it was militantly used during the 1980s. New central labor organizations, for which there had never been any room in the Estado Novo, were established. Under the new constitution, *sindicatos* no longer had to have government approval in order to function, and the government was granted no power to interfere in their internal affairs.

A publication of the Union of Drivers and Conductors of the Merchant Marine, a *sindicato* that did not belong to either the CUT or the CGT, expressed as well as anyone the transformation and aspirations of the trade union movement in the 1980s: "The maintenance of the *sindicato* as a bargaining or negotiating institution must prevail over any other function."

This article continued:

In reality the embryo of the first bargaining *sindicato* in Brazil appeared during the strike movements during the decade of the seventies in the dynamic sectors of São Paulo industry. Even so, in spite of all of the efforts of the leaders to transform the "new trade unionism" into bargaining institutions, it continued that the present trade union structure is vulnerable to the repression and intervention by the State. However, the penetration of *sindicatos* into the corporativist structure of the CLT [Consolidação das Leis do Trabalho], sooner or later, will contribute to consolidating the presence of bargaining unionism in the country. By this we mean to say that one of the ways to implant bargaining or democratic trade unionism in Brazil is through the organization of the workers at the level of the enterprise. In summary, it is only at the moment that the structure of the CLT will give way to rationalization of relations between the *sindicato* and the enterprise through collective bargaining.[97]

Obviously, the experience of Brazilian organized labor in the 1980s was markedly different from that of the labor movements of most of the Latin American countries in that period. Instead of being weakened by the victory of neoliberalism as the overwhelmingly predominant ideology of the region, the Brazilian labor movement gained great strength and to a large degree liberated itself from the government tutelage and control that had characterized it since the first administration of Getúlio Vargas a half-century earlier. It gained a large degree of independence and became more truly representative of the workers who belonged to it than it had been since 1930.

As Roque Aparecido da Silva wrote:

In spite of the economic crisis of the lost decade, together with elevated levels of inflation and constant wage policies that brought the reduction of real wages and their acquisitive power, which prevailed until the end of the decade, it is certain that on the organizational and political-institutional levels the conquests were important, principally impelled by the CUT, which at certain times allied with the other central labor groups.[98]

The labor movement was only to face the full blast of neoliberalism with the coming to power of the government of President Color de Melo in 1990. However, those events carry the story beyond the period of the present study.

NOTES

1. Interview with José Raimundo da Silva, member of Central Committee of Partido Comunista Brasileiro, in Rio de Janeiro, January 22, 1990.

2. Mario Morel, *Lula O Metalúrgico: Anatomia de uma Liderança*, Editora Nova Fronteira, Rio de Janeiro, 1989, pages 29 and 64–65.

3. For information on São Bernardo strikes, see ibid., pages 81–199; and John Humphrey, *Capitalist Control and Workers' Struggle in the Brazilian Auto Industry*, Princeton University Press, Princeton, 1982, page 160–207.

4. Humphrey, op. cit., pages 166–167.

5. Ibid., page 191.

6. Ibid., pages 191–192.

7. Ibid., pages 193–194.

8. Aparecido da Silva in Helem-Metley Kohler and Manfred Wannoffel (Coordinators), *Model Neoliberal y Sindicatos en América Latina*, Fundación Friedrich Ebert, Mexico, 1993, page 103.

9. See Anthony W. Pereira, *The End of the Peasantry: The Rural Labor Movement in Northeast Brazil, 1961–1988*, University of Pittsburgh Press, Pittsburgh, 1997, pages 58–59.

10. Ibid., page 58.

11. Ibid., page 195, footnote 3.

12. For a discussion of this violence, see ibid., chapter 6.

13. Rachel Meneguello, *PT: A Formação de um Partido 1979–1982*, Editoria Paz e Terra, São Paulo, 1989, page 40.

14. Morel, op. cit., page 117.

15. Meneguello, op. cit., page 61.

16. Ibid., page 60–61.

17. Ibid., page 62.

18. Interview with João Baptista dos Mares Guia, Partido dos Trabalhadores deputy in Minas Gerais State Assembly, in Belo Horizonte, May 28, 1984.

19. Morel, op. cit., pages 54–55.

20. Interview with João Baptista dos Mares Guia, op. cit.

21. For Trotskyist reaction to the Partido dos Trabalhadores, see Robert J. Alexander, *International Trotskyism 1929–1985: A Documented Analysis of the Movement*, Duke University Press, Durham, NC, 1991, pages 138–139.

22. Interview with Marcio Araujo, press adviser of Partido dos Trabalhadores in Chamber of Deputies, Brasília, January 24, 1990.

23. See Francisco C. Weffort, *PT: Um projeto para O Brasil*, Editora Brasiliense, São Paulo, 1989.

24. Interview with Marcus Vinicius, treasurer of Partido dos Trabalhadores in Federal District, in Brasília, January 24, 1990.

25. Interview with João Baptista dos Mares Guis, op. cit.; see also *1984 Yearbook on International Communist Affairs*, Hoover Institution, Stanford, Calif., 1984, page 89, and *Ligação*, magazine of Sindicato dos Metalúrgicos de São Bernardo do Campo e Diadema, May-July 1989, page 15.

26. Interview with Francisco Domingo Santos, president of Central Única dos Trabalhadores in Federal District, in Brasília, January 25, 1990; see also *1984 Yearbook on International Communist Affairs*, op. cit., page 89.

27. Ernest Harsch, "Union Maps Fight Against Dictatorship, *Intercontinental Press*, New York, December 10, 1984, page 737.

28. *Debate Sindical*, magazine of Corrente Sindical Clasista, trade union group of Partido Comunista do Brasil, São Paulo, November 1989, page 7.

29. *Estaturo CUT Central Única dos Trabalhadores*, São Paulo, n.d., (1989).

30. Interview with Paulo José da Silva, president, Confederação Nacional dos Trabalhadores em Establecimentos de Educação e Cultura, in Brasília, August 8, 1975.

31. Interview with Antonio José Reis, press adviser of Central Committee of Partido Comunista do Brasil, in São Paulo, January 31, 1990.

32. *Estatuto CUT Central Única dos Trabalhadores*, op. cit.

33. Interview with Francisco Domingos Santos, op. cit., January 25, 1990.

34. Interview with Maria de Fatima Moreira, secretary of trade union policy of Central Única dos Trabalhadores of São Paulo State, in São Paulo, January 30, 1990.

35. Ibid., and interview with Lawrence Doherty, director of Brazilian branch of American Institute for Free Labor Development, in São Paulo, January 30, 1990.

36. *Quadro Negro*, periodical of Sindicato dos Professores do Distrito Federal, Brasília, November 1989.

37. *CUT DF Informa*, periodical of Central Única dos Trabalhadores of the Federal District, extra edition of December 1989; for information on the evolution of the Partido dos Trabalhadores, see Sue Branford and Bernardo Kucinski, *Brazil: Carnival of the Oppressed: Lula and the Brazilian Workers Party*, Latin American Bureau, London, 1996.

38. Aparecido da Silva, op. cit., page 104.

39. Ibid., page 105.

40. *CGT*, magazine of Central Geral dos Trabajadores, São Paulo, April 1986, page 3.

41. Ibid., page 1.

42. Ibid., page 2.

43. Ibid., page 6.

44. Ibid., page 8.

45. Ibid., page 13.

46. Ibid., pages 15 and 18.

47. *Movimento*, generally left-wing Brazilian weekly newspaper, July 28, 1975, page 18.

48. Letter of Joaquim dos Santos Andrade, national coordinator of CONCLAT to "Prezados Companheiros," January 23, 1986 (mimeographed).

49. Interview with Lawrence Doherty, op. cit.

50. *Debate Sindical*, October/November 1989, page 11.

51. Ibid., page 51; and interview with Antonio de Palma, member of Central Committee of Partido Comunista do Brasil, in São Paulo, January 29, 1990.

52. *Diário Popular*, Rio de Janeiro, May 1, 1989, page 8, and *Jornal do Brasil*, Rio de Janeiro, May 1, 1989.

53. Ibid.

54. Interviews with Lawrence Doherty, op. cit., and José Siqueira, coordinator of courses of Instituto Cultural do Trabalho, in São Paulo, January 29, 1990.

55. Interview with José Sisqueira, op. cit. See also *CGT Brasil*, "informative organ" of Confederação Geral dos Trabalhadores, São Paulo, #3, page 3.

56. Interview with Walter Tesch, national adviser of Confederação Geral dos Trabalhadores, in São Paulo, January 31, 1990.

57. Ibid.

58. CGT: Confederação Geral dos Trabalhadores: Nacional: "Carta dos Presidenciáveis," September 30, 1989, signed by Antonio Rogerio Macri, Presidente (mimeographed), and CGT: Confederação Geral dos Trabalhadores, Nacional: "Ata da Plenaria Nacional de Entidades Sindicais da Confederação Geral dos Trabalhadores—CGT—Realizada no Dia 30/09/80."

59. Interview with Walter Tesch, op. cit.

60. Aparecido da Silva, op. cit., pages 107–108.

61. Antonio Carlos Granado in Manfred Wannoffel (Coordinator), *Ruptura en las Relaciones Laborales*, Fundación Friedrich Ebert (Mexico), Nueva Sociedad, Mexico, 1995, pages 63–64.

62. Ibid., page 64.

63. AMCONSUL SÃO PAULO: "Foreign Labor Trends in Brazil, end 1987—end 1988," March 1, 1989 (mimeographed), pages 5–6.

64. Interview with Lawrence Doherty, op. cit.

65. AMCONSUL SÃO PAULO, op. cit., pages 6–7.

66. *CGT*, periodical of Confederação Geral dos Trabalhadores, Year IV, No. 1, page 4.

67. Interview with Robert Blau, labor reporting officer of Political Section, U.S. Embassy, in Brasilia, January 26, 1990.

68. Interview with Walter Teach, op. cit.

69. Interview with Jorge Noman Neto, president of Federação dos Trabalhadores na Indústria Metalúrgica, Mecânica e Material Elétrico do Estado de Minas Gerais, in Belo Horizonte, May 28, 1984.

70. *Deprometal*, official organ of Departamento Profissional dos Metalúrgicos, Belo Horizonte, February 84, page 2.

71. Jorge Noman Neto, *Riscos de Doenças Profissionais no Setor Metalúrgico*, Departamento Profissional dos Metalúrgicos, Belo Horizonte, n.d.

72. *Estatuto CUT Central Única dos Trabalhadores*, op. cit; and interview with Antonio José Reis, op. cit.

73. *Jornal da Tarde*, March 30, 1989

74. *Diário Popular*, May 1, 1989.

75. Aparecido da Silva, op. cit., page 112.

76. Interview with Walter Tesch, op. cit.

77. Interview with Cassio Calvete, technical supervisor of Departamento Intersindical de Estudos Econômicos e Socio-Estatísticos, in Brasília, January 26, 1990; see also "Ja Pensou o Movimento Sindical Sem o DIEESE?," São Paulo, n.d. (a throwaway).

78. Interview with Robert Blau, op. cit.

79. Interview with Walter Tesch, op. cit.

80. Ligação, op. cit., page 5.

81. Ernest Harsch, op. cit., page 737.

82. *Conclat*, magazine of Coordenação Nacional da Classe Trabalhadora, São Paulo, January 1986, page 16.

83. AMCONSUL SÃO PAULO, op. cit., page 8.

84. *Jornal do Brasil*, August 3, 1984, page 4.

85. *Folha de São Paulo*, July 1, 1984, page 26.

86. *Conclat*, January 1986, op. cit., pages 16–17.

87. *Veja*, Rio de Janeiro, May 7, 1986, page 24.

88. *O Globo*, Rio de Janeiro, July 16, 1986.

89. *Veja*, May 14, 1986.

90. *Jornal do Brasil*, May 27, 1984, page 18.

91. *Granado*, op. cit., page 60.

92. *Veja*, November 11, 1985, pages 92–93.

93. *Esto E*, May 14, 1986.

94. AMCONSUL SÃO PAULO, op. cit., January 3, 1989, page 9.

95. *Ligação*, May-July 1989, pages 5–7.

96. Interview with Lawrence Doherty, op. cit.

97. *O Conductor*, newspaper of Sindicato dos Motoristas e Condutores da Marinha Mercante, Rio de Janeiro, July 1988, page 8.

98. Aparecido da Silva, op. cit., page 110.

Bibliography

BOOKS AND PAMPHLETS

Abreu e Lima, General. *Socialismo*, Typographia Universal, Recife, 1855.

Alexander, Robert J. *International Trotskyism 1929–1985: A Documented Analysis of the Movement*, Duke University Press, Durham, NC, 1991.

———. *Juscelino Kubitschek and the Development of Brazil*, Ohio University Monographs in International Studies, Athens, 1991.

———. *Labor Relations in Argentina, Brazil and Chile*, McGraw-Hill, New York, 1962.

———. *The ABC Presidents: Conversations and Correspondence with the Presidents of Argentina, Brazil and Chile*, Praeger, Westport, CT, 1992.

American Labor Year Book 1923–1924, Rand School Press, New York, 1924.

American Labor Year Book 1927, Rand School Press, New York, 1927.

American Labor Year Book 1931, Rand School Press, New York, 1931.

American Labor Yearbook, 1932, Rand School Press, New York, 1932.

Bandeira, Moniz, Clovis Melo, and A. T. Andrade. *O Ano Vermelho: A Revolução Rusa e Seus Reflexos no Brasil*, Editoria Civilização Brasileira, Rio de Janeiro, 1967.

Basbaum, Leoncio. *História Sincera da República, de 1930 a 1960*, Vol. 2, Editoria Fulgor Limitada, São Paulo, Terceira Edição, 1968.

Boletin da Commissão Executiva do 3° Congresso Operário, Confederação Operária Brasileira, Rio de Janeiro, n.d.

Branford, Sue, and Bernardo Kucinski. *Brazil: Carnival of the Oppressed: Lula and the Brazilian Workers Party*, Latin American Bureau, London, 1996.

Brazil 1939–1941, Ministry of Foreign Affairs, Rio de Janeiro, 1941.

Brito, José Saturnino. *O Socialismo Pátrio*, Rio de Janeiro, 1920.

Carneiro, Glauco. *História das Revoluçoes Brasileiras*, Volume I, Edições O Cruzeiro, Rio de Janeiro, 1965.

Chilcote, Ronald H. *The Brazilian Communist Party: Conflict and Integration 1922–1972*, Oxford University Press, New York, 1974.

Conclusões do 4° Congresso Operário Brasileiro, Realizado no Palacio Monroe no Rio de Janeiro de 7 a 16 de Novembre de 1912, Typographia Leuzinger, Rio de Janeiro, 1913.

Conferencia Nacional de Diregentes Sindicais Pela Defesa da Democracia e Bemestar do Trabalhador, Rio de Janeiro, GB – 6/7 de Junho de 1964, Rio de Janeiro, n.d. (circa 1965).

Conniff, Michael L. *Urban Politics in Brazil: The Rise of Populism 1925–1965*, University of Pittsburgh Press, Pittsburgh, 1981.

Consolidação das Leis do Trabalho, Comissão Técnica de Orientacão Sindical, Ministério do Trabalho, Indústria e Commercio, Rio de Janeiro, 1944.

Dulles, John W. F. *Brazilian Communism 1935–1945: Repression During World Upheaval*, University of Texas Press, Austin, 1983.

Encyclopedia of the Social Sciences, The Macmillan Company, New York, 1937.

Erickson, Kenneth Paul. *The Brazilian Corporative State and Working-Class Politics*, University of California Press, Berkeley, 1977.

Estatuto CUT Central Única dos Trabalhadores, São Paulo, n.d. (1989).

Freitas, J. V. Marcondes. *First Brazilian Legislation in Relation to Rural Labor Unions*, University of Florida Press, Gainesville, 1962.

Gómez, Alfredo. *Anarquismo y anarcosindicalismo en América Latina: Colombia, Brasil, Argentina, Mexico*, Ruedo Ibérico, Madrid, 1980.

Humphrey, John. *Capitalist Control and Workers' Struggle in Brazilian Auto Industry*, Princeton University Press, Princeton, 1982.

Jornal do Brasil. *Cadernos JB de IV Centernario, Dezembro 16, 1965*, Rio de Janeiro, 1965.

Kohler, Holm-Metlev, and Manfred Wannoffel (Coordinators). *Model Neoliberal y Sindicatos en América Latina*, Fundación Friedrich Ebert, Mexico City, 1993.

Lacerda Gustavo de. *O Problema Operário no Brasil (Propaganda Socialista)*, Rio de Janeiro, June 1901.

Los partidos comunistas de América del Sur y del Caribe y el Movimiento Sindical Revolucionario, Publicaciones 'Exige,' Barcelona, 1933.

Machado, Augusto. *A Caminho da Revoluçao Operária e Camponesa*, Calvina Filho, Rio de Janeiro, 1934.

Mendes, T. Teixeira. *A Ordem sociale e o comunismo anarchista*, Rio de Janeiro, 1893.

Meneguello, Rachel. *PT: A Formação de um Partido 1979–1982*, Editora Paz e Terra, São Paulo, 1989.

Meneses, Geraldo Montedonio Bezerra de. *A Justiça do Trabalho no Brasil, Relatório das Activadades de 1950*, Rio de Janeiro, 1951.

Moraes, Felix de, and Francisco Viana. *Prestes: Lutas e Autocriticas*, Vezes, Petropolis, 1982.

Morel, Mario. *Lula O Metalúrgico: Anatomia de uma Liderança*, Editoria Nova Fronteira, Rio de Janeiro, 1989.

Movimiento Obrero, Sindicatos y Poder en América Latina, Editorial El Coloquio, Buenos Aires, 1975.

Naft, Stephen. *Fascism and Communism in South America*, Foreign Policy Reports, Foreign Policy Association, New York, December 15, 1937.

Negro, Hélio and Edgard Leuenroth. *O Que e o Maximiso ou Bolchevismo*, São Paulo, 1919.

Niemeyer, W. *Movimento Syndicalista no Brasil*, Rio de Janeiro, 1933.

Noman Neto, Jorge. *Riscos de Doenças Profissionais no Setor Metalúrgico*, Departamento Profissional dos Metalúrgicos, Belo Horizonte, n.d.

Organizaçao Sindical, Ministério do Partido Socialista Brasileiro, Rio de Janeiro, 1933.

Pereira, Anthony. *The End of the Peasantry: The Rural Labor Movement in Northeast Brazil, 1961–1988*, University of Pittsburgh Press, Pittsburgh, 1997.

Pereira, Astrogildo. Formaçao do PCB, Editorial Vitória Limitada, Rio de Janeiro, n.d.

Piccarolo, A. *O Socialismo no Brasil—Esboço de su programma de acão socialista*, 3ra Edição, Editora Piratininga, Sao Paulo, 1932.

Pinheiro, Paulo Sérgio, and Michael M. Hall. *A Classe Operária no Brasil 1889–1930: Documentos*, Vol. I—*O Movimento Operário*, Editora Alfa Omega, São Paulo, 1979.

Poblete Troncoso, Moisés. *El Movimiento Obrero Latinoamericano*, Fondo de Cultura Económica, Mexico, 1946.

Price, Robert E. *Rural Unionization in Brazil*, Land Tenure Center, University of Wisconsin, Madison, August 1965.

Ravines, Eudosio. *The Yenan Way: The Kremlin's Penetration of South America*, Charles Scribner & Sons, New York, 1951.

Ridings, Eugene. *Business Interest Groups in Nineteenth-Century Brazil*, Cambridge University Press, New York, 1994.

Rodrigues, Leôncio. *Conflito Industrial e Sindicalismo no Brasil*, Difusão Européia do Libro, São Paulo, 1966.

Romualdi, Serafino. *Presidents and Peons: Recollections of a Labor Ambassador in Latin America*, Funk and Wagnalls, New York, 1967.

Santa Rosa, Virginio. *O Sentido do Tenentismo*, Civilização Brasileira, S.A., Rio de Janeiro, 1933.

Sindicato dos Operários nos Serviços Portuários de Santos. *Convenio Coletivo do Trabalho*, Rio de Janeiro, 1943.

Spalding, Jr., Hobart A. *Organized Labor in Latin America: Historical Case Studies of Workers in Dependent Societies*, New York University Press, New York, 1977.

Vargas, Getúlio. *As Diretrises da Nova Política do Brasil*, Libreria José Olympio Editoria, Rio de Janeiro, 1942.

Víctor, Mario. *5 Anos que Abalaram o Brasil*, Editoria Civilização Brasileira, Rio de Janeiro, 1965.

Vinhas, Moisés. *O Partidão: A Luta por um Partido de Massas 1922–1974*, Editoria Hucitec, São Paulo, 1982.

Wannoffel, Manfred (Coordinator). *Ruptura en las Relaciones Laborales*, Fundación Friedrich Ebert (Mexico), Nueva Sociedad, Mexico, 1995.

Weffort, Francisco C. *PT: Um Projeto para O Brasil*, Editora Brasiliense, São Paulo, 1989.

Wesson, Robert, and David V. Fleischer. *Brazil in Transition*, Praeger Publishers, New York, 1983.

Wiarda, Howard J. *The Brazilian Catholic Labor Movement: The Dilemmas of National Development*, Labor Relations and Research Center, University of Massachusetts, Amherst, 1969.

Young, Jordan. *The Brazilian Revolution of 1930 and the Aftermath*, Rutgers University Press, New Brunswick, NJ, 1967.

NEWSPAPERS AND PERIODICALS

Acão Direta, anarchist periodical, Rio de Janeiro.
A Classe Operária, Communist Party newspaper, Rio de Janeiro.
Allied Labor News, pro-Communist newsletter, New York.
A Plebe, anarchist newspaper, São Paulo.
Associated Press, news service.
CGT, magazine of Central Geral Trabalhadores, São Paulo.
CGT Brasil, "informative organ" of Confederação Geral dos Trabalhadores, São Paulo.
CIO News, periodical of Congress of Industrial Organizations, Washington, DC.
Communist International, official English-language magazine of Communist International.
Conclat, magazine of Coordenação Nacional da Classe Trabalhadora, São Paulo.
Correio da Manhã, daily newspaper, Rio de Janeiro.
CUT DF Informa, periodical of Central Única dos Trabalhadores of the Federal District, extra edition of December 1989, Brasília.
Daily Worker, Communist Party daily paper, New York City.
Debate Sindical, magazine of Corrente Sindical Clasista, trade union group of Partido Comunista do Brasil, São Paulo.
Deprometal, official organ of Departamento Profissional dos Metalúrgicos, Belo Horizonte.
Diário Carioca, daily newspaper, Rio de Janeiro.
Diário da Noite, afternoon newspaper, Rio de Janeiro.
Diário Oficial, official publication of Government of Brazil, Rio de Janeiro.
Diário Popular, daily newspaper, Rio de Janeiro.
El Libertario, publication of anarchist group, "Centro Internacional," Montevideo.
El Popular, newspaper of Confederación de Trabajadores de Mexico, Mexico City.
Esto E, weekly newsmagazine, Rio de Janeiro.
Folha Carioca, daily newspaper, Rio de Janeiro.
Folha de São Paulo, daily newspaper, São Paulo.
Inter American Labor Bulletin, periodical of Inter American Regional Organization of Workers.
International Press Correspondence, periodical of Communist International.
Jornal da Tarde, daily newspaper, São Paulo.
Jornal de São Paulo, daily newspaper, São Paulo.
Jornal do Brasil, daily newspaper, Rio de Janeiro.
La Correspondencia Sudamericana, periodical of South American Secretariat of Communist International.
Latin American Perspectives, scholarly review.
Le Mouvement Socialiste, Socialist magazine of 1880s and 1890s, Paris.

Ligação, magazine of Sindicato dos Metalúrgicos de São Bernardo do Campo e Diadema.

Monthly Labor Review, U.S. Department of Labor, Washington, DC.

Mother Earth, anarchist magazine edited by Emma Goldman, New York City.

Movimento, generally left-wing Brazilian weekly newspaper.

New York Post, daily newspaper.

New York Times, daily newspaper.

O Commerciario, newspaper of Liga dos Empregados do Commercio, Santos.

O Condutor, newspaper of Sindicato dos Motoristas e Condutores da Marinha Mercante, Rio de Janeiro.

O Cruzeiro, newsmagazine, Rio de Janeiro.

O Globo, daily newspaper, Rio de Janeiro.

O Trabalhador Graphico, organ of Sindicato dos Trabalhadores Graphicos, São Paulo.

Quadro Negro, periodical of Sindicato dos Professores do Distrito Federal, Brasília.

Revista da Associação dos Funcionarios Públicos do Estado de São Paulo, São Paulo.

Revista de Trabajo, publication of Ministry of Labor, Santiago, Chile.

The Call, Socialist Party daily, New York City.

The Labour Gazette, monthly periodical of Ministry of Labor of Canada, Ottawa.

Tiempo, weekly newsmagazine, Mexico City.

Tribuna Popular, Communist Party newspaper, Rio de Janeiro

United Press, news service.

Vanguarda Socialista, monthly newspaper, Rio de Janeiro.

Veja, weekly newsmagazine, São Paulo.

Viertel Jahres Berichte, periodical of Friederich Ebert Foundation, Bonn.

INTERVIEWS

[Brazilian names are often confusing. I have adopted the general policy of listing the names in this bibliography alphabetically according to the last name of each individual, except in cases in which the last word indicates family relationship (Senior, Junior, Son, etc.) or in a few cases in which the person is generally referred to by something other than the last name.]

Agostino, Sr., an editor of Communist newspaper *Gazetta Sindical*, Rio de Janeiro, March 21, 1956.

Alkmin, Ivan, vice president, Sindicato Nacional dos Aereonautas, Rio de Janeiro, August 21, 1959.

Almeida, João Baptista, president, Federação Marítima Nacional, Rio de Janeiro, June 3, 1953.

Amaral Peixoto, Alzira Vargas de, daughter of Getúlio Vargas, Rio de Janeiro, January 10, 1966.

Andrade, Joaquim dos Santos, president, Sindicato dos Trabalhadores Metalúrgicos do São Paulo, New Brunswick, NJ, April 28, 1968.

Araujo, Hilton Silva, executive secretary, Confederação Nacional dos Trabalhadores no Comércio, Brasília, August 7, 1975.

Araujo, Joviano de, Brazilian representative of International Confederation of Free Trade Unions and ORIT, Rio de Janeiro, June 13, 1953.

Araujo, Marcio, press adviser of Partido dos Trabalhadores in Chamber of Deputies, Brasília, January 26, 1990.

Assis, José Benedicto de, president, Sindicato dos Trabalhadores em Empresas de Radiodifusão do Rio de Janeiro, and of Federação Nacional dos Trabalhadores em Empresas de Radio e Telivisão, Rio de Janeiro, October 27, 1965.

Andrezzo, Orli, one of the editors of Communist newspaper *Hoje*, São Paulo, August 3, 1946.

Baker, Herbert, U.S. Embassy labor attaché, Rio de Janeiro, August 5, 1965.

Barata, Agildo, onetime *tenente*, onetime treasurer of Partido Comunista, Rio de Janeiro, August 20, 1965, September 6, 1965.

Barreto, Caio Plínio, labor lawyer, son of Plínio Barreto, São Paulo, August 22, 1946.

Blum, Rudor, secretary of international relations, Confederação Nacional dos Trabalhadores na Indústria, Rio de Janeiro, August 10, 1965.

Brandão, Domingo, first secretary, Sindicato dos Estivadores do Santos, Santos, April 25, 1956.

Brentano, S.J., Ludwig, national ecclesiastical adviser of Confederação Nacional de Círculos Operários, Rio de Janeiro, March 12, 1956.

Calvete, Cassio, technical supervisor of Departamento Intersindical de Estudos Econômicos e Socio-Estatísticos, Brasísilia, January 26, 1990.

Campello, José Ferreira, president, Federação dos Trabalhadores nas Indústrias de Química e Farmácia do Estado de Rio y Distrito Federal, Rio de Janeiro, July 6, 1954.

Campista, Ary, secretary general, Confederação Nacional dos Trabalhadores na Indústria, Rio de Janeiro, June 13, 1971.

Campos, Rui, official of Federação dos Trabalhadores na Agricultura do Estado de Paraná, New Brunswick, NJ, November 3, 1978.

Candia, Luiz Fuuza, president, Federação dos Trabalhadores na Indústria de São Paulo, São Paulo, July 7, 1954.

Cardoso, Fausto, president, Confederação Nacional dos Trabalhadores no Comércio, Rio de Janeiro, March 15, 1956.

Careja, José Lopes, administrative secretary, Sindicato dos Oficiais Alfiates, Costureiras e Trabalhadores na Indústria de Confecções de Roupas do Pôrto Alegre, September 19, 1946.

Cascardo, Heroclinio, ex-*tenente*, onetime president of Aliança Nacional Libertadora, Rio de Janeiro, January 3, 1966.

Cavalcanti, Diocleciano de Holanda, president, Confederação dos Trabalhadores na Indústria, Rio de Janeiro, March 9, 1956, June 1, 1968.

Cerqueira, Benedito, secretary of Confederação Nacional dos Trabalhadores na Indústria, Rio de Janeiro, August 15, 1962.

Coelho Filho, Manuel Lopes, official of Metallurgical Workers of Rio de Janeiro, later secretary general of Confederação Geral do Trabalho Brasileiro, Rio de Janeiro, August 29, 1946.

Costa, Carlos Alberto, executive secretary, Confederação Nacional dos Trabalhadores no Comércio, Rio de Janeiro, August 24, 1959.

Costa, Paschoal F. da, president, Federação dos Trabalhadores na Indústria of Santa Catarina, in Florianópolis, December 6, 1965.

Costa e Silva, Bernardino da, president, Sindicato dos Motoristas e Condutores em Transportes Fluviais no Estado de Pará, Belem, February 13, 1956.

Coutinho, Cherubim Mendes, secretary, Federação dos Trabalhadores na Indústria de Vestuário do Estado de São Paulo, São Paulo, August 26, 1959.

Crimmins, John, U.S. ambassador to Brazil, Brasília, August 9, 1975.

D'Agazio, Antonio, head of office staff of Sindicato dos Trabalhadores de Fiação e Tecelagem, São Paulo, June 17, 1953.

Damore, Pascuele, secretary, Federação dos Trabalhadores na Indústria de Vestuário, São Paulo, April 18, 1956.

De Fazio, Paulino Humberto, ex-president, Sindicato dos Trabalhadores nas Indústrias Gráficas de São Paulo, São Paulo, August 22, 1946.

Devichiatti, Julio, president, Sindicato dos Trabalhadores de Tecelagem e Fiação de São Paulo, São Paulo, August 27, 1959.

Dias, Antonio, communications adviser, Confederação Nacional dos Trabalhadores na Agricultura, Brasília, August 8, 1975.

Doherty, Lawrence, country program director, American Institute for Free Labor Development, São Paulo, January 30, 1990.

Dutra, Maria de Graça, secretary general, Federação Nacional de Jornalistas, an editor of Communist daily *Imprensa Popular*, Rio de Janeiro, June 10, 1953.

Fatima Moreira, Maria de, secretary of trade union policy of Central Única dos Trabalhadores of São Paulo State, São Paulo, January 30, 1990.

Fonseca, Nivaldo, second secretary, Sindicato dos Trabalhadores na Indústria de Fiação e Tecelagem de São Paulo, São Paulo, April 20, 1956.

Forli, Remo, president, Sindicato dos Trabalhadores Metalúrgicos de São Paulo, São Paulo, June 16, 1953, August 27, 1959.

Fraga, Heitor Nunes, adviser to Delegation of Confederação Nacional dos Trabalhadores na Indústria de Pôrto Alegre, Pôrto Alegre, December 10, 1965.

França, Luiz Augusto de, treasurer, Confederação dos Trabalhadores no Comércio, Rio de Janeiro, June 11, 1953.

Freitas, José de Patrocinio, president, Sindicato dos Operários de Fiação e Tecelagem de São Luís de Maranhão, São Luís, April 15, 1966.

Galardi Filho, Pedro, president, Sindicato dos Trabalhadores nas Indústrias de Construção Civil de São Paulo, São Paulo, June 17, 1953.

Gamboa, Vicente, Venezuelan trade union leader recently returned from Brazil, Caracas, July 21, 1947.

García, José Alonso, president, Electric Power Workers Union of São Paulo, São Paulo, July 8, 1954.

Gatto, Dacyr, president, Federação dos Trabalhadores na Indústria de Vestuário de São Paulo, São Paulo, September 26, 1959.

Gonçalves, José, president, Sindicato dos Operários nas Serviços Portuarios de Santos, Santos, April 25, 1956.

Gouves, Jaime, president, Sindicato dos Trabalhadores na Indústria do Açucar do Estado de Pernambuco, Recife, August 5, 1975.

Guia, João Baptista dos Mares, Partido dos Trabalhadores deputy in Minas Gerais State Assembly, Belo Horizonte, May 28, 1984.

Gurgel, Sr., member of Diretorio of Sindicato de Empregados Bancários do Distrito Federal, Rio de Janeiro, March 15, 1956.

Hewitt, Cynthia Naegele, Columbia University graduate student studying Brazilian rural unions, Rio de Janeiro, September 1, 1965.

Hirschley, Josef, executive secretary, Sindicato dos Empregados em Establecimentos Bancários de Pernambuco, Recife, May 4, 1966.

Jorgenson, Harold, agrarian reform expert of American Institute for Free Labor Development, Recife, May 2, 1966.

José, Nassim, administrative secretary, Sindicato dos Empregados no Comércio de São Paulo, São Paulo, July 6, 1954.

Lacerda, Carlos, ex-governor of Guanabara, onetime leader of Brazilian Communist youth organization, Rio de Janeiro, February 6, 1966.

Lacerda, Celio Dinardo L., head of Registration Section of Serviço de Organização e Registro Sindical of Ministry of Labor, Rio de Janeiro, April 5, 1956.

Laluce, Centino, secretary of public relations, Federação dos Círculos Operários do Estado de São Paulo, São Paulo, August 28, 1959.

Leão, Octavio de Sousa, president, Conselho Superior de Previdência Social, Rio de Janeiro, March 12, 1956.

Leite, Hilcar, Socialist journalist, Rio de Janeiro, June 19, 1953.

Leite, Luís Antonio, member of Conselho Fiscal, Sindicato dos Trabalhadores nas Indústrias Metais, Mecânicas e Materiais Elétricos de Barra Mansa, Volta Redonda, April 3, 1956.

Leuenroth, Edgard, onetime leader of Confederação Operária Brasileira, São Paulo, September 2, 1946.

Liebof, Jack, consul and labor reporting officer of U.S. Consulate General of São Paulo, São Paulo, October 7, 1965.

Lima, José Ferreira, vice president, Federação dos Trabalhadores na Indústria de Amazonas, Manaus, February 28, 1966.

Lins, Evandro, member of Brazilian Supreme Court, Brasília, March 17, 1966.

Lisboa, Luis Augusto de Castro, president, Sindicato dos Empregados em Establecimentos Bancários de Pôrto Alegre, Pôrto Alegre, May 7, 1956.

Lombardi, Aldo, secretary general, Sindicato dos Trabalhadores nas Indústrias Metalúrgicas, Mecânicas e de Material Elétrico de São Paulo, São Paulo, April 17, 1967.

Lopes, Aurélio, functionary of Sindicatos dos Empregados Bancários do Distrito Federal, Rio de Janeiro, March 15, 1956.

López, Arthur, head of American Institute for Free Labor Development in Pernambuco, Recife, May 2, 1966.

Loureiro, Jarbas, administrative chief of Federação dos Trabalhadores de Construção Civil de Minas Gerais, Belo Horizonte, March 28, 1956.

Ludovico, Pedro, governor of Goiás, onetime *tenente*, Goiânia, October 3, 1965.

Macedo, Isidoro Belmonte de, president, Círculos Operários Católicos Portoalrgrande, Pôrto Alegre, April 30, 1956.

Maceio, Jaime, president, Sindicato dos Estivadores da Bahia, Salvador, March 1, 1956.

Magaldi, Antonio Ferreira, president, Federação dos Trabalhadores no Comércio de São Paulo, São Paulo, July 30, 1975.

Maghenzani, Helcio, secretary general and Director, Instituto Cultural do Trabalho, São Paulo, July 30, 1975.

Manlaes, Hermes, president, Sindicato dos Trabalhadores na Indústria Gráfica do Campos, R.J., Campos, February 6, 1966.

Mariano, Djalma A., director of Rio de Janeiro office of ICFTU-ORIT, Rio de Janeiro, August 24, 1959.

Marques, Delveaus Sissenanda, secretary, Junta Governativa of Federação dos Trabalhadores nas Indústrias de Espírito Santo, Vitória, February 11, 1966.

Martina, Marina, secretary, Federação dos Trabalhadores nas Indústrias de Santa Catarina, Curitiba, December 1, 1965.

Masckio, Gervasio Eliseu, secretary, Sindicato dos Trabalhadores Gráficos de São Paulo, São Paulo, June 17, 1953.

Matteo, Mario, secretary, Sindicato dos Trabalhadores na Indústria de Metal, Mecânica y Materiais Elétricos do Distrito Federal e Estado do Rio de Janeiro, Rio de Janeiro, April 9, 1956.

Maura, Dr. Raimundo, president, Tribunal Regional do Trabalho, Belem, February 8, 1956.

Mello, Plínio, a leader of Partido Socialista Brasileiro in São Paulo, ex-Communist, ex-Trotskyist, São Paulo, June 16, 1953.

Mello Sobrinho, José Machado de, secretary general, Sindicato dos Armadores de Santos, Santos, April 25, 1956.

Mendes, Heitor Teodoro, president, Sindicato dos Trabalhadores nas Artefatos de Papel de São Paulo, São Paulo, August 27, 1959.

Miranda, Valentin, delegate of Sindicato Nacional dos Trabalhadores Ferroviarios in Cachoeiro de Itapemirim, Espírito Santo, February 9, 1966.

Moreira Junior, Delfim, president, Tribunal Superior do Trabalho, Rio de Janeiro, March 13, 1956.

Morena, Roberto, leading Communist trade unionist, subsequently member of Chamber of Deputies, Rio de Janeiro, August 28, 1946, June 10, 1953.

Motta, Nelson, president, Sindicato dos Empregados do Comércio de Rio de Janeiro, Rio de Janeiro, August 14, 1946.

Moura, Wilson, president, Junta da Intervenção of Confederação Nacional dos Trabalhadores de Crédito, Brasília, August 7, 1975.

Muller, Felinto, onetime *tenente*, senator, Brasília, March 18, 1966.

Neves, Paulo Baete, president, Confederação Nacional dos Trabalhadores no Comércio, Rio de Janeiro, June 9, 1953.

Nunes, Jaime Wallace, Socialist leader in Sindicato de Chofers Autônomos do Rio de Janeiro, Rio de Janeiro, August 21, 1959.

Oiticica, José, old-time anarchist labor leader, director of *Acão Direta*, Rio de Janeiro, August 30, 1946.

Oliveira, Alrino Martins de, grievance secretary of Textile Workers Federation of the State of São Paulo, São Paulo, July 8, 1954.

Oliveira, Francisco Patricio de, lawyer of Sindicato dos Trabalhadores na Indústria de Energia Hidroelétrica de São Paulo, São Paulo, April 14, 1956.

Omans, John, U.S. Embassy labor attaché, Rio de Janeiro, June 11, 1971, June 8, 1972.

Orlando, Vicente, president, Federação dos Trabalhadores na Construção Civil, Rio de Janeiro, June 10, 1953.

Paiva, Pedro Chavier de, president, Sindicato dos Trabalhadores na Indústria de Fiação e Tecelagem de Recife, Recife, February 24, 1956.

Paiva, Sebastiao, secretary, Confederação Nacional dos Trabalhadores no Transporte Terrestre, Rio de Janeiro, March 16, 1956.

Pedrosa, Mario, editor of *Vanguarda Socialista*, ex-Communist, ex-Trotskyist, Rio de Janeiro, August 13, 1946.

Pedrosa, Ruy Brito de Oliveira, president, Confederação Nacional dos Trabalhadores nas Empresas de Crédito, Rio de Janeiro, June 2, 1972.

Peixoto, João, vice president, Sindicato de Bancários da Bahia, Salvador, March 3, 1956.

Pereira, Isaltino, editor of *Voz Metalúrgica*, organ of Metal Workers Federation of Federal District, Rio de Janeiro, August 26, 1959.

Pereira, Ramon, secretary, Federação dos Trabalhadores Metalúrgicos do Rio Grande do Sul, Pôrto Alegre, May 3, 1956.

Pinheiro, José Carpintero, president, Sindicato dos Trabalhadores de Luz e Força do Rio de Janeiro, Rio de Janeiro, March 23, 1956.

Portcarrero, Alceu, president, Confederação Nacional dos Trabalhadores nas Comnicações, Rio de Janeiro, June 11, 1971.

Powers, Tom, official of U.S. Department of Labor, Rio de Janeiro, September 27, 1965.

Prestes, Luiz Carlos, secretary general, Brazilian Communist Party, Rio de Janeiro, August 22, 1946.

Previatti, Olavo, president, Federação dos Trabalhadores nas Indústrias do Papel, Papelao e Cortiças do Estado de São Paulo, Rio de Janeiro, May 27, 1966.

Prieto, Arnaldo da Costa, minister of labor, Brasília, August 7, 1975.

Puggina, Adolfo, Partido Democrata Cristão member of Rio Grande do Sul state legislature, organizer of rural unions, Pôrto Alegre, December 10, 1965.

Quintana, Gabriel Marcelo, president, Sindicato dos Trabalhadores nas Indústrias Graphicas de Pôrto Alegre, May 4, 1956.

Rama, Luisanto de Mata, president, Sindicato dos Comerciários do Rio de Janeiro, Rio de Janeiro, August 1, 1975.

Ramos, Américo, country program director in Brazil of American Institute for Free Labor Development, Washington, DC, June 30, 1975.

Ramos, José Calixto, vice president, Confederação Nacional dos Trabalhadores na Indústria, Brasilia, August 7, 1975.

Reis, Antonio José, press adviser of Central Committee of Partido Comunista do Brasil, São Paulo, January 31, 1990.

Ribeiro, José, member of Executive Committee of Federação dos Trabalhadores na Indústria de Paraíba, João Pessoa, April 20, 1966.

Rizzo, Santos, secretary general, São Paulo Metallurgical Workers Union, São Paulo, July 5, 1954.

Rocha, João Francisco da, president, Sindicatos dos Empregados no Comércio Hoteleiro e Similares do Rio de Janeiro, Rio de Janeiro, August 27, 1946.

Rodrigues, José Albertino R., director of Departamento Intersindical de Estatística e Estudos Socio-Econômicos, São Paulo, August 27, 1959.

Romualdi, Serafino, assistant secretary general, ORIT, Washington, DC, December 9, 1953.

Salert, Irving, U.S. Embassy labor attaché, Rio de Janeiro, June 8, 1953, March 5, 1956, March 9, 1956.

Salles, Manuel Buies de, secretary, Federação Marítima Nacional, Rio de Janeiro, June 13, 1953.

Salles, Padre Eugenio, apostolic administrator of Archdiocese of Bahia, former Bishop of Rio Grande do Norte, Salvador, May 16, 1966.

Sampaio, José Soares, president, Sindicato dos Trabalhadores na Indústria do Fumo do Rio de Janeiro, Rio de Janeiro, August 30, 1946.

Santos, Abreu Egydio dos, president, Federação dos Trabalhadores nas Indústrias Metalúrgicas, Mecânicas e Materiais Elétricos do Estado de São Paulo, São Paulo, July 30, 1975.

Santos, Francisco Domingo, president of Central Única dos Trabalhadores in Federal District, Brasília, January 25, 1990.

Santos, José Airton dos, president, Confederação Nacional dos Trabalhadores en Transportes Terrestres, Brasília, August 6, 1975.

Santos, Valmyr Rafael dos, president, Sindicato dos Empregados no Comércio de Londrina, Londrina, November 29, 1965.

Segadas Viana, José, former director general of Labor, Rio de Janeiro, August 26, 1946, March 16, 1956.

Sfair, Raquel, secretary, Teachers Union of state of Rio Grande do Sul, New Brunswick, NJ, September 12, 1968.

Sgubin, Antonio, president, Sindicato Têxtil Americano, and secretary of Federation of Textile Workers of São Paulo, São Paulo, July 8, 1954.

Shaw, Paul Van Orden, American-Brazilian newspaperman and teacher, Rio de Janeiro, August 25, 1946.

Shea, James, U.S. Embassy labor attaché, Brasília, July 28, 1975.

Silva, João Francisco da, president, Confederação Nacional dos Trabalhadores Agrícolas, Brasília, August 8, 1975.

Silva, José Raimundo da, member of Central Committee of Partido Comunista Brasileiro, Rio de Janeiro, January 22, 1990.

Silva, Manoel Francisco da, president, Federação dos Trabalhadores na Indústria de Alimentação; secretary, CNTI, Recife, February 22, 1956.

Silva, Paulo José da, president, Confederação Nacional dos Trabalhadores em Establecimentos de Educação e Cultura, Brasília, August 8, 1975.

Singer, Paulo, member of Inter Union Strike Committee of Metal Workers Union of São Paulo, São Paulo, June 18, 1953.

Sisqueira, José, coordinator of courses of Instituto Cultural do Trabalho, São Paulo, January 29, 1990.

Sisson, Roberto, onetime secretary of Aliança Nacional Libertadora, Rio de Janeiro, September 8, 1965.

Street, Ernesto, economist of Confederação Nacional da Indústria, Rio de Janeiro, March 6, 1966.

Sussekind, Arnaldo, legal adviser of Confederação Nacional dos Trabalhadores na Indústria, Havana, Cuba, September 10, 1949; Rio de Janeiro, April 5, 1956.

Talarico, José Gomes, a leader of Journalists Union, Rio de Janeiro, June 9, 1953.

Tesch, Walter, national adviser of Confederação Geral dos Trabalhadores, São Paulo, January 31, 1990.

Torres, Juvenal Guerreiro, president, Sindicato dos Trabalhadores nas Empresas Elétricas de Campos, R.J., Campos, February 6, 1966.

Torres, Walter, treasurer, Sindicato dos Trabalhadores nas Indústrias Graphicas do Rio de Janeiro, Rio de Janeiro, August 22, 1959.

Tubbs, Guillermo, president, Federação, dos Trabalhadores na Indústria de Fiação e Tecelagem de São Paulo, São Paulo, August 20, 1946.

Vico, Francisco Ramon, secretary general, Sindicato dos Conferentes de Carga e Descarga do Porto de Santos, Santos, September 4, 1946.

Vinicius, Marcus, treasurer of Partido dos Trabalhadores in Federal District, Brasília, January 24, 1990.

Wagner, Heracy, secretary, Confederação Nacional dos Trabalhadores na Indústria, Rio de Janeiro, August 25, 1959.

Xausa, Leonidas, former leader in Rio Grande do Sul of Christian Democratic Party and Acão Popular, Pôrto Alegre, December 6, 1965.

Zanino Junior, Armando, a leader of Marine Officers Union and of 1953 maritime strike, Rio de Janeiro, July 1, 1954.

Zanino Senior, Comandante Armando, a leader of 1953 maritime strike, Rio de Janeiro, June 18, 1953.

MISCELLANEOUS

Alexander, Robert J. Letter to Jay Lovestone, September 25, 1959.

Alexander, Robert J. "Observations on São Paulo Textile Union, April 24, 1956" (typed).

AMCONSUL São Paulo: "Foreign Labor Tends in Brazil, end 1987—end 1988," March 1, 1989 (mimeographed).

Barreto, Vicente. "Carta de Rio de Janeiro: Brasil y Sus Problemas Concretos," publication of Press Service of Congress for Cultural Freedom, Paris (mimeographed).

"Brazil—Volta Redonda Steel Works 1959: Collective Agreement Entered Into by the Metal, Mechanical and Electrical Industries Union of Barra Mansa and the National Steel Company" (typed manuscript in English).

CGT: Confederação Geral dos Trabalhadores, Nacional: "Ata da Plenaria Nacional de Entidades Sindicais da Confederação Geral dos Trabalhadores—CGT—Realizada no Dia 30/09/80.

CGT: Confederação Geral dos Trabalhadores: Nacional: "Carta dos Presidenciáveis," September 30, 1989, signed by Antonio Rogerio Marci, Presidente (mimeographed).

Decreto N. 1637 de 5 de Janeiro de 1907: Crea Sindicatos Profissionais e Sociedades Corporativas, Soc. Coop. Resp. Limitada, Banco de Petrópolis, Rio de Janeiro, 1928.

"Departamento Intersindical de Estatística e Estudos Socio-Econômicos: "10 Anos de Política Semanal," São Paulo, August 26, 1975 (mimeographed).

Erickson, Kenneth Paul. "Corporative Controls of Labor in Brazil," paper presented at 1971 Annual Meeting of American Political Science Association.

French, John D. "Industrial Workers and the Origin of Populist Politics in the ABC Region of Greater São Paulo, Brazil, 1900–1950," Ph.D. dissertation, Yale University, 1985.

Hall, Michael, and Paulo Sérgio Pinheiro. "The Control and Policing of the Working Class in Brazil, Paper for the Conference on the History of Law, Labour and Crime," University of Warwick, 15–18 September 1983.

Hewitt, Cynthia Naegele. "An Introduction to the Rural Labor Movement of Pernambuco" (manuscript).

"Ja Pensou o Movimento Sindical Sem o DIESSE?" São Paulo, n.d. (a throwaway).

Letter of Joaquim dos Santos Andrade, National Coordinator of CONCLAT to "Prezados Companheiros," January 23, 1986 (mimeographed).

Meade, Teresa. Community Protest in Rio de Janeiro, Brazil During the First Republic 1890–1917," Rutgers University Ph.D. dissertation, 1984.

Naft, Stephen. "Labor Movements in South America," unpublished manuscript

"Relação das Entidades Membros do Departamento Intersindical de Estatística e Estudos Socio-Econômicos," typed, n.d. (circa 1959).

Stein, Barbara Hadley. Unpublished manuscript on Brazilian labor.

Yearbook on International Communist Affairs, Hoover Institution, Stanford, Calif.

Index

About the Author

ROBERT J. ALEXANDER is Professor Emeritus of Economics at Rutgers University. His most recent books are *A History of Organized Labor in Cuba* (Praeger, 2002), *A History of Organized Labor in Argentina* (Praeger, forthcoming in late 2003), and *Maoism in the Developed World* (Praeger, 2001).